HOW TO WRITE IN PSYCHOLOGY

HOW TO WRITE IN PSYCHOLOGY

A Student Guide

John R. Beech

WILEY-BLACKWELL

A John Wiley & Sons, Ltd., Publication

This edition first published 2009

Blackwell Publishing was acquired by John Wiley & Sons in February 2007. Blackwell's publishing program has been merged with Wiley's global Scientific, Technical, and Medical business to form Wiley-Blackwell.

Registered Office
John Wiley & Sons Ltd, The Atrium, Southern Gate, Chichester, West Sussex, PO19 8SQ, United Kingdom

Editorial Offices
350 Main Street, Malden, MA 02148-5020, USA
9600 Garsington Road, Oxford, OX4 2DQ, UK
The Atrium, Southern Gate, Chichester, West Sussex, PO19 8SQ, UK

For details of our global editorial offices, for customer services, and for information about how to apply for permission to reuse the copyright material in this book please see our website at www.wiley.com/wiley-blackwell.

Library of Congress Cataloging-in-Publication Data
Beech, John R.
How to write in psychology : a student guide / John R. Beech.
p. cm.
Includes bibliographical references and index.
ISBN 978-1-4051-5693-6 (hardcover : alk. paper) – ISBN 978-1-4051-5694-3 (pbk. : alk. paper)
1. Psychology–Authorship. I. Title.

BF76.8.B425 2009
808′.06615–dc22

2008014316

A catalogue record for this book is available from the British Library.

Set in 10.5/13pt Minion by SPi Publisher Services, Pondicherry, India
Printed in Singapore by Markono Print Media Pte Ltd

6 2013

CONTENTS

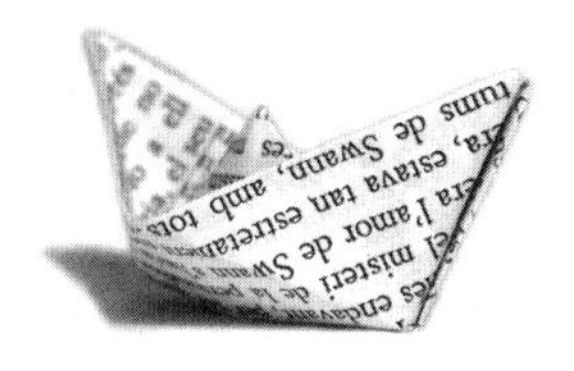

ILLUSTRATIONS

Cartoons

Figures

ACKNOWLEDGEMENTS

Every effort has been made to contact copyright holders. However, should there be any omissions, we will be pleased to make any necessary corrections in future printings. We wish to thank the following for their permission to use copyright material.

Figure 6.1 is based on data from Beech, J.R. (2001). A curvilinear relationship between hair loss and mental rotation and neuroticism: a possible influence of sustained dihydrotestosterone production. *Personality & Individual Differences, 31*, 185–192, with permission from Elsevier.

Figure 6.7 is based on data from Beech, J.R. & Harris, M. (1997). The prelingually deaf reader: A case of reliance on direct lexical access? *Journal of Research in Reading*, a journal of the United Kingdom Literacy Association (UKLA), *20*, 105–121. This has been produced with permission from UKLA.

Table 6.3 is based on Beech, J.R. & Mackintosh, I.C. (2005). Do differences in sex hormones affect handwriting style? Evidence from digit ratio and sex role identity as determinants of the sex of handwriting. *Personality and Individual Differences*, *39*, 459–468, with permission from Elsevier.

INTRODUCTION

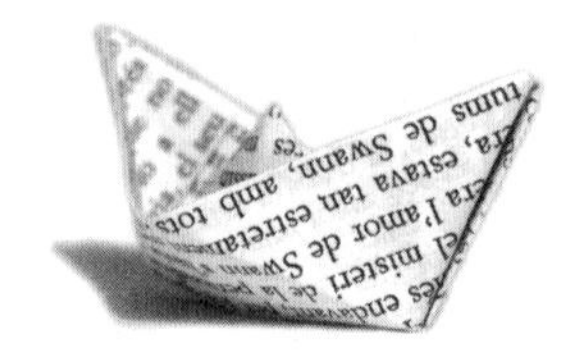

The discipline of psychology attracts students for various reasons, and like students in most academic disciplines, they soon have to start writing in a particular style. This can be a different experience from other types of writing. Some take to this kind of writing like ducks to water, others are shy to venture to the water, some simply flounder and one or two decide to give up altogether and search for another pond. (Early lesson: metaphors can sometimes be taken a little too far.)

This book describes in detail writing an essay and writing a research report with an emphasis on how to plan, to organise and to keep motivated. Writing for both quantitative and qualitative research reports is covered. Other areas include: writing examination essays and preparing for multiple-choice exams; how to format essays and lab reports; how to create tables and figures; and how to write for other purposes, such as writing items for questionnaires. In addition, chapter 11 outlines the basics of grammar and includes an examination of words that can create confusion.

The final chapter is designed to improve your own proofreading and editing skills. It consists of chunks of text taken from students' writings and you are invited to work out what is wrong. My own analysis follows each sample. The appendices contain a sample student essay and a lab report, along with commentaries. Both of these provide useful models of the kind of writing that is expected.

The process of writing is difficult for most of us. I remember my early struggles and frustrations learning to write in the discipline. It is a long time ago now, but I also remember thinking: why do I have to write in a particular way and why are studies referenced in the way that they are? I have experienced writing blocks and the difficulty of getting across the precise meaning of something. Over time, this process has changed.

Writing is a little bit like exercising. With exercise, one becomes stronger as muscles develop, but the demands similarly change. The same applies to writing: in some ways, it gets a bit easier; but is always challenging. It has been my aim in writing this book to be sympathetic to the struggles of the apprentice writer; but at the same time, I have tried to ease the pathway in places with a light-hearted approach.

It is important to use this book along with the advice received from your lecturers or instructors. You have probably been given a 'style manual' written by them that outlines how to set out your writing. Whatever your lecturers tell you has to be given priority and overrides any information given in this book. However, in contrast to them, this book is available for consultation at any time. Besides, it may well go into much more detail in various ways.

Treat this book any way that suits you. You may want to dip into individual chapters to deal with problems that are relevant at the time, or even most urgent. Alternatively, you may want to settle down and have a good long read. I am not going to give any guarantees, but if after reading this book you follow up with suitable action, it could improve your grades!

I would like to end this introduction by thanking those who have been influential during the course of writing this book. The inception of the book involved me writing a few chapters and then for one reason or another it languished. Andrew McAleer from Wiley-Blackwell encouraged me to continue with the task and Elizabeth-Ann Johnston, also from Wiley-Blackwell, has been instrumental in helping me to sustain this effort to fruition (in the nicest possible way). I am very grateful to them both. I also would like to thank the anonymous reviewers for the very helpful comments they made on an earlier draft. Finally, I would like to thank my wife Liz and daughter Harriet for their good humour and forbearance during the writing of this book.

John Beech

1

SOME PRELIMINARIES

In this first chapter, we have an assortment of 'tasters' that need to be borne in mind when approaching coursework assignments. We begin by examining the different needs of essays and lab reports. It is important to be aware of the contrasting aims of these two major types of assignment. You also need to understand what type of writing is needed in psychology. For example, do psychologists like to put quotations in their writing? Are there any underlying assumptions that distinguish it from other disciplines? We will also consider the importance of making satisfactory preparations, including discussing whether it is better to write on paper or to use a computer. The final part considers 10 different ways to get your writing started.

Essays and Lab Reports

While essays and lab reports have many similarities, it is important to know the different expectations for each. Let's begin with the essay. The essay is as an exercise to find out our skill in examining a particular issue relevant to psychology. This means that we are going to study a controversy or subject area and analyse the available evidence. This needs an assimilation of the evidence and the construction of an argument to support our analysis. We want to produce a work that interests the reader and one with a coherent structure that will be easy to understand.

The aim of the essay setter is not only to see how well writers can examine an issue, but also to see how skilled the writers are in expressing themselves. To achieve this the writer needs a good plan of the essay structure. One needs to show skills in self-expression as well as displaying good critical appraisal of the research that is being described. The language should be precise, have a continuous flow, be free from ambiguities and modern in style.

Writing up the lab report involves different processes. The report presents a particular research problem and the aims of the experiment with specific hypotheses. It then describes the research that has been undertaken in enough detail that anyone else could perform the same experiment. This is followed by an analysis of the findings and a discussion of these findings in the context of the earlier hypotheses in the report.

Clearly, this is research not undertaken in isolation. There are invariably findings from other psychologists that have a bearing on these hypotheses. The introductory section is the place to describe this work. The writer returns to other work in the discussion as the new findings from the current experiment are assimilated into the existing body of knowledge. The report then reaches a conclusion.

There are, of course, similarities and contrasts between the two types of assignment. For example, they are similar in that both need good organisation, which includes an introduction and a conclusion, and the writing needs to be logical, clear and concise. However, there are also contrasts. The essay involves a description and assessment of other people's research work, whereas the lab report incorporates your own research. This consists of a limited research exercise to study a particular hypothesis or hypotheses. Another contrast is that the area of study in a practical report is usually narrowly focused. An essay can afford to take a more general look at a particular question.

Problems with lab reports and essays

There may be a few areas of difficulty with the lab report. (However, don't worry as these problems are all surmountable.) For example, one of these problems is how to create a hypothesis, which is dealt with in detail in chapter 3.

Let me pause for a moment to explain that in this book, I will have a conversation with a (usually polite) fictional student (yes, I have a split personality) and here is the first question:

> *Student:* Suppose that I run my experiment and the actual result is completely different from my initial hypothesis: I was anticipating a difference between two groups, but actually found no significant difference between them. Do I therefore change my hypotheses in my introduction and state that no difference is expected between the two groups?

John: You have my sympathy if this happens to you. Suppose that from your reading you find that previous research suggested that a difference between the two groups would have been expected. It would look odd in your introduction if you then stated that you were expecting no difference between the two groups.

There is no point in leaving out relevant evidence from the research literature (indicating that a difference would be expected) in your introduction either. This would be unethical and the marker will probably know about that research anyway. Instead, use this evidence to build up a case to put forward the hypothesis that a difference is expected. Then in the discussion explain that the hypothesis has unexpectedly not been confirmed. ”

Continuing this discussion, you may wonder why you can get unexpected results in your own research. This is something that just happens. If results always came out as expected, psychology would be a dull science. Unfortunately getting an unexpected result this way can be difficult to explain.

It could be that your non-significant result is the correct one, and later researchers may publish similar non-significant results. In other words, the finding of a significant difference by a previous researcher may simply have been a chance result. On the other hand, if there had been many more participants in experiments that had previously found a difference, it is more likely that you have just got a fluke result. Another possibility for discussion is that your experimental design is slightly different from previous research. Could this change account for the different result?

Writing an essay also has challenges. One of the most important of these is being sure the essay you are planning to write is going to answer the question. One concern may be that you are not covering all the areas the marker requires. Another is that you might think the title is ambiguous. If so, get in touch with the essay setter for more help. We will go into much more detail about essay writing in the next chapter.

“ *Student:* How can I squeeze all this information in my essay and still come up with a product that is going to get a high mark?

John: It is important to learn to express yourself concisely and still leave room in the essay to provide sufficient analysis of the issues involved. ”

The Importance of Preparation

Preparation for the longer term

'Sharpen the saw' is a phrase meaning that preparation can save effort. When a woodcutter tries to cut wood with a blunt saw it takes a tremendous amount of effort and time. By contrast, if the saw is first sharpened, the wood can be cut through much more easily and in a fraction of the time. According to Covey (1989), people often go about their work without sharpening the saw, because they think that they are just too busy. Nevertheless, if they found the time to perform the kind of task represented by this simple operation, they would create more time and subsequently work much more efficiently.

Applying the sharpening principle
How would this principle be useful for you coursework assignments? The fact that you are reading a book like this is not because you are trying to delay writing up that essay. Instead, it is saw-sharpening. By working out the best way to write assignments, you are not wasting time writing them in inappropriate ways. You will save time and avoid disappointment by finding out what is needed as soon as possible.

Another way to sharpen the saw is by improving your writing craft. Writing is a skill that can be developed. Part of that improvement comes about by reading as much as possible and noting the ways that psychologists express themselves. This can also help to improve vocabulary both in terms of word meanings and spellings. This is an efficient saw-sharpening activity because it means that in the future less time will be spent looking up words in the dictionary, and more importantly you will not be interrupted mid-sentence while hunting around for the best word. If you do find yourself trying to think of a suitable word, leave a blank. Alternatively highlight a word of nearly the same meaning and just continue writing and return later. This is better than breaking off from a train of thought.

Learning how to reference is saw-sharpening. Learning about how psychologists format their work and lay out their references should save time by reducing the need to rearrange or correct references. Learn to touch-type so that you can look directly at the screen while you type. This is also saw-sharpening.

Regular saw-sharpening is better
As with all such advice, take this in the way that is most suitable for your situation. If one is 3 days away from an essay deadline, it would be foolhardy to start working to improve word power. Get down to writing that essay immediately

and drop everything else to get it handed in on time. Saw-sharpening is for the longer term, but should be integrated into the daily routine, to give a real sense of making definite progress over time. Do not use saw-sharpening as an excuse for not getting on with more urgent assignments.

Preparation for the shorter term

Planning your time

Link your short-term goals to your forthcoming assignment deadlines. This means planning carefully so enough time is spent on each assignment. If time is tight, you will have to give up some leisure time to get everything done. If time is not so tight, plan suitable rest times for doing other activities.

Getting the evidence

When the assignment details are given out, first think about the exact requirements of the topic. Then hunt around for suitable material to provide background reading. This would include going to general textbooks, encyclopaedias, books in the library, accessing the web, and accessing databases such as PsycINFO and Web of Science. It would also be useful to look up the topic and associated terms in a psychology dictionary.

This should not imply mindlessly gathering information like a squirrel. Get down to learning and understanding your topic. It can be helpful to talk to friends about the topic, especially as it can mean explaining technical topics in a way that they can understand. Work out the issues involved and evaluate strengths and weaknesses. This will improve further reading as it will provide more focus.

You need to be focused during this search. Although reading material that is 'off topic' will help with general knowledge about psychology, it is not going to help to get that background reading completed. You need to be disciplined with yourself if this leads to too much time-wasting. Engaging with the topic will develop a positive mindset. Work out why the topic question could be interesting and go from there.

Planning your assignment

You then need to think about the structure of your essay or lab report. Some like to think of a structure immediately without any further reading, while others prefer to do some background reading to get a 'feel' for the topic before starting on the planning stage. It does not matter which way you advance, as the plan is likely to be adjusted as work progresses. Nevertheless, it is important to have a plan to direct these activities and to act as a reminder about what has to be done next.

How Psychologists Write

The approach of most academic disciplines

Each academic discipline has its own philosophy and writing style. However, most of these different academic styles have the common element that the writing style is formal. This is in contrast to chatty informal writing, as when writing a letter or sending an e-mail to a friend. For example, psychologists would not write: 'The student didn't choose the right one'. We do not use *contractions* such as 'don't', 'it's', 'there's' and so on.

Informal or colloquial writing is a habit that some students find difficult to shake off. If you cannot help writing this way, at least go back and edit your chatty style afterwards to make it suitably formal. A handy tip is to do a computer search for a single quote (') to find contractions such as 'can't' afterwards.

> *Student:* But you haven't written this book in a formal style; for example there are occasional contractions. You're not setting a very good example.
>
> *John:* I'm sure the odd book reviewer will enjoy pointing this out as well! However, in this book I aim to explain in a friendly, approachable way how to write well in psychology. It is not in itself a technical report or academic essay.

We also write concisely. We would not write, as one student did for me in an abstract, '... it was therefore decided to explore this effect by presenting participants with…' Instead, we might write, 'Participants were therefore given….' Writers in psychology write formally for an audience that expects the writing to be concise.

Our writing should also be unambiguous and have continuity. Some examples of avoiding ambiguity in certain words can be found in chapter 11 (e.g. see the entry for *since*), but ambiguity can also be created by using fuzzy descriptions. Turning to continuity, there is the expectation that there should be a logical progression in the arguments that are presented. In practice, this is not always going to be easy: sometimes blocks of information must be included that do not need to be placed in any particular order.

In the scientific disciplines, including psychology, there are more assumptions and the writer is expected to be aware of them. For example, this includes formulating hypotheses and testing them by experimentation. All academic disciplines discourage broad, unsupported statements. Thus if a statement is made, experimental evidence with the names of the investigators (and years) needs to back that statement.

Students can get into difficulty when discussing these hypotheses in relation to the experimental outcomes. They might refer (mistakenly) to a hypothesis being 'proved' by their experimental result. This implies that the evidence has settled the truth of the matter. However, the scientific endeavour is about approaching the truth about the world. We cannot be certain, based on one experiment, or even several experiments, that we have reached our goal. Instead, we should write that the hypothesis was *confirmed*, *supported*, *substantiated* or some equivalent term. There will be more on this topic in chapter 3.

The approach of psychology

Over the years in psychology we have developed our own notion about what is acceptable writing. An important facet of our discipline is that we have a scientific approach, but this orientation is tailored to our particular requirements. This means that we develop hypotheses and test them, just as in other scientific disciplines. In contrast to a discipline such as chemistry, our interest is not in inert substances, but in living participants, who need to be treated accordingly. We often refer to people taking part in our experiments as 'participants', rather than 'subjects', as we want to treat such people with respect.

There have been other gradual changes in the way that we write in psychology, reflected partly by the changes in attitudes within our society. We now try to avoid any hint of prejudice and bias in our writing. For example, we avoid sexism. Thus, the participant was not '… told to press the key with *his* preferred hand'. Instead, participants '… were asked to use *their* preferred hand to press the key'. This avoidance of sexism is a two-way process and means avoiding sexism against men as well, such as by continual reference to *she* without the corresponding *he*. The greatest difficulty in removing sexist language is avoiding the use of third person pronouns such as he or she. Occasionally they may need to be bundled together as 'he or she' (see the entry for *s/he* in chapter 11).

Similarly, we should be careful not to cause offence to any individual with any particular characteristic. As an example, we should not write 'A group of 9- and 10-year-old dyslexics were tested on the reaction time task.' The experimenter here is testing a group of children who happen to have a condition called dyslexia. The identity of these young people is not their dyslexia. A more suitable way might be 'A group of children aged 9 to 10 years diagnosed with dyslexia were tested . . .'. Try also to be sensitive to the use of colour terms, as they may be construed to be similar to skin colour, so avoid terms such as 'pure white' and so on. However, political correctness has to be treated sensibly and should not go to such laughable lengths as 'Snow White and the Seven Vertically Challenged People'. The main criterion is whether the term you are using is likely to cause someone somewhere embarrassment or offence.

Because of our scientific ideals, we are concerned with being 'objective' when collecting data. (However, see chapter 5 on the qualitative report for a different perspective.) In other words, we should focus on our hypotheses, rather than refer to our personal views, and try to express ourselves in formal objective language. Although these objectives are laudable, it has sometimes led to prose that is dry to read. Now a slightly more relaxed approach is considered suitable, with the writer being allowed to express views more directly.

An aspect of scientific writing in the past was its excessive use of the passive voice. For instance, the sentence beginning 'The copper sulphate was placed in the test tube . . .' is in the passive voice, whereas 'The experimenter placed the copper sulphate in the test tube' is in the active voice. Expressing yourself in the active voice makes you understood more easily, but there will be situations when the passive voice will be preferable. If the grammar checker is on permanently while you write, it will usually alert you to passive constructions. But be aware that the checker does not always get it right. There is further discussion on this topic in chapter 11 (see *active vs. passive voice*). As a footnote, do not get obsessed with this aspect because when writing Method sections in particular it is very difficult to avoid writing in the passive voice.

The use of quotations (that is, when quoting written sources rather than direct speech) is an area of interesting contrasts between disciplines and within psychology. For instance, if studying history one would include quotes from authorities (leading historians) within the field of history to back up the interpretations of historical events. In English literature academics would be expecting to see the author's quotation used by the student as a basis for a critical appraisal.

In psychology, the quotation is used far less often and the language that is used by an author to express an idea is not considered as important as the idea itself. We do find quotations used much more in student essays, but probably by students steeped in the traditions of other disciplines. As a rule of thumb, if more than 4–6 per cent of the text consists of quotes, there is probably an overuse of quotations. As a footnote, if you have been given an essay or report to write that is oriented in a qualitative way (see chapter 3 for an explanation, or chapter 5 about writing a qualitative report) then quotations will be used much more.

The Case for Writing Up Using the Computer

Should you write up directly on to your computer, or would it be better to start writing up on paper? The advantages of using a computer for your write-up are as follows:

1. There is no final draft to type up.

One problem for those who write on paper is that time then has to be spent transcribing the whole handwritten piece on to a word processor before handing in the work.

2. Cutting and pasting is easy.

One can keep on 'cutting and pasting' to rearrange chunks of text until satisfied with the final arrangement.

3. Finding a keyword is quick.

Accessing any particular word in the text is fast. If you work in Microsoft Word, the control key and the 'F' key finds keywords quickly. One can also 'find and replace', meaning that if there is a need to change a word or something several times, it is easy to do (again accessible by Control + F). However, it is wise to check each individual change, rather than doing a 'universal change' in which all instances of the word are changed to something else in one push of a button.

4. It is faster than writing by hand.

If you learn to touch-type, your typing speed should become faster than writing speed. You can type up more text without experiencing as much strain as when you write by hand. Incidentally, it is well worth learning to touch-type. There are books available that have typing exercises as well as programs on the web to help you achieve this. The best way to start is first to do the basic exercises to learn which finger covers which keys. As soon as possible, you should then type everything by touch-typing. *Never* look at the keyboard – except perhaps for numbers. It will be agonisingly slow to begin with, but with perseverance typing speed will build up. This is an excellent saw-sharpening activity. A reasonable speed can be achieved within about 2 weeks as long as you persevere.

5. You can use dictation software.

There is software available into which one can dictate and this is simultaneously converted into text on the screen. This needs some time and effort to set up, but eventually could prove useful.

6. There is no bulky paper storage.

When typing on computer there isn't the problem of bulky paper storage; so you will find it increasingly easy to retrieve documents from your computer compared with paper storage, unless you have enough filing cabinet storage for your paper. Journal papers and other documents can be stored in PDF form on computer, which also helps speed of access.

If a computer is used, it is important to be well organised with your documents. If you use Microsoft Word, then Windows Explorer should be used for your file organisation. Each document is typed into a file and these files are stored within a folder. This allows the organisation of the files into a hierarchy. It is a good idea to limit the size of any particular folder (perhaps to 20–30 files). As the number of files increases, consider whether certain folders could be usefully subdivided. Occasionally a document may be accidentally filed in the wrong place. It is possible to do a limited search by looking up your history of document retrievals within Word (click 'File'), or a more extensive search, focusing on particular folders, by using 'Search' in Explorer.

The Case for Writing Up on Paper

Some people find it difficult to compose what they want to write directly on the computer. They prefer to plan their work and then write it out on paper and then either to redraft it or cut and paste the paper until it is in a form that is acceptable. The work is then typed in and printed off only at the final stage. There are two main advantages of this approach. First, there is flexibility in where you write, as pen and pad are portable, and second, you can access what you have written more easily as you can lay out your sheets of paper to look at. Some disadvantages with using a computer are as follows:

1. Computers can lack flexibility in location.

If you have not got a laptop or portable device such as a PDA, you may be restricted to using the computer in one particular location.

2. Computers have a restricted field of view.

You have a restricted field of view on the screen. Printing out the text can help overcome this problem.

3. Typing is too slow to keep up with thoughts.

This is perhaps a Catch-22: because you are used to writing on paper, you are slow at typing on the computer. Therefore, some people never make a switch-over to typing.

Starting to Write: Ten Ways to Get You on Your Way

At last, you are able to start writing. Let's suppose that you have already worked at understanding what the question is asking. (There is more about how to unpack a question at the beginning of the next chapter.) Unfortunately, you have a problem starting or you have stopped soon after starting. Most of us have been there. You are looking at a blank computer screen and your mind is equally blank; but you need to write. You have to write. Suddenly you feel overwhelmingly compelled to get up and perform some trivial task that is going to waste yet more time. Do not despair. Here are 10 ways to get going:

1. Gather enough information.

Probably the most important task that can be done is to gather sufficient evidence so that there is enough to write about. If you have not found enough on the topic, it is not surprising that you are going to run out of ideas.

2. Begin by writing anything that springs to mind.

Go to your computer, or get your writing pad. Sit down and write anything that comes into your head. You might start by typing a letter to a friend or relative about what you are doing, or about a film you have seen. Anything will do. After doing this for a while, try to steer round to the topic that you have to write about and start writing about this.

3. Develop a positive mental attitude.

Do not worry at this stage if you feel that what you write is terrible. If you have this attitude, this could be why you find writing difficult. You need to convince yourself that what you are doing is acceptable and that you are doing fine. Even better – suspend that editor in your head while writing the first draft.

4. Set up a routine for writing.

For some, getting up early and writing for 2 or 3 hours each day, no matter what, is an excellent way to tackle any writing assignment. However, you do not need to cut yourself off from the world when writing, which leads on to the next point.

5. Your writing environment does not have to be perfect.

Do not use the excuse that your working space needs to be silent before you can write. As Stephen King (2000) wrote: 'At times I'm sure all writers feel the same… if only I were in the right writing environment… I just KNOW I would be penning my masterpiece' (p.279). In fact, the interruptions during writing can be helpful. As King puts it: 'It is, after all, the dab of grit that seeps into an oyster's shell that makes the pearl' (p.279). In an experiment on distraction Reisberg and McLean (1985) played tapes of the comedian Joan Rivers to participants which they had to ignore while doing the main task of adding up columns of numbers. They found that if they gave participants enough financial incentive they were able to ignore Joan and get on with the task. So imagine yourself working in the library and trying to write that essay, but you are getting distracted by that talkative, smelly, fidgeting, finger-tapping person who insists on sitting as close as possible. Remember that if you are motivated enough you should be able to ignore most happenings. But, on second thoughts, there are limits – I would go and find somewhere else to sit!

6. Do not procrastinate.

Do not even allow the luxury of any self-doubts; get down to writing straight away. We will see how getting an early draft completed well before the essay deadline will help the quality of the final product. If I want to go running on a cold winter day, I 'just do it' – I put on my kit and get out there. Similarly, when it comes to writing – just do it.

7. Take a break.

This is just the opposite of the last point and not the way to get going! The point here is that much time might have been spent on the essay and you are getting into a rut. This is a good time to take a break, either by doing something different for a while, or by switching to another assignment for a while. That is, as long as the time is available, of course.

8. Tackle lethargy.

Your lethargy might be simply because your room is too warm and comfortable. It could be because of a lack of sleep. You could consider embarking on an exercise programme, starting with regular walks, developing into something more strenuous. Give this continuous writing project (already suggested in point 2) a serious try every day and it could well overcome the problem.

9. Give yourself incentives.

Do not allow yourself to watch a favourite television programme, or have any other treat, until you have achieved a sequence of set goals in your self-imposed writing assignments.

10. Park on the slope.

The idea here comes from skiing – if you park temporarily but still on the slope, you can resume down the slope whenever you wish. Using this analogy, don't feel that you need to complete the section you are writing by the end of your session. Leave the rest of a section unwritten, or if you do complete it go on to make a start on the next section. This way you can pick up from where you left off the next day and carry on down that slope. In other words, finish that uncompleted section and go on to the next. Incidentally, just in case someone is planning to sue me, this is not actually a good tip for skiing as you might find that your skis have gone the next morning.

Chapter Summary

We began this chapter by considering the two major types of assignment in psychology: the essay and the lab report. Both have their problems, but these are surmountable. All academic essays in most disciplines, including psychology, involve writing a discussion and argument around a topic in a more formal language than that used in everyday speech. However, psychology has its own distinctive approaches to academic problems that need to be recognised by students. One common mistake of the beginner is to imagine that academic writing needs to include many quotations from leading authorities. Psychologists usually are not so much concerned with how other psychologists express themselves, but more about other people's findings, interpretations and theories. We also discussed the importance of developing suitable skills for essay writing, using the analogy of 'sharpening the saw'. In the closing part of this chapter, we discussed the advantages of writing your essay directly on your computer versus on paper. If you convert to using your computer for essay writing, this would be a good saw-sharpening activity as you will develop a skill that will make essay writing increasingly easy to fulfil. We finished by looking at 10 different ways to get you writing or to keep it going.

2

WRITING THE ESSAY

We need motivation to do well. However, motivation alone is not sufficient. It is important to learn the craft of writing. If you can learn this, it will make the writing of essay assignments, exam essays, lab reports and other forms of writing so much easier and more enjoyable. Along the way, put yourself into your writing to breathe life into it. Towards the end of this chapter is a checklist of things that need to be done to make sure the essay does not have any problems.

Some people produce a finished product that is poor, many can produce a reasonable piece that can be improved, and a few achieve excellence. This distribution of marks would be radically different if everyone knew how to write properly and were motivated enough. It is not so much innate ability that helps people to write excellent essays, but intelligent application. Everyone studying psychology at college or university who is willing to undertake the necessary degree of work will do well.

The Minimalist Approach

What is the best way of collecting information for the essay and then organising it? Perhaps your preferred style is minimalist. The writer finds the nearest textbook and a few other relevant sources, and then tries to pull out anything that is considered appropriate. The writer then types it up. Perhaps the writer moves some of the content around a little and then the essay is submitted. This may produce an essay swiftly, but this approach would be unlikely to achieve good marks, although sometimes one may get lucky.

The Value of Effort and Motivation

This introduces an important side of academic work. If you put more effort and time into the essay, you will be likely to achieve higher marks. However, this effort has to be applied intelligently. There is not a one-to-one relationship between time expended and marks awarded. Instead the relationship is probably not linear but exponential. If it requires (say) 6 hours to produce an essay at a sufficient level to pass, this time can increase exponentially if we wish to improve on our grades. If you want to achieve the highest grade, this can require a substantial amount of time.

“*Student:* But I can't put in all those hours – I've got to do part-time work to make my way through college. Besides, I've also got to find time to enjoy myself as well.

John: All I'm saying is that if you can't afford the time, it might impact on the quality of your work. I've known students with spectacularly difficult lives and circumstances who have done extremely well. They somehow had the fortitude to overcome their personal problems and keep themselves well motivated and organised.

Another way of arranging your affairs is to try to do more part-time work when your college/university work does not count so much (such as in the first and second years of a 3-year course) and perhaps save up so that you can afford to do less part-time work during the final year. Also, try to avoid shift work that could induce sleep deprivation, even if it is much better paid.”

It helps considerably to be motivated and have good self-organisation so that each day can be planned and appropriate time allocated. For example, start work on your essay as soon as you get your title. This will mean the first draft can be completed comfortably before the deadline. There is then time to put it to one side for a while before doing the final revision. Having this delay should produce a better final product as the perspective will be fresher. There are plenty of excellent books that can provide help on self-organisation, motivation and confidence that are worth reading (e.g. Allen, 2002; Bryant, 2004; Covey, 1989, Fiore, 2007). (Do not be put off by the garish covers and the snappy titles of some books in this field.)

Tools for Writing

Before examining the different ways of collecting information for essays, it is useful to consider some useful tools to have while consulting sources. These are:

- a first-class general dictionary;
- a thesaurus (or synonym finder); and
- a good dictionary of psychological terms.

A pocket dictionary might be useful for checking spelling. However, a 'heavy' dictionary is indispensable for looking up difficult words to help understanding of the trickier passages of text. The psychology dictionary is helpful for finding terms that have not found their way into the main dictionary.

You might like to put each new word into a notebook or schematic mind map for future reference to help build up your vocabulary. The thesaurus is not obligatory, but can help if you struggle to find the right word occasionally. Of course, the web is also a good source for finding a good dictionary and thesaurus suitable for your needs.

Methods of Collecting Information from Published Sources

Before we get into detail about the planning stage, we need to look at where to go for sources of information. We will also examine the more mechanical aspects of note taking.

You probably have notes from your lectures as a starting point. These will provide sources to find further information. As these come from the lecturer, they are obviously important, but not necessarily the only sources of information. Most information in psychology comes from articles (often called 'papers') in journals. These can be accessed within databases by computer and often a PDF file can be retrieved or else the paper is available in printed form within your library. If a lecturer has recommended any books, it is highly likely that they will be available in the library, subject to demand from fellow students. Your library will have printed versions of major journals in its stocks. However, library catalogues normally only list the journal titles, not the papers within these journals. To find particular papers you will need to search a database.

Searching a database is the best way of accessing the information that you need. You might want to search these databases by subject (e.g. sibling rivalry) or to search for a paper by a certain author published in a particular year. At the least, you will be provided with a full reference (author names, date, title of paper, journal title, etc.), and most of the time an abstract (or summary) of each paper will be available. Depending on the database, you will have different levels of success in obtaining a PDF copy of the full paper. If all else fails, sometimes authors have their own websites that have PDF copies of all their published papers.

The main computer databases to access papers in psychology are PsycINFO and PsycARTICLES. PsycINFO contains information on papers in about 2000 journals in psychology or related to psychology. It also includes books, book chapters and dissertations. This database can provide the majority of your needs. PsycARTICLES is much narrower in focus and consists mainly of the full articles in American Psychological Association journals (about 60 at the time of writing). This information can be accessed from within the PsycINFO database.

The Social Sciences Citation Index and the Science Citation Index are both available through the Web of Science. These two useful databases can be searched simultaneously, and they cover disciplines wider than just psychology. The bonus with the Web of Science site, apart from its size, is that it also enables you to examine the citations of papers, which can be a measure of a paper's importance. (PsycINFO does this too, but is currently more limited.) To explain this further, all research papers have a list of references at the end, also known as citations. These are collated by Web of Science so that subsequent citations of the journals in its database can be monitored. A minority of research papers attract a substantial number of citations, whereas the majority attract hardly any.

Google is a useful search engine, particularly Google Directory. This can be accessed by means of Google Scholar (available from their front page), or by going to this link: www.google.com/Top/ (this web link ends with the final slash '/'). On this page should be a list of main headings, one of which is 'Science' and beneath this is 'Psychology'. Clicking this provides a listing of categories, and then further categories are listed within this, and so on. This can provide additional material that could supplement your search. Wikipedia is also a very useful source of information for definitions and for providing a wider context, but it has to be used with care. However, much of this material, if it is not in a published journal, has not been through a reviewing process.

Your write-up should rely on information from journals and books. However, your tutor may have a different view on this.

Assuming that you have found appropriate sources of information from books and journals, there arises the question of how to process them. The way to do this for your essay is a matter of individual style. Here are some possibilities.

Often people photocopy or print out their source texts and mark up bits that they think could be useful later for their essay. This is a method of distilling all the information down to just the relevant parts. From there, some students put the text into their own words while others copy selected texts verbatim into their notes. Occasionally some people just cut out relevant passages and paste them into some kind of arrangement.

These methods involve to different degrees getting involved in the text and understanding what it means. At this stage, there can be a problem of plagiarism (i.e. copying). Copying an unaltered chunk of text into your notes carries the danger that it will later be mistaken for your own writing. Thus, it is important to be meticulous and surround any such material by quotation marks.

Box 2.1 An Anecdote

I knew a student when in my first year at university who got into difficulties over photocopying. He photocopied all relevant sources and then cut out the relevant bits. Instead of rewriting, he simply presented the pasted photocopies. By way of explanation, he said that the authors expressed themselves far better than he could! At least he was honest about what he was doing, but his stay at university was brief.

Verbatim copying from sources is almost like photocopying, except the transcription is by hand. Although it saves the cost of photocopying it is time-consuming. The writer is making notes without necessarily having a full understanding of the text, and without assessing its relevance to the essay question. Therefore, it means painstakingly copying material from an extensive range of sources. People who do this may think that they will somehow understand the material better. Perhaps they do. Others with obsessive tendencies may feel that they have to raise their note-taking to this level, as everything has to be covered. Perhaps for others it is a form of writer's block – a mind-deadening activity that delays the write-up.

Focused searching

A much better way of proceeding, which can save time, is to think beforehand carefully about the essay question. Consult the lecturer's notes and recommended sources. These should be skimmed, seeking out only material that is directly relevant to the question. At this point one should start taking notes. However, it is up to you whether you choose to write out what is relevant literally, or to write the gist of the text in your own words. It will also save time to note the exact reference to put in the References section at a later point and to note the page number, if quotations are going to be used later. One slight drawback with this approach is that you may become too selective and not end with enough material. You will then need to go back to get more information. This more focused method needs mental effort by being more involved with the essay question early on.

“*Student:* I'm not sure I agree with you. It seems to me that making notes on everything and focussed searching are both extremes. Surely, it is better to take a middle course that avoids the disadvantages of both?

John: Yes, both approaches have their pros and cons. The focussed searching approach while being efficient could filter information so much that there is not enough material left to include in the essay. The other approach of taking thorough notes means that you are less likely to miss out something that might turn out to be important later. The important thing is not to be too wasteful of your precious time while taking notes. However, some time-wasting and some false starts are going to be inevitable.”

We have just looked at the issue of the problem of how far to go when taking notes. Before leaving this more mechanical aspect of preparing for essay writing, we also need to consider a different form of note taking – mind mapping.

Mind mapping

One method strongly recommended by Buzan (2002) is the use of 'mind maps' to represent topics. These topics are written out on paper and are enclosed by ovals. Properties or aspects of these topics emanate from these ovals like spider's legs. We need a large piece of paper. (Wallpaper is ideal, but preferably not still stuck to the wall.) Then our diagram can develop organically in whatever direction.

Mind maps sometimes need a much larger area . . .

This is useful for those of us who like to think in visual terms. It is an excellent way for memorising information for an examination. One problem with it, though, is that if it is on paper it is difficult to change its structure once started. There are, however, computer programs available that can get round this. Some of the software for mind mapping is free from the web. For example, one way to find out what is available currently is to look up 'mind mapping' in Wikipedia.

An alternative way to mind mapping is simply to type up a plan of the topics on the screen. Under the topic headings, we can nest subheadings and features. If we need to rearrange, we 'cut and paste' and thus move the headings around. Topics can be expanded by adding information directly into your file. Another way, this time without using a computer, is to put ideas down on cards. We can then lay out these cards in whatever way we wish. New information can be added to any card, but this is obviously limited by space. Each of these ways allows us to set down some working plan of what we want to write. As the essay progresses adapt the plan as necessary.

The Planning Stage

Read the question set

It sounds obvious, but the essay must answer the question. This is integral to deciding the plan. Some people just read the question quickly and misinterpret it by mistaking a particular word for another. It is well worth taking the time to study the question carefully, making sure to analyse its complete meaning. Try to understand the problem, concept or topic. If necessary look up any words or terms that you think you may not understand. Is the question putting an emphasis on a key aspect? Further reading should lead to a greater insight into what the question requires. To make sure you are following the question, write it at the top of your screen or sheet of paper and keep it firmly in your mind. Here is an example of how to interpret a question:

Box 2.2 An Example of Interpreting an Essay Question

If you are given a question such as 'Explain the role of the cerebellum as a cause of dyslexia', you should first note that 'explain' means that you are required to give an explanation. You might consider here the evidence for the cerebellum being a cause of dyslexia; but you should also note the argument of Bishop (2002) suggesting that to the contrary, the state of the cerebellum could be a consequence of dyslexia. The second aspect to note about the question is the word 'dyslexia'. This obviously means that you are going to be writing about the subject of dyslexia, and therefore you would be wise to define this term. Finally, you note that 'the role of the cerebellum' means that you are required to give emphasis to the topic 'the cerebellum', and not to some other part of the brain, although other areas of the brain might be mentioned in the appropriate context.

Some students can get confused about their essay topic. For instance, when writing about dyslexia, it is possible to start writing about learning disabilities. However, these are different subjects. Those with learning disabilities have a general problem with learning about language, whether written or oral and about other aspects of cognition. By contrast, those with dyslexia may have a problem with reading (and perhaps spelling) but a problem with intelligence is not one of them. Problems with dyslexia might, however, be referred to as a specific learning disability.

Think carefully about the concepts that you are writing about. If you do not understand one particular writer's definition, keep hunting until you find a writer whom you understand.

Types of essay question

Most questions fit into four broad types: descriptive, evaluative, explanatory and 'compare and contrast'. Some questions can be a combination of one or more of these types.

1. The descriptive question

An example of a descriptive question might be: 'Describe Piaget's theory of cognitive development. What are its implications for teachers?' The first part of this question is obviously descriptive as it has the word 'describe' in it. Simply describe Piaget's theory of cognitive development. Thus, the descriptive type of question might include words or phrases such as 'outline', 'describe', 'sketch', 'depict', 'delineate', or 'illustrate'. These words do not all mean the same thing, so be careful to look up keywords in the dictionary to make sure you understand what they mean.

At first glance, this sort of question presents no difficulties. You simply have to cover the topic and that's that. However, one problem is there may be too much information to do this topic justice within the available word limit. Obviously, you would need to reduce the information to keep the most important parts.

Another problem is that it is might be difficult with such questions to gain high marks because they are not challenging. By contrast, if the question has the word 'discuss' in it, this is an invitation to be more critical and evaluative when answering the question. Even though it is not implied by the more neutral 'describe' type of question, try to include criticism and analysis (which are dealt with later) without making these too prominent.

2. The explanatory question

The explanatory essay allows one to get to grips with an issue or theory or even events, if a historical perspective is being taken. The explanatory question is the most common question asked of students. The question would usually include words or phrases such as 'causes', 'explain', 'account for', 'effects of', 'reasons', 'examine', 'why' and may include phrases such as 'aims of', 'sources of', and 'origins of' (see Box 2.3).

Box 2.3 Examples of Explanatory Questions

Explain how the dual-route model of reading works
What are the causes and effects of autism?
What are the reasons for conformity to wrong majority opinion when in a group pressure situation?
Account for the rise and fall of behaviourism

Be careful of the term 'account for' in this last question. In this case, it pays to think about the question. This is asking for an explanation as to why behaviourism emerged and why it later lost its popularity. It is not asking for 'an account of'. 'An account of' would be about giving a description of events, although in this particular instance an account of events would play some part in the answer.

3. The evaluative question

The evaluative essay is asking for your assessment of something. It would include words and phrases such as, 'do you agree with', 'comment on', 'evaluate', and 'elaborate the deficiencies in' (see Box 2.4).

> **Box 2.4 Examples of Evaluative Questions**
>
> Critically evaluate Freud's theory of psycho-sexual stages
> Examine gender stereotypes. Do you think they are disadvantageous to women?

If you have to tackle an evaluative question, a significant part of your answer will be about your views on the topic in question. However, be aware that this needs to be backed up at every stage, with evidence. If, for example, it is a theory that you are examining, you should pose questions such as: Has it got any internal inconsistencies?

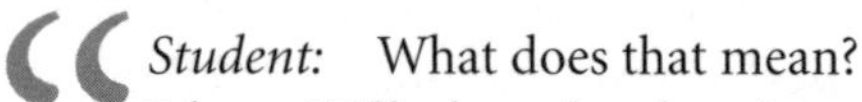

Student: What does that mean?

John: Well, does the theorist suggest something in one aspect of the theory that sits uneasily with something else within the same theory? This can arise if the theory is trying to be too eclectic by incorporating too many ideas from other theorists. To continue with the evaluative question …

Can the theory be falsified? Is it poor at predicting new scenarios? When evaluating the theory look for rival theories or explanations. For instance, if evaluating the dual-route theory of reading, point out how a connectionist model can explain some of the same phenomena.

4. The 'compare and contrast' question

This is perhaps the most challenging, but also can be potentially the most rewarding for getting high marks. Sometimes essay setters do not think out carefully beforehand about the implication of their question, and the topics being compared and contrasted may be too dissimilar to afford much in the way of comparison. In such circumstances walk away and find another topic. Unfortunately, some markers may have rather fixed views about how such a question should be tackled. Therefore, if you can, it might be as well to check with the marker first that your particular approach is acceptable. 'Compare' and 'contrast' mean, respectively, show the similarities and show the differences. Clearly, these operations cannot be undertaken simultaneously or we would rapidly get twisted into a tight knot. There are in practice at least three ways we can go:

a. Show all similarities then all differences This is the most common structure for such an essay. Thus, an essay comparing and contrasting topics A and B would be arranged as follows:

Box 2.5 An 'All Similarities Then All Differences' Structure

1. Introduction
2. Ways in which A and B are similar to one another
3. Ways in which A and B are different
4. Conclusion

b. Arrange by each aspect An equally valid structure is as follows:

Box 2.6 A Structure Arranging by Each Aspect

1. Introduction
2. Aspect 1 – compare and contrast A and B
3. Aspect 2 – compare and contrast A and B
4. Aspect 3 – compare and contrast A and B
5. And so on …
6. Conclusion

This is a more difficult kind of 'compare and contrast' essay, and probably to be avoided. This is because for each aspect you choose, you need to find a likeness and a matching contrast. Whereas, in the previous structure, one aspect might get chosen which is used as a basis for a similarity, but we do not necessarily need to go on and use that same aspect for a contrast. An illustration of this second structure is shown in Box 2.7.

Box 2.7 An Example of Planning a 'Compare and Contrast' Essay Arranged by Aspect

Suppose we had to answer a question asking us to compare and contrast how the cognitive therapist and the behavioural therapist conceptualise the treatment of anxiety. The first aspect chosen might be mental events associated with anxiety. The contrast between the two therapies is easy, as mental events are the basis of cognitive therapy but supposedly not for behavioral therapy. The cognitive therapist will be working to break down and eliminate negative automatic thoughts that are generating the state of anxiety. By contrast, the behavioural therapist would theoretically deny the importance of such mental events, when for example using systematic desensitisation. However, there could be construed to be a similarity in the treatment used by the behavioral therapist that involves relaxation and gentle acclimatisation to an anxiety-provoking stimulus. This is because the process of relaxation will involve inducing an appropriate mental state and the avoidance of certain mental events. This would then be elaborated.

c. Arranging by topic A third structure is this one.

Box 2.8 A Structure Arranged by Each Topic

1. Introduction
2. Description of Topic A
3. Description of Topic B
4. Comparisons and contrasts between A and B (optional)
5. Conclusion

In this arrangement, each topic is described in turn. An optional section compares and contrasts the two topics. This is the easiest arrangement to write. However, there is less interaction between the topics, so this structure is unlikely to gain high marks. The similarities and the differences between the topics in this arrangement are much more implicit, if the optional section is missed out. Although this third way is the easiest to write, it is not to be recommended.

These then are the major ways to tackle essay questions. You may, however, not be given an exact essay question to answer. Instead, you need to decide on your own topic.

Finding your own topic for an essay

Instead of being supplied with a set of topic questions, sometimes we may be invited to set our own question and answer within a prescribed area. This poses different challenges.

Breaking the subject down

We first need to be aware of how topics are organised. At the more general level, we could have topics such as memory, or learning, or selective attention. Within these subjects are subcategories. For example, within memory is the topic of memory for smell. This in turn can be broken into subtopics such as the time course of its decay, the effects of age, comparisons and contrasts with other modalities such as touch, its relation to emotion and so on. Thus, one helpful start is to have a look at textbooks or the web or access an encyclopaedia to find out more about the subject. Then move to topics within that subject. Thinking carefully about the organisation and the distinctions between categories and subcategories allows us to make a start on deciding what ground we want to cover.

Selecting a suitable topic

We need to generate several possible topics without too much self-censoring at this stage. Refer to the earlier section on types of essay question. Do you want to explain a topic or perhaps compare and contrast two topics?

Part of your task will be to cover the topic and produce material that is going to interest the reader – and yourself. One way to do this is to 'follow the fire engines' and try to find one of the 'fires' of controversy within psychology. These might be found by looking at book review sections, scanning more popular journals (e.g. *Psychology Today*), or scanning titles of papers in academic journals. We then need to narrow down our choice of topic.

Essays that are too general and try to cover too much in the available space are unsatisfying to write and ultimately to read. It can be a mistake to think the best essays cover the most ground. Conversely, if we decide on too narrow a field it may not be interesting.

Other aspects to consider in finding a suitable topic include: Are there enough resources available in your library, or available in computer searches, to do this topic justice? Is the subject going to be too easy or too difficult? An easy subject is not challenging. Alternatively, a difficult subject may be too demanding within a tight schedule. You need to steer the moderate course.

Interacting between incoming evidence and the plan

Collecting information should be an iterative or recursive process. We think about the essay question, decide on the likely main topics, consult the sources, write, readjust what we cover within these topics and then go back to further sources. This process can go back and forth as our knowledge becomes more refined, so do not expect the structure to remain static. Some people carry around a notebook or an electronic notebook and make notes as ideas arise. This notebook could also have a 'to be done' list of what is needed to achieve the various goals working towards completion. As the writer progresses, each is ticked off. Thus, it is useful to devise a tentative plan of the sequence of main topics early on.

> “*Student:* My approach is usually just to start writing. This seems to generate new ideas and gradually my essay gets written.
>
> *John:* That method certainly works, particularly if it gets you writing. Eventually though, some degree of planning and reorganisation will be required. Certainly, the process of writing makes you more creative and you can always keep adjusting the plan during writing. An advantage of a plan is that it can steer you back on course. A difficulty with 'just writing' is that you can spend too much time and effort in one area that is a bit too 'off track'; however, this is only a minor problem compared to the great advantages this approach can bring.
>
> Whichever method you choose, it is a good idea to begin writing as soon as possible, as the writing process enables you to engage creatively with the subject matter. You don't have to be 'ready' before you can start writing. Just write what seems at the time the best place to start writing.”

Paragraphing and Planning the Essay Structure

Sometimes I have come across an essay in which a new paragraph starts neatly every four or five lines, irrespective of content. Occasionally in the past, I have had an essay that had no paragraphs at all. I know in such circumstances that

I am reading the work of someone who has not understood the idea of a paragraph. A paragraph contains a complete topic and probably therein is one of the misunderstandings. What is a topic?

“*Student:* Yes, what do you mean by a topic? How will I know what it is if it hits me in the eye?

John: Well it wouldn't hurt you very much as it's an abstract concept. What I mean is that each paragraph you write should boil down into a nutshell.

Student: You can't boil down nutshells.

John: You're right – sorry about the mixed metaphor. However, to illustrate, try this for an exercise. Find a book in psychology and pick at random any paragraph and see if you can summarise it into one topic or idea. If the writer is any good, each paragraph should have a kernel. If it has two or more topics in the same paragraph, then perhaps the writer should have broken it down into further paragraphs. This is not to be confused with a paragraph containing subtopics around one over-riding topic. That would be perfectly acceptable. To continue ...”

How general or specific does a paragraph have to be?

“*Student:* I can divide my 1000-word essay into 50 topics, so why can't I have 50 paragraphs?

John: Well you could, but ask yourself: Would it be enjoyable to read or would it be dull? Would it not lack continuity? Now stop interrupting quite so much and let me continue ...”

When planning our essay we should organise it into broad topics and assign each to a paragraph. Each paragraph should have at the beginning a topic sentence that describes the content of that paragraph in general terms. Occasionally this topic sentence can be close to the beginning or even at the end; but do this carefully. We are getting ahead of ourselves, as first we need to examine the introductory paragraph of the essay.

“*Student:* Do I really need to have a topic sentence at the beginning of all my paragraphs? I've had a quick look at what some psychologists have written and they don't appear to do this very consistently.

John: This is true. Nevertheless, my aim here is to help you to develop a good writing style. Therefore, it does no harm in your early stages to aim to construct topic sentences consistently before your paragraphs. As you progress, you'll find that they are not always necessary; but topic sentences definitely make things easier for the reader. Perhaps too much of a good thing can lead to monotony in the long run. You'll have to judge this for yourself. ”

The introductory paragraph

Some essays I mark do not begin with an introductory paragraph; instead, the writer wades straight into the topic. Occasionally the introductory paragraph is deep into the essay. This may be because the writer wants to begin with an attention grabber. This involves introducing something unusual about the topic that will help attract the reader's curiosity and get them reading our essay. Some writers then get sidetracked for a few paragraphs.

Journalists often start with attention grabbers, beginning perhaps with an ambiguous title. The material is organised in order of sensationalism, with each sentence getting successively more boring. It may end perhaps with the ages of the participants. There is nothing wrong with this way of starting the essay, but it is not to everybody's taste. Be warned: the reader of a psychology essay is expecting an introduction near to the beginning.

The introductory paragraph needs to be a clear, but limited, statement about the content of the essay. Expanding this term 'limited' in the previous sentence, you should not give away too much information at this early stage. This is the point to whet appetites. It is also a suitable place to show that you understand the question and so you should define key terms. Finally, do not make the mistake of being too general in the opening statements. Keep to the confines of the area of the question.

The topic sentence and the rest of the paragraph

The introduction to our essay normally would begin with a general introductory sentence that is about the subject of the essay. The rest of the paragraph consists of sentences that are relevant to this opening general sentence. Immediately at the end of the introductory paragraph, a transition into the first topic would be useful. This can be by the final sentence, or by the first sentence of the second paragraph, or it may just be a word or phrase. A transition sentence helps the reader move easily into our next paragraph.

The following paragraphs

In the paragraph immediately after the introduction, we have now started the first main topic of the essay and need another topic sentence. This topic sentence should give the reader an idea of the direction of the paragraph. It is a statement in general terms about the topic covered in the paragraph. The following sentences will be related to the topic sentence and subordinate to it.

Box 2.9 An Example Topic Sentence

As an example of a topic sentence, if we are going to cover sleep deprivation, we could open with: 'We can do without sleep for a surprising length of time. However, sleep deprivation will eventually have some psychological consequences.'

Some students fail to have any topic sentence in their paragraphs. Occasionally a student starts nearly every paragraph in this way: 'Smith (2003) found that . . .', followed by a dry description of some experiment and the finding. Almost without pausing for breath, this is followed by the next paragraph: 'Jones (1998) found that . . .'. It goes depressingly on. Without the topic sentence, there is no sense of direction, less form and no continuity.

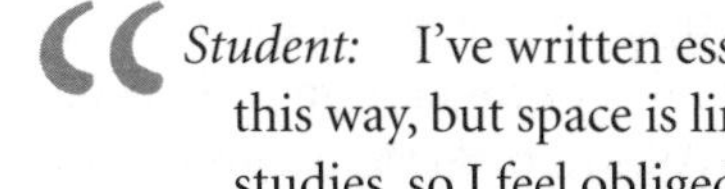

Student: I've written essays in the past that cover a lot of studies in this way, but space is limited. The essay setter has referred to these studies, so I feel obliged to put them all in. There's no space left for this 'analysis'.

John: In my experience, students who get high marks often seem more willing to take a greater risk, or at least are more self-confident. In this case, instead of including all the 'essential' studies, they might be more selective in order that they can incorporate newer or better material and also so that they can include their own interpretations and criticisms.

When does a new paragraph begin?

No one likes to read a solid bank of text. It is much more pleasant to the eye if there is reasonably frequent paragraphing. This means working with enough topics to avoid solid pages of text without paragraphs.

Starting a new paragraph is useful for providing the opportunity to cover a new important point. (This allows their importance to be emphasised by putting them near the beginning or end of a paragraph). New paragraphs also give the chance to emphasise a contrast or a change in time or place. Our essay will then continue with further paragraphs and their topic sentences until the conclusion.

“*Student:* You talk about emphasising points by their placement in a paragraph. **But why can't I just use bold type to make my important points**?

John: The American Psychological Association (APA) style guide is the basis for the writing style of most psychologists. This guide specifically discourages the use of the bold or italic typeface to emphasise points. Instead, provide emphasis by the way that you express yourself (e.g., 'It is particularly important to consider . . .') and you can think carefully about the placement of your important points. This is not going to make your writing less interesting.”

The conclusion

(No, I'm not ending the chapter yet, this is about essay conclusions.) This is the opportunity for us to sum up our main points within a paragraph, and to bring closure to the reader. At this point, provide some sentences reviewing the main points, avoiding the temptation for a literal restatement of our earlier topic sentences. We may want to make one or more of these statements in strong terms. We need to give a final perspective, especially if we have been writing an evaluative essay. Therefore, the best form of conclusion reviews the main points stating our thesis or theme. This is drawn from the accumulation of the previous points.

The conclusion, like the introduction, sometimes can be missing in student essays. What is the point of taking readers through a topic without giving them something to think about and go away and savour at the end? An essay without a conclusion suggests a lackadaisical approach: 'Here's the information – draw your own conclusions.'

Many psychologists believe that you should not introduce any new information within the conclusion. The introduction of a new topic at this late stage would be considered odd, but this can be a matter of judgement. For instance, if you suggested a practical implication from the research (e.g. that children should be taught phonics from an earlier age) that you had not mentioned before, this could be construed as new information. It will depend on the discretion of the marker.

An outline of the essay structure

An overview of your essay might look like the following:

Box 2.10 An Overview of an Example Essay Structure

Introduction	
Paragraph 1:	General introductory sentence Rest of sentences (including definitions) Transition statement
Main body	
Paragraph 2:	Opening topic sentence Rest of sentences Transition statement
Paragraph 3:	Opening topic sentence Rest of sentences Transition statement
Paragraph 4:	Opening topic sentence Etc.
Conclusion	
Final Paragraph:	Opening topic sentence Rest of summarising statements The conclusion constitutes the thesis of the essay

Of course, this is idealised and the final product would not be as neat as this. When the word count is tight, for instance, transitional statements may be something of a luxury. As mentioned before, not all topic sentences may be located at the beginning of the paragraph.

The Topic and the Thesis of the Essay

Either you have a question to answer or you have decided on your own question. The question, in the sense we are looking at it here, is the topic of your essay. We have already examined the kinds of topics that can be covered. However, the topic is not to be confused with the thesis or theme of the essay. The thesis, sometimes called the theme, is the heart of the argument of the essay in the course of answering the topic question. The thesis may develop at a late stage in the writing. If you are unsure what the thesis is, it can help to try writing out several different theses and then decide which one fits the best. To understand this better, consider an example of a topic and then an example of its associated thesis. Box 2.11 illustrates a topic.

Box 2.11 Topic: Is Visual Imagery Equivalent to a 'Picture in the Head' or Is It a Propositional Representation?

Defining these terms ('visual imagery' and 'propositional representation') is difficult as there is disagreement between researchers about what they mean. Roughly speaking, the term visual imagery is the experience of 'perceiving' an image in the mind's eye, whereas the term 'propositional representation' in this essay title means producing a set of statements that are representations of entities in the mind.

For example, suppose you were asked to imagine your neighbour's cat. This might on the one hand evoke a vague internal visual experience of the image of a cat. However, from another perspective what might be happening is the construction of a configuration of neural firing (equivalent to the construction of propositional statements) that evokes the same experience. Of course, both events might be happening.

Most people can relate to having the experience of mental imagery. However, is that experience better understood as being analogous to a 'computer program' in the brain consisting of numerous statements that generate a 'picture' similar to what might be seen on a computer screen?

When we write about this topic, our thesis might emerge as follows.

Box 2.12 Thesis

There is a controversy about the nature of imagery, but the resolution could be that the processes involved in mental imagery are very similar to the processes that are involved in visual perception.

In the example above the topic is a controversy about the nature of visual imagery. The essay would run through the major arguments of this controversy, but in finishing this argument, the thesis will be the culmination of the points made in the conclusion. Thus in answering the topic question, you have produced your statement of your thesis. This thesis represents your own analysis of the question. The thesis or central argument might be expressed in much more detail than shown in Box 2.12. In good novels, authors have a story to tell, but at the same time, the reader should come away with a message or theme. One example of a theme, taken from a novel I've just read, is that sudden success brings temptations and false friends. However, if that success suddenly vanishes, the false friends also disappear and one reaps the consequences of falling for those temptations. Similarly, in the non-fiction essay, the ideal is for the reader to come away with the central thesis.

Putting Yourself into Your Writing

It is not your job as an essay writer just to be a pure information gatherer, fitting the relevant information together like a jigsaw into a neatly structured essay. It is much more. Your essay needs YOU.

Description and analysis

Following from this need to be proactive, the interaction between description and analysis is an important part of transforming the essay from a good one to an excellent one. To put it crudely, essays essentially consist of chunks of information, usually the descriptions of experiments, theories and so on. However, if they are just about this they are soulless. This is where you, and your brain in particular, are needed. Our analysis of these chunks is what provides the glue that makes the essay hang together. This is one of the most important paragraphs in this book. Keep it to the forefront of your thoughts when writing.

“*Student:* But there just isn't the space for putting in all that analysis!
John: It might be difficult, but part of this process means being more selective and excluding information that is not relevant, or being more concise about describing the chunks of information that you wish to include. In any case, I'm not implying that every chunk of information needs your evaluation, as usually there just isn't the space available, as I was going on to elaborate ...”

One limit on this idea is that it gives the impression that all these descriptions require analysis. If you tried this literally, the essay would be over-evaluative, stodgy and possibly repetitious. Also, bear in mind that providing analysis should not mean that you should be egotistical. There is no need to make statements that impose you on the reader, (e.g. 'I believe that…'). Instead, your analysis helps to provide a perspective and aids the transitions from one part to the next.

“ *Student:* How does this analysis, as described here, relate to the concept of the thesis of the essay?

John: The thesis of your essay is the core message that emerges from your essay. In one sense, it is the same as analysis, as they both require your interpretation of the essay topic. However, the theme is a special, summarising analysis of the topic. The other type of analysis is your critical appraisal, probably grounded in your thesis, which you use to provide a running perspective throughout your essay, wherever appropriate. As you can see, although analysis and theme are distinct, at the same time there is a relationship between the two as the theme can determine your critical perspective, which we now examine… ”

Perspective

Whatever topic or issue we are writing about, it is important that we develop a perspective (or viewpoint). Suppose we are writing a 'compare and contrast' essay about two topics. If the essay is lacking in viewpoint, the reader will find it dull. Instead, do we prefer one theory to another, and if so why? Can we hold this position consistently or do we recognise points that can be made for the opposing view? Obviously, we will rarely be able to take a position in which all the evidence convincingly supports our viewpoint. We have to try to resolve awkward parts of the evidence, and we should not try to sweep them under the carpet. Try to reread the essay after completion, looking at the evidence from the contrary view. This can counteract your taking on a stance that has not adequately considered the other position.

“ *Student:* Isn't there a danger in taking a perspective that the essay becomes unbalanced?

John: It could indeed lead to an unbalanced essay if the writer gives only a cursory examination of the opposing case. It will depend on the subject matter. If the evidence is overwhelmingly pointing in one direction, probably little can be said against the thesis.

However, is it worth writing an essay on this topic if this is the case? Usually, the opposing arguments can have sufficient weight to make the essay more stimulating to write. So yes, there has to be a degree of balance to give sufficient attention to the opposing view. ”

Developing an Argument in an Essay

Part of the skill in writing a good essay is to bring together the evidence in a logical sequence and in a balanced manner to arrive at the conclusion. The writer sets down piece by piece aspects of the topic. At each stage, the argument for the thesis is made with a presentation of the accompanying evidence. Then the counter-argument is presented and the evidence for that presented. Alternatively, it re-examines or reinterprets the same evidence, but from the other perspective.

These pieces of evidence need to be arranged in a logical sequence. In addition, it helps to have good connections, or transitions, between these pieces of evidence as they are described. This is what is meant by presenting information in a logical sequence.

“ *Student:* I'm sorry but I simply don't get this. Couldn't there be situations in which the topics can be presented in any old order – there is nothing logical about how they follow one from the other?

John: You're asking, I presume, if there could be a situation in which there is no intrinsic logical order in which topics could be presented. This is possible, but unlikely. I'm not saying there is only one particular order that will fit and that your task is to sit down and work it out – just like solving an anagram. However, as you develop your subtopics you will probably find that it is helpful to move their order around until you find a sequence of the description that for you makes the most sense. If you can also introduce good transitions between each subtopic and the next, you will approach what should be a logical development of the topics. ”

To achieve this logical progression it means that you have to have a good understanding of the topic and the two opposing viewpoints. For each aspect of the theory, you will need to think about how the opposing theory would deal with this same aspect. If the alternative theory is not sufficiently understood, there is a danger of making a misinterpretation.

“*Student:* Suppose I was writing about two plausible theories and as I looked at each aspect, sometimes one theory would be better and sometimes the other?

John: You like dreaming up awkward questions, don't you?

Student: That's what I'm here for! But wouldn't you agree that arriving at a perspective would be very difficult?

John: If we took your situation literally, it would be unlikely that we could reach a perspective. Interestingly, there are disputes that break out between researchers. Each takes a perspective and thinks that they are completely in the right. It might be hard for the outsider to take a perspective as there is usually good evidence for each view. However, on most occasions after you had read thoroughly about the research in the area, you would be likely to reach a viewpoint.”

The result of your argument is that you should have explained to the reader that your perspective is the better of the two. You will be much more convincing if you can show that you have examined the opposing view as thoroughly as possible. This will show that the presentation of the arguments and the evidence has been balanced.

The Editing Process and its Interaction with Writing

When do we start to edit the essay?

Editing involves assessing and changing what you have written; but when does it begin? The best principle is to edit as little as possible initially while you are writing, because it can impede the generation of ideas and development of argument. Instead concentrate on the writing in the beginning.

This means that we have started by reading and making sure we understand the question. We consult our notes from lectures and the references provided. A preliminary plan has been devised. One useful approach from here would be to write up the essay directly as the paragraphs (i.e. the topics) develop. We might hop from one topic to the next preserving their spatial order in the plan, but not necessarily completing them in the order of the plan. We should not bother too much at this stage about the best way to express something or other aspects of editing.

However, a vital part of writing is editing, so a point comes when this process has to be given full attention. Some writers delay carrying out the editing until late on. Others like to write a chunk of text and then go back and revise as they go along. Whether or not you have done any early editing, it will help your writing, if you have enough time, to go back to it a week or two later to revise it. If you have been sufficiently well organised to be able to achieve this, it will allow time for you to forget the thoughts and the mindset that you had when you originally composed the text. At this later point, you are now reading it in a mental state similar to somebody who is reading the text for the first time (that is, unless you have an excellent verbatim memory). This way you will spot errors and ambiguities more easily. If you are like me, you may find yourself asking at several points: 'What did I originally intend to write here?'

Checking spelling and grammar

Run through the spelling checker, but be aware that some spellings of words in the wrong context may escape the checker, such as homophones (e.g. here/hear). Most writers have it on all the time, so typing errors are corrected automatically (e.g. changing 'hte' to 'the') and misspelled words are highlighted. The grammar checker can also be useful and at least can alert one to long sentences.

Other checks

Some of the checks that should be made are to do with points already made: Are there an introduction, main body and conclusion? Does the essay flow with suitable transitions between sentences and between paragraphs? Is the essay interesting to read? Grammar will be dealt with in chapter 11. For example, does each sentence have a subject? The sentence 'Posted the letters.' has no subject. Do the subject and verb agree, for instance in singular versus plural? 'The postal worker post the letters' has disagreement. Is the tense of the writing consistent or is there too much alternation between past and present? You can do some extra checks. Read the essay aloud to hear how it sounds. Check also that the style is not too chatty or colloquial. As mentioned previously, one can try looking at the essay from the opposite view that one is trying to take, to see if the criticisms from one's own perspective are valid.

Now we need to check for the following aspects shown in Box 2.13.

Box 2.13 Final Aspects to Check About Your Work Before Handing It In

1. Your name or reference number. Have you put your name or reference number on, or if filling in a form to be submitted with your essay, have you answered all the questions on the form?
2. Page numbering. Have the pages been numbered?
3. Title. Have you copied it correctly?
4. Appendices. Have these been included?
5. Margins. Are the margins suitable?
6. Font. Is there a good font and font size (e.g. Times New Roman, size 12, for Microsoft Word)?
7. Line spacing. Are the lines 1.5 spaced or double spaced (depending on the required format)?
8. Word limit. Have you written the essay within the required word limit?
9. All boxes ticked? The final overarching question: have you managed to fulfil all the requirements?

Try to allow enough time to elapse before doing the final editing. Experiment to see if the paragraphs could be arranged into a better order. Check for spelling, grammar and essay structure. Check there are no colloquialisms. Finally check that your own perspective is clear.

Chapter Summary

Achieving excellence in writing needs not only hard work, but also hard work that is intelligently focused. We began by looking at the essential tools to begin the business of writing; then we looked at the main databases that can provide material for the basis of your essay. Focussed searching is probably the best way to process the information you acquire, rather than extensive note-taking over many sources, some of which may turn out to be irrelevant. This means taking notes from sources only when this information is considered directly relevant for your purposes.

We have been given the essay question and after some investigation feel reasonably confident about understanding what it involves. During this early stage, we examined the main types of essay questions that could be asked and what this entailed in order to answer them properly. Alternatively, we have had to choose our own question, basing this decision on a number of factors. We have some preliminary information about the subject and the topic and we understand the nature of the subcomponents of the topic. We are aware that we will want to develop a thesis that will emerge as the writing progresses.

During the planning stage, we have outlined the topics that are going to be covered. However, we are also aware that as we progress that this structure will probably need to be changed several times in the light of the information that is collected from published sources. The order of the topics may require further experimentation to produce the most satisfactory sequence. A key element in improving the essay is to provide an analysis of the information that is presented. This will include having a perspective, for instance, by deciding which of two competing views gives a better account of the evidence. This does not mean that the opposing view should not given sufficient consideration.

The essay needs to have a structure in the form of an introduction, a main body and a conclusion. The introduction should introduce the key subtopics of the essay and the conclusion will round off the key topics and should culminate in the statement of the thesis of the essay. It consists of a number of topics and these are arranged in as logical an order as possible with appropriate transitions between them. Another aspect is that these topics are each arranged within one or more paragraphs. These paragraphs normally begin with topic sentences to guide the reader on the content of each paragraph.

The editing process is a key element to improving the essay. It is probably better not to try to edit during the active process of developing the first draft, because the processes of writing and editing can compete too much with each other. One is creative while the other requires being so judgemental that it may hinder progress. However, there is variation among writers, with some preferring to go back frequently over what they have written, while others wait until later. It is best to leave a few days between drafts so that you can come back to edit more thoroughly and with a fresh perspective. Various checks are suggested to improve the quality of the writing, both during the process of writing and during the editing process. There is a lot to remember but over time and with a lot of practice and feedback the quality of the writing should improve considerably.

3

PRELIMINARIES TO WRITING THE LAB REPORT

Before going into detail about carrying out and writing up the lab report, dealt with in the next chapter, we need to cover some background material. This means examining the basics about hypotheses and variables, how to formulate hypotheses, ordering presentations, as well as examining effect size and power. We will also cover the ethos of psychology and ethics. Some of this material will need to be supplemented by reading an introductory statistics book, if you are just starting in psychology.

Hypotheses and Variables

Creating a hypothesis is the first step in a scientific study. Hypotheses often describe how a change along one variable (the independent variable) will affect another variable (the dependent variable). For instance, in economics an increase in interest rates usually leads, after a lag, to a reduction in the rate of inflation. In psychology, as IQ gets lower, reading skill usually becomes poorer.

A hypothesis is made testable by describing specifically how it works in terms of its underlying variables. To help this, the hypothesis needs to be clearly described and care needs to be taken in defining the associated variables. The variables are often *operationally defined*. To give a simple example, the degree of hunger in a rat can be defined in terms of the time that has lapsed before it was last fed. In some experiments psychologists use tests to measure variables. For example, a test may measure the extent of someone's depression.

Psychological tests are created beforehand by creating many test items relevant to the dimension being studied. For example, 'I often think about my past failures' could be one of a bank of items for a test on depression. Then participants are given these items. (The participants should be representative of the population if the test is going to be used appropriately in a wider context.) The analysis of the individual items forms the basis for the eventual test. To achieve this, a proportion of items are removed (e.g. half of them) because they do not satisfy certain criteria. One of these is that each item should correlate with the overall score for all the items. There is no point having items within a test that have little or no correlation with what the test is supposed to be measuring overall.

Criteria used for evaluating tests are reliability and validity. An example of reliability is that the test should be reasonably consistent in performance if given on two separate occasions. For instance, a test of depression should be able to pick out roughly the same people with problems of depression in two successive testing sessions. Validity, as the name suggests, is examining the validity, or soundness, of the test. For example, does it produce the same findings as other tests designed for this purpose? Do the items of the test intuitively measure what we would expect for this particular test? This second aspect is called *face validity*.

We are examining hypotheses in more detail throughout this chapter, but as far as this part is concerned, you have to consider the variables used in the experiment carefully. This also means that when writing about these variables you need to reassure the reader that your measurement of these variables is sufficiently effective. For example, if describing a test of happiness, you need to provide information on its reliability and validity. Always do this – there are no exceptions.

Hypotheses, Theories, Models and Laws

A hypothesis can be an explanation of a phenomenon (e.g. 'the information in the memory store rapidly decays …') or it can be a description of the likely outcome of an experiment (e.g. '… an inverse relationship between level of frustration and self-rated happiness was predicted'). In everyday use it implies a tentative aspect: it is only a suggested explanation. However, as far as scientists are concerned, this does not in the least reduce the status of the hypothesis. Hypotheses are the building blocks for developing their science.

Sometimes hypotheses are classified further. One such classification is based on an assumption of statistics: the *null hypothesis* and *alternative hypothesis*. A null hypothesis states that no difference between two conditions is expected. The alternative hypothesis, as its name implies, is expecting the opposite: a statistically significant difference between the two conditions. The example in Box 3.1 explains this further.

Box 3.1 The Distinction Between the Null and Alternative Hypotheses

Whenever we do an experiment we are taking a sample of participants and taking a sample of measurements. Suppose that we make two lists of words. One consists of emotive or so-called vulgar words (e.g. 'bottom') and the other is a set of normal words, matched in word frequency. We then present these randomly and measure the reaction times to say the words.

In this experiment the null hypothesis would be that there will be no difference in reaction time between the normal and emotive words. Statistically this means that any differences between the reaction times would be just random. So even if there were a difference between the averages or means of these two groups of words, this difference would just be because of error. The alternative hypothesis is that there is a real difference between the two word sets. The two hypotheses are set up against each other and only one can win.

The normal criterion for deciding which is correct is the 5 per cent chance level. If the difference between the means could only have happened on average once in 20 experiments (i.e. 5 per cent of the time), then we conclude that there is a statistically significant difference. The alternative hypothesis is supported and the null hypothesis is correspondingly falsified.

Some instructors like students to write up their hypotheses in terms of the null and alternative hypotheses. Perhaps this is because they believe that making this explicit for students helps them to understand the underlying theory behind many statistical tests. By contrast, experiments that are published rarely do this. So unless directed otherwise, it would be better, referring now to Box 3.1, to propose the experimental hypothesis that there should be a significant difference between emotive and normal words. You may also wish to go further than this and predict the direction of this difference. Thus we could write: '... emotive words should take significantly longer to process than normal words'.

Let us move on to theories and models and start with the idea of the theory. Theories are broader generalisations than hypotheses, but are nevertheless just as tentative. However, the concept of the properties of hypotheses and theories can vary according to different theorists and philosophers. The theory might consist of several statements that try to describe the interrelationships among some concepts. These concepts in turn describe processes or situations that are either directly observable or unobservable (i.e. hypothetical). Theories vary in the scope of what they can explain, from general statements to something that is specific. This should become clearer by looking at an example of a theory, as shown in Box 3.2.

Box 3.2 An Example of a Theory

Seligman (1975) proposed a theory of learned helplessness that can be expressed in three main statements:

1. The first condition is for a person (or an animal) to be in circumstances in which whatever occurred was not influenced by their own behaviour.
2. Because of being in this first condition, an expectation is induced in this person that their own behaviour will not affect these circumstances.
3. Finally, this expectation causes psychological problems which in turn make that person feel like that they do not have control over their circumstances.

A model is more specific than a theory and can be more complex in its detail. The parts of a model might be mathematically defined in relation to one another, or the model may be a complex computer simulation. The model may have started life as a theory with a simple formulation. Having survived the first few experimental onslaughts it became a 'working model' awaiting further work and then it changed into a more sophisticated form.

The idea of a model has several connotations to the lay-person including the architectural idea of some small-scale construction to represent something larger. This can be a good analogy for a model as used in science – the idea of something that can be represented. However, in science the model can be less tangible or easy to visualise. Although a model may be complex, in another sense it may also be a simplification of a seemingly confusing array of data.

Both models and theories may disintegrate under the weight of contradictory experimental evidence at some later point. Their demise could have a dramatic reaction in the scientific world.

Eventually theories can turn into laws. This means the work on this theory has been verified to a great extent. Perhaps it is funny that psychologists in the late 19th and early 20th century had a tendency to write about their 'laws' after hardly any experimentation. However, in psychology this rarely happens now. Back then this tendency to make laws would have been partly because theirs was a developing science and so, politically, psychologists wanted to show their scientific credentials.

"*Student:* I'm still a bit confused about how all this relates to explaining *why* variables interrelate in the way they do, as compared with describing *how* they interrelate. You mentioned that hypotheses can do both. What about theories and models?

John: It's useful whenever looking at someone's hypothesis or theory to try to understand if it is just describing *how* concepts or variables are related versus *why* these relate together. Take Seligman's theory described in Box 3.2. At one level it is explaining how the mechanism for inducing learned helplessness is produced. So that ticks the descriptive box – it provides an insight into how learned helplessness works. Seligman's theory can also be considered explanatory, as learned helplessness can help to explain how depression can occur. Finally, to answer your question, theories and hypotheses can cover description or explanation or both. Models, on the other hand, tend to work only descriptively."

Formulating Hypotheses for Yourself

The psychologist develops hypotheses, tests them with an experiment and then analyses the results of the experiment by a statistical analysis. To make sense of these results the writer needs to interpret what the results mean in terms of the hypotheses that have been formulated. The results are not obvious; instead they need explanation. In this section we examine the business of developing those hypotheses. So far we have looked at other people's hypotheses, but when writing your own report you obviously have to put forward your own hypotheses. Let us examine the case of a student who started off by wondering why there are variations in people's body images.

Kim did not have a detailed knowledge of her area, nor did she have a particular perspective to begin with. She found by a computer search a test that measures body image, but wondered if dissatisfaction with one's own body image is related to personality. For example, perhaps more neurotic people worry more about their body image? She also wondered what the psychological effect of changing one's body image would be. For example, she thought about persuading people with a poor body image to undergo some intervention treatment. She would then test their attitudes to their body image.

Whatever you want to explore, try writing out a statement about how the experiment is going to turn out. In this case Kim might have written: 'I am expecting that those who are more neurotic are more likely to be dissatisfied with their body image.' In doing so, she has essentially written her hypothesis. This is a specific hypothesis as it is relating directly to the variables involved in the experiment. It is not pitched at a more theoretical level. For example, it is not addressing the issue of why there should be this connection.

Working out your hypotheses should come easily. If not, try discussing the problem with one or two friends. Just explaining what you are trying to achieve with someone else should make it clear what the expectations are for the experiment. In Box 3.3 is a scenario of Kim thinking aloud about her experiment before she even starts it. Note that the account below includes the hypotheses, but it also covers more experimental detail and weighing up possible pitfalls:

Box 3.3 A Rough Outline of an Idea for a Study

Suppose I did an experiment in which I gave a number of participants a questionnaire on their satisfaction with their body image, a test of their

(cont'd)

Box 3.3 *(cont'd)*

neuroticism and a test measuring their general self-worth (excluding opinions of their body). I will also measure their height and weight. I will take a photograph of their entire (clothed) bodies and will subsequently blur out facial features as I don't want these to influence outcome. I will then get a small group of raters to rate all my photographs for body image or shape (ignoring clothing), perhaps on a few dimensions (e.g. athleticism, maleness vs. femininity) to include attractiveness of their body.

In the next phase, I will enter for analysis all the final scores on the body image questionnaire and the rated attractiveness for each participant based on their photos. I will examine the difference between these two measures. (To be technical, both measures would be converted to z scores before being subtracted from each other.) I will rank these scores, so that at the top would be the individual with the greatest disparity between satisfaction with body image and rated body attractiveness by others. In other words, this individual hates his or her body, but according to others, it is relatively attractive. I will choose the top quarter of this group for further testing. It would be a good part of the design to have a control group, which could be the bottom quarter where there is the least disparity.

I will show both groups, perhaps a week after the original testing, how they were rated by their disparity between their body image self-ratings and their actual ratings in a graphic form. They will also inspect themselves in a full-length mirror. Afterwards I will test them again for their body image and all the previous measures. I'm expecting (even hoping) for several outcomes:

1. By doing this the low-esteem group will have improved images of their body. An improvement in the other group would not be expected. Because one is showing the other group in this second part that they have an expected level of satisfaction approximately equal to their body image.
2. The estimation of the low-esteem group of their general self-worth might improve.
3. There could be a relationship between neuroticism and a low estimate of body image.

Box 3.3 (*cont'd*)

One problem with (1) and (2) is that even if I do get an improvement in the low-esteem group, I suspect that this may be just because they want to somehow please me. A further risk with the experiment is that the disparity used for the basis of ranking and for deciding group membership may in practice be very small.

The expectations (hypotheses) are laid out towards the end of this description. This is a feasible experiment, except that it is a bit ambitious and perhaps too complicated for a student project. Participants are shown the disparity between their own body image and objective ratings by others of their body. The student is expecting that this treatment will lead to an improvement in self-image. The student is also aware that even if the hypothesis is confirmed, this result may have been because of the participant wishing to please the experimenter (i.e. due to the demand characteristics of the study). Another problem is that a disparity between ratings of self and ratings by others may not happen. However, these concerns do not need to be aired in the introduction.

Incidentally a further problem not mentioned in this scenario is 'regression to the mean' effects. This simply means that if you select a group of people based on a test, then test them again on the same test, there is a statistical tendency to go back to the mean. So if selecting a group of people chosen because they have a poor body image, when they are retested they will tend to rate their body image as slightly better than before, on average.

Experimental Controls

An important aspect of planning your experiment is a careful consideration of the experimental controls you are going to use. For instance, you may decide that you want an experimental group who will experience some intervention. There will also be a matching control group who have an equivalent intervention, but one designed to be neutral. For example, an experiment examining caffeine effects compares performance of an experimental group given caffeine dissolved in orange juice versus a control group who are also given orange juice but without the added caffeine. Performance on a psychological task is then compared. In this situation the intervention (drinking orange juice) is the same experience for everyone. They are all told that there is a 50 per cent chance they will be getting caffeine in their drink. They may be asked after the experiment is over to assess whether they thought they had been given caffeine.

Another control is to do with the counterbalancing, or pseudo-randomisation, of the stimuli. Counterbalancing the order of the participants who were assigned to different conditions would also be necessary. Randomisation is always a worthwhile objective, but may be awkward to achieve if the experiment is not controlled by a computer.

“*Student:* I want to give my participants about five small questionnaires for my project. I'll bundle them together, and then get them printed off and stapled. It would be a huge effort to have these arranged in different orders.

John: You could do that, or better still you could arrange them into two different orders (e.g. 1, 2, 3, 4, 5 in the first order, could be 4, 5, 2, 1, and 3 in the second order) and give half the participants one order and the other half the other order.”

Many educational studies that examine some intervention (e.g. teaching letter-sounds to beginning readers) fail to assign the children randomly to their groups before the intervention, mainly because it is organisationally difficult. But if the study is being run in a lab, then this is much easier to do. Work out the randomisation before beginning testing to ensure equal numbers in each group. In a more complex design, perhaps involving more than four groups, it might be better to use a Latin square design (see Table 3.1).

“*Student:* Latin square – what's that?

John: It's a square …

Student: Yes, I've worked that much out.

John: Thanks for that – it's a bit like a solution to a Sudoku puzzle. Each column and each row in the square has each number in it exactly once. It is used to run through subsets of participants in a fixed sequence.”

There are four groups of people and four experimental conditions. The first group of participants has the four conditions in the order A, B, C then D – reading downwards; the second group has the order D, A, B then C, and so on. It is not an ideal solution, but it is one way round the problem.

Table 3.1 A Latin square for four groups

		Groups			
		1	**2**	**3**	**4**
Conditions	**A**	1	2	3	4
	B	2	3	4	1
	C	3	4	1	2
	D	4	1	2	3

The design may not involve different groups of participants, but they still need some counterbalancing. For instance, suppose that all the participants had to go through an imagining condition and a condition that involved verbal recall. This would need to be counterbalanced so that half received the imagining condition followed by the verbal recall, while the other half would have the reverse order. Thus whatever the counterbalancing, this needs to be reported.

Effect Size, Sample Size and Statistical Power

A description of how to calculate and interpret statistical tests is beyond the scope of this book. However, we will briefly look here at dealing with effect size in the statistical analysis. You may need to read this bit with the help of an introductory statistics book. When you have computed some statistics on your experimental results it is important to examine the effect size of what you have found as it gives another dimension to the findings.

In essence, an effect size is the size of an effect measured in units of variability. Specifically, we can measure variability by standard deviation and we can measure the separation of two averages (or means) by this same standard deviation. For example, an effect size of 1.5 indicates that there is a separation between two means of 1.5 units of standard deviation. To take our emotive words experiment, let us suppose that we had found the results shown in Table 3.2.

Table 3.2 shows that it takes longer to respond to emotive words compared with normal words (532 ms on average for one group vs. 462 ms for the other group). We can work out the effect size by calculating Cohen's *d* from this and this would give 0.981. This means the difference between the means (532–462) divided by the pooled variance of the two samples produces a difference of

Table 3.2 Means (and standard deviations) of reaction times (in ms) to normal and emotive words

Word type	*Mean*	*SD*
Normal	462	67.8
Emotive	532	74.8

nearly one standard deviation between the means. Thus the overall variability is used as a basis for measuring, or calibrating, the difference between these two sets of reaction times. Cohen (1988) proposed that we can judge the extent of this difference in relation to three points on a scale: small, medium and large, corresponding to 0.2, 0.5 and 0.8 standard deviations. So our SD of .98 is within the large category as it is over 0.8 standard deviations.

Some people occasionally try to make something of the level of significance of their results. If one gets a significant difference at the 5 per cent level there is a natural tendency to think that this is not such an important result as one that goes beyond the 1 per cent level. Although they may be right, this inference cannot be made based on the statistical test alone. This is where effect size is so important. Armed with this you can give a measure of the importance of the effect you are studying.

“*Student:* Well that sounds odd. Why can't I say anything about the level of probability of my t test?

John: I didn't quite say that. You can discuss the probability level of your test, especially if you have just missed getting significance. For example, this could be in the context of the statistical power of your test, which in turn is related to the size of your sample. A study might, for instance, report a high level of significant difference (e.g. $p < .001$), but this could be because they had tested 1000 participants. The actual effect size might be 0.13 of a standard deviation, which in Cohen's terms would be small. It all depends on context.

A standard deviation of 0.13 may be important from a medical perspective. Suppose that research found the effects of a drug had an effect size impact of 0.13. This would mean that it could save the lives of tens of thousands of people. In the psychological context it would normally be considered to be unimportant.”

All this is relevant to the statistical idea of power. It is important that an experiment has enough power to give a reasonable test for the hypothesis. Suppose an experimenter is half-hearted, or is simply unfortunate, and does not recruit enough participants. The testing will be weak and potential effects will not come out as statistically significant. On the other hand, one could be over-enthusiastic and collect an enormous sample of participants. An experimenter might, for example, conduct an experiment on the web and publicise it in a popular magazine so she gets a huge response from the public. However, because of the immensity of the sample size, even the most trivial effects become statistically significant. Furthermore, there might be an ethical concern that too many people had been put to inconvenience for too little extra gain.

As far as the question of statistical power is concerned, the experimenter wants to collect enough to test the hypothesis comfortably. A test is considered to have enough power if there is an 80 per cent or more chance of finding a difference. Your tutor will be able to give you advice about how many participants you need for your study. Alternatively, if you know a bit more about the subject you can calculate the number of participants required for your experiment using one of several available websites. For example, put 'G*Power' into Google to gain access to a free site so that you can work out the number of participants you will need.

The Ethos of Psychology

Report writing can be helped if you know something of the accepted reasoning about doing research in psychology. However, as this is not an essential first step to doing the lab report; this section could be skipped, but at the risk of making certain errors.

“*Student:* Look, I just want to get on with writing up my report. Why is this so important that you want to tell me about this first?

John: Return to this section later if you like, but it's really useful to know about the kinds of expectations that most psychologist have in mind when they do research in psychology. If you are unaware of these it won't exactly do much damage to your performance, but it could suggest to the reader that you have only a limited grasp of the subject.”

First, think of psychology as a science. This means that it is important to understand how hypotheses explain the area you want to study. For example, we can study the movements of the eyes during reading and notice certain characteristics. From these observations we can then think about explanations, or theories about why these phenomena happen. These explanations are often simplifications that can make the data more understandable, although sometimes it may not seem like it. These explanations transcend the variations and errors in the data across studies and try to come up with beautifully simple statements about the way something works. This is sometimes referred to as 'Occam's razor'.

> *Student:* Who is Occam and why isn't he or she using an electric shaver?
>
> *John:* So you've decided to read this section after all? The short answer is, because there wasn't any electricity in his day. The longer answer is a bit off-topic, but William of Ockham was an English logician and a friar living in the 14th century. He recommended *parsimony* or simplicity in theories. The 'shaving off' part was to do with the paring away of as many assumptions as possible to get down to the simplest possible explanation.

In ideal conditions, when it comes to conducting an experiment one is trying to see if a particular hypothesis is going to work. The philosopher Sir Karl Popper proposed that the purpose of the scientific effort was to falsify hypotheses. So if the hypothesis worked it should survive each experimental assault. Because of this process the hypothesis would be substantiated or supported. Conversely, if the hypothesis did not work, and if it had been tested by the properly designed experiment, it would be considered to have been falsified.

Students occasionally write that they have proved their hypothesis. If you were to do this it could make the late Sir Karl Popper turn in his grave, and you wouldn't like that to happen, would you? Hypotheses are never proven. Unlike mathematical proofs, we cannot prove anything by data collection and analysis. We can only get nearer to the 'truth'. That is, we can gradually come closer to understanding the workings of underlying processes working within the mind, brain and body. Similarly we learn how the interrelationships between people and between animals work, and so on.

Consider the point when we might have our 'Eureka!' moment and our hypothesis appears to work. We may fleetingly even be tempted to say that our hypothesis is now proven. However, we cannot predict the future, because someone more brilliant than us may come along and design an even better experiment. Perhaps this person will show that we had not previously taken something critical into account and our hypothesis will be falsified. That is the nature and fascination of science: it is always tentative.

“*Student:* OK, OK, I won’t write that I ‘proved’ the hypothesis. But surely it’s being a bit dogmatic if when I ‘falsify’ the hypothesis, I state that it is falsified. In other words that it is gone, dead as a Monty Python parrot, ‘kaput’ for good.

John: Yes, I get your point. A hypothesis falsified in one experiment isn’t necessarily dead and gone for ever. Popper’s critics have pointed out that the falsification of a hypothesis is based on probability and is therefore just as tentative as when a hypothesis is confirmed. Therefore, we can’t make such an absolute statement. It might be that this is one of those hypotheses that is not strong enough to reach significance. It may just have a weak effect size and the experiment didn’t have enough power to detect the effect. Poletiek (1996) notes that in practice psychological research rarely falsifies a hypothesis; instead, the vast majority of effort goes into the confirmation of hypotheses. To be fair to Popper, in one of his books (1959) he does acknowledge that ultimately it is the consensus among scientists that resolves the conflict between hypotheses and experimental findings.”

Popper was mindful of experiments in physics or chemistry that could produce clear-cut demonstrations that the hypothesis was not working. (Nearly everyone now agrees, for example, that the earth is not flat.) So if a hypothesis does not work it is more correct to write that: ‘... the hypothesis was not supported’. Anyway there are some instances in psychology in which some experiments cannot support a hypothesis, whereas others can. Usually over the course of research, however, this situation will become clearer.

“*Student:* Aren’t you making this out to be very simple, whereas couldn’t it be much more complicated than this? For example, are there not many theories that can explain things, but it is impossible to falsify or disprove them?

John: Yes. Sometimes these are called ‘frameworks’ as they can provide an explanation for the data. However, it would be difficult to think up an experiment that could actually falsify them. Some might argue the theory hasn't been seriously challenged because you or anyone else so far hasn't been able to think up the right experiment. So it is an arguable point. ”

When making a hypothesis, you should aim to make it an explanatory hypothesis, but do not worry if you can only manage to be descriptive. Returning to eye movements, we could just hypothesise that the eye will fixate in the middle of a word. This is just a simple observation, nothing more. It would be better to think instead of something more explanatory. For instance, we might think that there are two systems at work. One of these could be an occulomotor part that controls the direction and movement of the eyeballs in a mechanical way. The other part could be the cognitive processing of visual features during reading. Having thought about the properties of these two systems, we might design an experiment to test some aspect of this model. This particular model might turn out to be another framework model; but no matter, it can still stimulate useful experimental work.

“ *Student:* You have been talking about the ethos of psychologists – are there any other viewpoints?

John: There is a branch of philosophy concerned with the theory of knowledge called epistemology. Any research method we use involves taking a particular epistemological position. The scientific method with its use of quantitative statistics that we have just examined is psychology's main approach, but this is by no means the only one.

One example from the past was the Introspectionist approach. Its supporters, such as Wilhelm Wundt, working mainly in the 19th century, believed the best way to study human thought was experimentally. Investigators asked people what they had been thinking about during an experiment or after it was over. Many psychologists may not consider this to be a scientific approach. ”

More recently feminist psychologists have disagreed with some aspects of psychological practice. For instance, some have argued that to use terms such as *control* and *subject* (i.e. control as in a *control group* and subject as in a *participant*), which have been used in the traditional core of the discipline, are masculine and thus unsatisfactory.

Most psychological research is *quantitative*, meaning, as it says, that what is being studied can be quantified – that is, variables can be measured (e.g. in terms of reaction time, by ratings, and so on). *Qualitative* analysis is different from quantitative analysis in that it is usually text based. There is much more weight placed on what people are saying or writing, with an emphasis on the quality of the material rather than on measuring it. This material is then analysed in a different manner. This does not mean that qualitative research does not formulate hypotheses as well. The epistemology of the qualitative method is explained in more detail in chapter 5. Psychologists can use a mix of quantitative and qualitative methods, as shown in Box 3.4.

Box 3.4 An Example of a Quantitative and Qualitative Approach

In our study (Beech & Mackintosh, 2005) we were looking at gender differences in handwriting so we displayed samples of people's handwriting, one at a time on a computer. We had raters judge whether each sample was written by either a male or female and to give a rating of confidence. The computer gave feedback after each rating as to whether they were correct or not and then showed the next sample, and so on. While doing this our raters learned to tell what distinguished the two types of writer. At the end of their session they were each asked to describe these differences and they made statements such as 'the men's handwriting was messier' and 'women's handwriting can be more ornate'. This was the qualitative part of the experiment. We grouped these responses into broad headings and displayed the results in a table. It is difficult with such analyses to test any particular hypothesis; but they are useful in that they can provide fresh insights, such as forming the basis for a future questionnaire. The other part of our study, the major section, involved quantitative analysis. Here we examined whether certain psychological and physiological characteristics were associated with the degree to which their handwriting was masculine or feminine.

When getting instruction in the psychology lab you may find that different instructors have different epistemological approaches to psychology, so you need to have a flexible attitude.

Ethical Conduct

Psychological experiments are conducted under ethical guidelines and these will have been supplied by your tutor. Your tutor will also advise you on the extent to which you should mention the ethical details of your study in your write-up. Ethical aspects would be included if relevant. You may need to inform the reader of your report about how much participants knew about the experiment before they started. It would be necessary to describe the extent to which there was deception, if this was part of the design. There are several main areas that need attention during the conduct of the research:

1. Handling deception

Deception is occasionally used in psychology experiments. For instance, people are given a task to do and then afterwards unexpectedly they might be asked to recall information as part of an incidental learning paradigm. They were not warned beforehand about this. In a social conformity experiment other participants, unknown to the others, may have been coached to act in a particular way. After the experiment sometimes participants can be displeased that they have been treated in this way. Try to avoid this design if an alternative way can be found to do the same experiment.

2. Informed consent

Participants need to give consent to doing the study on the basis of sufficient information, which is referred to as 'informed consent'. This might be difficult as you will not want to affect their performance with this information. For this reason it is permissible to restrict disclosure to what is accurate enough for the participant to be sufficiently informed. In any case, more detailed information can be given in the later debriefing session. However, this disclosure should not be so restricted that you fail to tell them of anything that might potentially challenge their self-esteem or anything that involves any kind of discomfort (such as using a chin rest, having vision temporarily distorted, etc.). If there is anything such as this that is potentially difficult from an ethical view, you would need to get advice. For children or adults with limited understanding you will need to get permission from the appropriate parent, guardian or authority. Naturally, there should be no element of compulsion to get consent.

One has to be very cautious about how much to reveal as part of this process because it is so easy to affect the outcome. This is illustrated by Abrams, Eller and Bryant (2006) who deliberately gave subtly different instructions to two groups of older people (who ranged from 59 to 89 years of age). One group was told (in a 'high threat' condition) that: 'It is widely assumed that intellectual performance declines with age, so the purpose of this study is to see whether old people do perform more poorly on intellectual tasks than young people. Both older and younger people will be taking part in this research' (p.694). The less-threatening condition removed the 'intellectual tasks' part so that the purpose of the study was explained to the other group as: '... to see how people differ in their responses on different tasks. Different types of people will be taking part in this research' (p.694). As a result of these instructions the two groups produced significantly different patterns of performance.

3. Withdrawal from the study

All participants have the right to withdraw at any time and they should be told this at the beginning. They also have the right to withdraw their previous consent and in this instance all their data should be destroyed or removed.

4. Debriefing

At the end of the experiment all participants should be told about the purpose of the experiment. This is easy for an ethically neutral experiment as the purpose can be explained verbally. However, care has to be taken that the participant does not leave the experiment in a negative mental state because of the design of the experiment. We will come back to the debriefing phase later in chapter 9.

5. Confidentiality

All information about a participant is confidential. For example, data for particular individuals are published; no participant should be identifiable. Names of participants should not be in their corresponding data files.

Departments have an ethical committee to refer to that deals with all experimental designs. They consider whether each one may be problematic, particularly those using deception. Your tutor or faculty adviser will be available to discuss these matters further and provide you with more information about this.

Chapter Summary

We examined the concept of the hypothesis as a means of understanding the underlying assumptions of the scientific enterprise in psychology. Take care when you describe your hypotheses. Typically you will have done a literature review in your introduction in such a way that your hypotheses will logically emerge. We first noted there is a relationship between hypotheses and variables. The variable is a means of describing an underlying psychological dimension and manipulating or observing these variables is a means of testing hypotheses.

One aspect of the hypothesis is the distinction between the null and alternative hypotheses, which is useful for understanding the underlying basis of statistical testing. One of the defining characteristics of hypotheses, theories and models is that hypotheses are simpler whereas theories and models are more complex. Hypotheses and theories can be descriptive and explanatory. Models are more descriptive than theories and concerned with a more precise representation of the mechanism involved. Some guidance was given on how to formulate hypotheses by looking at an example of a student planning a project. As part of the planning process we examined an example in which randomisation was an essential control as part of the design.

We briefly covered effect size and statistical power. This is because it is not just important to describe the statistical test and whether it was significant; but it is also useful to know, for instance, the degree of separation between two means. This not only applies to tests of difference, but also extends to tests of association. However, you will need to consult a book on statistics to find out more.

The final part of the chapter covered the ethos of psychology as well as a description of the main aspects of ethical practice. Most of psychology takes a scientific view that we formulate hypotheses and that these should be capable of falsification. It was accepted during this discussion that sometimes it seems as if the theory is not falsifiable. I also stressed that if the experiment has gone your way and each of the hypotheses has worked, you should not decide that the hypotheses have been proved – they can only be supported. The quantitative method in statistics is not the only method of analysis in psychology. Chapter 5 covers how to write a qualitative research report.

Finally we looked at the main areas in which your experiment should be ethically conducted. You will need to find out what precise instructions on ethics are provided by your tutor. Here I advise you just to mention ethical aspects only where they might be relevant to the experimental outcome. However, the experiment would nevertheless have been performed ethically.

4

WRITING THE QUANTITATIVE LAB REPORT

This chapter deals with writing up a practical report, in other words, a report that you have been assigned to do as part of a lab class. It also covers writing reports that require statistical analyses, such as *t* tests (hence the term 'quantitative'). These are the majority of reports that are written in psychology. If you are writing a qualitative report, for instance, one analysing text in an interview, you need to refer to the next chapter. However, there is a lot of relevant information in the current chapter for the qualitative report as well. If you are doing a research project in which you need to think up your own topic, design the experiment, collect data and then write it up, you will also need to read chapter 7.

One of the most helpful ways to get the ball rolling with writing a research report is to start with the easy parts, such as the Method section. Even better, try to get a rough version of the whole piece typed out in a long hard session, or over several sessions within a few days.

There are different ways you can write the report. You can plan an outline of all the various sections and then write, or you can use a 'headlights' approach in which you plan just a little way ahead and then get writing. (Just like night driving – looking just as far ahead as what is in the headlights.) If you use 'messy writing' – by which I mean, you lock out the editor in your head that tells you sometimes that you are writing rubbish – you have a good chance of getting a rough draft done quickly. This will also create ideas for you along the way. Then go back and edit. But keep in mind that you want a report that has a unity with the parts nicely interrelated and connecting to the hypotheses – the nub of the paper.

The Title

The title is important for the published paper as it is the first way of attracting the reader. It is also an important element of your lab report. It needs to encapsulate the central concern of the paper as concisely as possible. Often titles will give the independent and dependent variables, such as 'The role of episodic structure and of story length in children's recall of simple stories'. Occasionally they may be in the form of a question at a more theoretical level, such as 'Consistency based compliance: When and why do children become vulnerable?' Avoid titles that do not give enough information, such as 'The effects of age and fitness' or 'An investigation into prosocial behaviours'. Try to be as concise as possible. As a rough guide, if your title is over 25 words in length, this is probably getting too long.

Method

The easiest place to start, as just mentioned, is with the Method section. This part is much like keeping a diary. Recount all the activities that were needed during the experiment. Part of getting the method right is to make sure to put information in the right subsection. Do not, for instance, put a description of a questionnaire in the Apparatus subsection instead of in the Materials part.

Divide the method into the following subsections (some of which are arbitrary and may be in a different order to that provided by your tutor or lecturer):

1. Participants;
2. Apparatus and Materials;
3. Design; and
4. Procedure.

Participants

Selecting participants

Before we get into the writing involved for this subsection, it is useful to consider the planning stage when we have to decide:

1. How many participants will I need?
2. What population will I select these from?
3. How will I get these participants? (This may be supplemented with: How will I select them?)

The question of how many participants to use is related to the statistical notion of power. We have already discussed this in chapter 3 and noted that it is possible to calculate how many participants are needed based on the expected effect size. As an alternative, look at similar experiments in the field to see how many participants are normally tested.

Usually student experiments are based on other students, either people in the same class, or from a participant pool based on students on the course, or similar courses. Students have been in the educational system longer than normal and because of their current experiences are not representative of the general population. In other words, they are a biased sample. This means that findings of research based on students may be limited when generalising to the national population.

“*Student:* Of course I know this, but what, if anything, should I do about it?

John: It depends on what you're looking at. If it is an experiment on a visual illusion, then it is reasonable to suppose the results will apply to the general population of the same age as the sample. In this case, there is no need to mention the problem of generalisation, although where you got your participants from should be mentioned. However, suppose you gave these students a test on schizophrenia to learn more about this condition, then the problem of applying your results to the population of people with schizophrenia would be discussed later in your report. Similarly, suppose you were looking at anything that is to do with cultural, linguistic or socio-economic norms. A student sample, on average, is likely to come from a more economically advantaged background and may show bias in this regard and this will need discussion.”

If you have the choice of where to get participants, naturally it is going to be tempting to look for them in places where they are most readily accessible. Conversely, it will be more difficult to find those who have a particular psychological or physical profile, such as being obese. However, it may make the study more interesting because it is not on students (no offence intended to students, but most of our psychological knowledge is based on them).

It is easy to obtain participants if there is a participant pool already set up from which you can draw as many people as you wish. There are many alternative sources that could be sampled, but we will just look at testing children. To test a group of schoolchildren you will first need to approach the head teacher of one or more schools. In my experience, the best way is to send a letter that briefly describes the research and asks whether an appointment could be made to see the head to discuss this further (see chapter 9 for further advice about letter-writing). If you manage to get an interview, this will increase your chance of getting approval to go ahead. There are other things to do before making such an approach, such as getting ethical approval. In the UK, you will also need to arrange screening for the absence of a criminal record by the police. This can be a slow process, so it needs some planning. Refer to the last part of chapter 3 on ethical conduct on getting suitable permissions (e.g. from parents) before testing.

Describing participants

Returning to the write up-of the experiment, we now examine how to write up the subsection on the participants. To help this, see Box 4.1 for a checklist of the information that needs to be included.

Box 4.1 A Checklist for Describing Participants

The subsection should include:

- the number of participants in each condition;
- participant details: gender, age, education (where relevant), area of testing (if relevant, e.g. children in school in a disadvantaged area). Other details if relevant: corrected vision, good hearing acuity, English as first language, handedness, and so on;
- details of the population they came from (e.g. 'first-year students studying psychology . . .'); and
- how they were selected and other information (e.g. What was the rate of pay, if they were paid? Was this for a course credit? Did they volunteer? Were they randomly selected?)

There may be details about the participants that may be important for explaining the results in the later discussion, so you need to have planned what information you require from them.

As stated in Box 4.1, report their ages (in years if about over 15 years in age and in years and months if younger) and their gender. So put down the mean age and the standard deviation of the age of the group. If you have the space, then the range would be useful as well (e.g. 'the range was 18 to 23 years of age'). You should report gender. For example, 'There were 23 males and 45 females who were tested and their mean ages were 19.50 years (SD = 1.23 years).' Two groups could be written up as follows: 'There were two groups of participants that were initially created by random assignment of 20 participants to each group. This resulted in mean ages of 18.57 (SD = 1.45) and 19.67 (SD = 2.3) years, for Groups 1 and 2, respectively.'

Another possibility is that you start with one group and then test them on some measure and then subdivide based on this measure. For instance: 'Participants were tested on the Blogg's Imagery Scale (BIS, Blogg *et al.*, 1967) and using the 50th percentile as the basis of the cut-off, they were then divided into two groups. These consisted of the High Imagers versus the Low Imagers, with all the Low Imagers below the 50th percentile on the BIS. The participants were split into two groups of 22 with 9 and 13 males in the Low and High Imager groups, respectively.' Then you would report the ages of the participants within each group.

How much should you reveal about the participants? If there is a tight word budget, one would give just age and gender. However, on longer projects or in qualitative reports it is better to ask participants further questions on the detail of the experiment, such as: (if it needs a certain linguistic competence) is English the participants' first language? Or (if the test needs reasonable visual acuity), do they normally wear glasses and did they wear them for the experiment? If the experimental task needs manual dexterity, ask if they have drunk alcohol in the past 24 hours and try to get an estimate of the units drunk. If there is something that may potentially affect the results, make sure to ask the participants about it.

Occasionally a participant will be inappropriate for the experiment (e.g. flagrantly not following the instructions). The preferred action would be to save conflict and just run the participant, but discard the results and report what was done. Occasionally there are people who soon refuse to do the experiment, or, for whatever reason, decide that they do not want to continue later in the experiment. If a questionnaire experiment is being run and people on the street are being asked to complete it, one should log and report the circumstances in which people were approached and the number of people who refused. Similarly if running a study in a classroom, the parents would have been asked beforehand for permission and some children might have been excluded because permission had been withheld. All these instances need to be reported.

As already mentioned, an important aspect of finding participants is the issue of sampling. It may be that particular results are found because of the way that participants were sampled. For example, questionnaire gathering may be in a rundown area of a city, which may attract a different response compared with somewhere else. Similarly the area in which schools are selected will affect the educational standard of the children being tested. This is why it is so important to specify how the sampling was achieved in this Participants subsection.

Apparatus and Materials

This is a subsection that comes after the subsection on the participants and is usually called Apparatus and Materials, but the two parts can be put into separate subsections, or if there is no apparatus, just use the heading Materials.

Apparatus

In this part give only a description of the apparatus that was used (and its layout, if relevant). Do not describe what you did with it, as this would belong to the subsection on procedure. The apparatus might be something simple such as a stopwatch, but it will still need to be noted. It may be something constructed for the experiment. Suppose we were doing an experiment in which people had to judge the weight of tins and these tins varied in weight and volume. The subsection on the apparatus would consist of a description of their dimensions and their weights. Similarly if testing on an instrument to measure galvanic skin responses, or on a computer to get reaction times, these instruments would need to be described by giving as much detail as possible. This might get technical, for example if the design needs a display to come on briefly (e.g. <20 ms), it would be important to give the refresh rate of the computer screen. If the computer is running special software, this needs to be described.

If apparatus has been used, I hope the information about it is available from your tutor or you took down details before it was packed away. The idea here is that another person somewhere else can get hold of your 56-year-old piece of junk (sorry, apparatus) and reproduce the experiment on the same piece of cranky machinery. Occasionally the apparatus may be specialised and has usually got a maker and a model identification number on it that you can report. For instance, 'a Weston tachistoscope, Model 2k' might have been used by Galileo.

Materials

A subsection on materials is invariably necessary as all experiments are going to have materials that have been presented to the participants. These can be a list of words, the description of visual stimuli, a puzzle, a standard questionnaire (i.e. one already created and in common use), a new test that has been devised by you. There are three important considerations here. First, obviously there is a need to describe these materials. Second, if the test has been made specifically for the experiment an explanation has to be given about how it was made. Third, the tests' properties need to be outlined concerning reliability and validity, as will be explained.

Description of materials

We begin with the description of tests that have already been invented. This should become clear from some examples, which include the fictitious Blogg's Imagery test referred to before. The description might start with: (a) 'The Blogg's Imagery Scale (BIS, Blogg et al., 1967) was given to all participants to measure their ability to generate visual images.' That is simple. But this might be one of several tests, so the beginning might instead be: (b) 'Several tests were given to the participants, all in the same sequence as follows: . . .' Of course, this would have been nicer if the sequence had been randomised for each participant. Then this could be followed with a list of the tests and a description of their purpose. Then the next part, (c), would follow: 'The first of these was the Blogg's Imagery Scale (BIS, Blogg et al., 1967), which described various scenes (e.g. "imagine you are looking at a full moon"). Participants were asked to rate on a 7-point scale the vividness of the image that each scene evoked.' Note that one does not just give a simple list of materials used in the experiment. Instead it is necessary to describe the materials in detail and their purpose, if this is not obvious from the description.

If the test was made specifically for the experiment

In this case explain how this test (e.g. a questionnaire on attitudes to recycling waste materials) was constructed. It may be thought that this is unnecessary if all the items were just created and then one just went ahead with the experiment. This would not necessarily impress the marker (although the fact that the experimenter had invented his or her own questionnaire could count for something). Instead the experimenter should have been a little bit more thoughtful than this. Before doing the main experiment, a larger pool of items (say 30) could have been created with a view to removing the worst ones. This experimenter would then have given these items to perhaps 20 participants. There is a statistical method that can be used that removes items one at a time depending on the extent to which Cronbach's alpha is improved. This statistic is a measure of internal reliability.

More complicated designs

The materials used may have been involved in selecting items as part of a more sophisticated design. For example, it may be that a design has a 2 × 2 manipulation of word frequency by word regularity, as shown in Table 4.1. (Note that this particular table is not in APA format and has been constructed this way for illustrative purposes.)

This table represents a 2×2 arrangement (i.e. the four blank cells in the bottom right-hand corner) with the top left cell (of the 2×2) representing words that are high in word frequency and regular in spelling. The top right cell represents words low in word frequency and regularly spelled, and so on. You might describe where you got these word frequencies from, as shown in Box 4.2:

Box 4.2 An Example of a Description of a 2×2 Design

A pool of 200 words was randomly selected from Kucera and Francis (1967) consisting of either words high in word frequency (WF; between 50 and 200 instances per million) or low frequency (equal to or below 20 words per million). Any plural words, proper nouns, words below three letters in length or above seven letters were removed to get this pool. The author and two other raters then rated each word on a 5-point scale for its degree of spelling regularity. Based on the means of these ratings 16 words were assigned for each of the 4 conditions of (1) high WF-regular, (2) low WF-regular, (3) high WF-irregular and (4) low WF-irregular, to produce 48 words in the test. Eight extra words were included to put at the beginning to allow for practice. The test items then followed in a pseudo-random order to ensure a degree of randomness, but at the same time allowing each of the four conditions to occur reasonably close together.

Table 4.1 A table of a design involving two independent variables: word frequency and spelling regularity

		Word frequency (WF)	
		high	*low*
Word regularity (WR)	regular		
	irregular		

As can be seen when the construction of the materials is more complicated, there is a need to explain carefully step by step what was done as part of the construction.

Properties of the test

Remember from our discussion of hypotheses in chapter 3 that these tests are measuring variables. In the case of the BIS, just examined, it is measuring a person's reported vividness of mental imagery. As such, readers need to have information here on the reliability and validity of these tests that have been devised by others. This will enable the reader to judge whether the test you have used is fit for the purpose of the experiment. You should find this information either in previous papers or in the original test manual. The manual should give any information on the test's reliability and validity. This could be written as: 'The test–retest reliability of the BIS is .86 and it correlates well with the XYZ test of mental imagery ($r = .89$).' This means that the test's deviser had given the BIS twice to the same respondents, perhaps separated by a week and the correlation between the two sets of scores was .86. The correlation with the XYZ test of imagery served to show the validity of the test. In this case it correlates with a well-established test of imagery (actually I lie, it is another fictitious test – but you get the idea).

Manuals can go on at length with such information, in which case be selective. Sometimes, for whatever reason, the manual is unavailable. If you have time, try a search with PsycINFO or Google and find any papers that used the test and have a look at what information they reported about the test in question. Sometimes it can be difficult or impossible to find any such information; but at least you tried.

With a self-constructed test you will need to work out the internal consistency for yourself. First enter the response of each participant on every item in the test. In this way the internal consistency can then easily be computed using SPSS, for example, to work out Cronbach's alpha.

“*Student:* If I make my own test and then test it out on some participants before I decide on my final items, surely the results of this particular analysis ought to go in the Results section, not the Method section?

John: No, not in my book (or in this book either). You don't want to clutter up your results with this detail. So you can legitimately write in the Materials subsection something like: 'The Cronbach's alpha was .86, which was calculated based on the preliminary testing and selection of the test items on 20 participants.' You might want to do a further analysis if you have space: 'In the main experiment, the Cronbach's alpha of the test was .83.' ”

Design

This subsection describes the variables, the groups and how participants were assigned to groups. The variables will be described in terms of the independent and dependent variables. For example, a study of the effects of age on speed of response would have age as the independent variable and reaction time as the dependent variable. Not all experiments have independent variables; for instance, a correlational study consists only of dependent variables. When describing the independent variables describe the different conditions, or levels. For example, this might be three levels of chronological age, so the different age ranges need to be given. Similarly, for the dependent variables the units of measurement need specifying, such as milliseconds, seconds, percentage of correct responses. If the design needs to divide participants into groups this should be described in detail. Some tutors might expect you to specify your hypotheses within this subsection. However, most would prefer that the narrow perspective is taken of just describing the design and that the rationale for doing the experiment should be placed instead in the end part of the introduction. Sometimes the subsection on design is omitted because it potentially overlaps with other subsections. For instance, most or all variables might have already been described within the Materials subsection. Similarly, the design of something like an analysis of variance can be described succinctly within the results (see Appendix 2 for an example).

Procedure

This describes what the participants did (and if relevant, what the experimenter did). It usually helps to start at the beginning and describe what took place. This will consist of describing anything that you did as an experimenter and precisely what the participants had to do. Be thorough so that everything is included that would be necessary for someone else to replicate the experiment. For example, in a social psychology experiment a 'stooge' may have been involved, so you would describe the training of the stooge and how this person was introduced to the participant. As far as responses are concerned, vocal reaction times might be examined, for example. Thus you would describe how responses were recorded and transcribed for later analysis.

Any problems that arose during the testing would be described; for example, one person might have asked to leave the experiment midway. However, the problem would be described in the appropriate subsection, so that an equipment problem would be mentioned in the Apparatus subsection. You might also mention the debriefing session immediately afterwards that explained the purpose of the experiment as part of the ethical code of practice. With more complex procedures consider using a diagram to explain clearly what is happening and if space is tight, this is an excellent way of saving on precious words. Sometimes it is difficult putting the method into these artificial separate compartments. The Procedure subsection is an area in which it is easy to make blunders, such as: 'She sat with her head on the stand and her eyes fixed to the screen.' So take care.

The description of an experiment can sometimes confuse readers. Unfortunately, if the reader is unsure about what happened, then the rest of the write-up may be difficult to comprehend.

Instructions and practice trials

We begin here with a few considerations that are not strictly relevant to the write-up process, but more relevant to running your experiment. Before

The participant's head was placed on the stand and clamped firmly in place

your experiment think about how to formulate your instructions carefully (we examine how to do this further in chapter 9). Also, when participants start, it would be good to say how much you appreciate them giving their time and effort and that you hope they will enjoy doing the experiment. In this opening stage you will tell participants that they are free to leave at any point in the experiment. When it comes to writing up the instructions, they do not need to be given literally in the report. A clear and concise outline should be enough.

After the instructions the participants need some practice trials, unless the task is simple. These can serve several purposes: (a) they allow the participants to warm up; (b) they let the occasional participant who does not understand the instructions have a second run through, if the task is complex; (c) they give time for the more nervous participants to feel more relaxed about what they are doing; and (d) if they have just been involved in one part of the experiment that needs a different type of response, then the practice trials allow them time to adjust to another task.

Occasionally the experiment might need performance to improve up to a certain criterion. For example: 'Participants were given a sequence of practice trials and were only allowed to proceed to the main experiment when they were correct on more than 80 per cent of a running sequence of the last 20 trials. On this basis three participants were excluded as they failed to reach this criterion within 100 trials.' (Or, they failed to reach the criterion before the building was closed up for the weekend.) But seriously, no matter what you do, faithfully report what you did for your practice trials. If there was any counter-balancing (see chapter 3) this needs to be described, except that the actual sequences do not need to be given.

Which section should you do next? This would be a good point to go straight to the results and continue to leave that Introduction section unwritten. This is probably what many investigators do as it gives them an immediate idea of what the findings are. An added advantage is that the Method and Results sections are less flexible in what can be removed. When you have completed these, it will help you to write the rest of the sections knowing how many words remain.

It is not necessary to follow this particular order; you might alternatively want to turn to the introduction next. If so, the entire introduction does not need to be written at this stage. It could be useful to start the planning and writing and therefore to begin clarifying your research hypothesis or hypotheses. (It might also be useful to chase up references earlier rather than later.)

Student: But I thought that you are supposed to know your hypotheses as well as the justification for them (as described in the introduction) *before* you do the experiment. Then when see your results you can discuss them in the light of the hypotheses.

John: Just because you're writing up your Method and Results sections before the introduction doesn't mean that you don't already know what your hypotheses are. Knowing your hypotheses will determine how you approach the Results section. The statistical analysis of the data can't take place without the experimenter having hypotheses in mind. This is not to say that hypotheses are carved in stone. Some adjustment may be useful when the results are revealed. ”

Returning to the question of the order of writing, there may well be some experimenters who write their whole report from beginning to end in the correct order. They may even be so well organised that they have most of the introduction written before experimenting begins and never change a thing in the light of the results. However, there are many others who will have a clear idea about what they are expecting to find, but who prefer to do a thorough analysis of their Results section before getting down to the introduction.

Results

In this part we are going to cover the Results section in the context of the rationale of the Results section and the approach you should take. Results sections also have potential formatting issues such as deciding on the format to present numbers and statistical results. You need to choose whether to present data in the text, in tables or in figures, and so on. (These aspects about the best presentation of the data are examined in chapter 6.)

The following points outline the main aspects of what should go in a Results section.

Box 4.3 A Checklist of What Should Go in the Results Section

- This section is a summary of the statistical results of your experiment.
- This is not the place to discuss in any way the results. The Results section does not refer to the experimental hypotheses and does not interpret the findings – this will come later.

(*cont'd*)

Box 4.3 *(cont'd)*

- Report everything relevant to your hypotheses and then anything else (within reason) of interest.
- Always give descriptive statistics of variables in terms of measures of central tendency (means, medians or modes; I would advise just giving the means in most cases) and variance (standard deviation normally). A summary table is generally used for this purpose.
- Other statistical analyses (statistical tests of difference, association, or trend) need to be described. For each analysis the following needs to be included:

  1. the name of the test (e.g. *t* test);
  2. the obtained value of the test statistic;
  3. the degrees of freedom, or number of participants, where relevant; and
  4. the significance level in terms of the p-value.

- Report if necessary whether the test was directional (e.g. one-tailed) and the direction of the result if it is significant (e.g. if a correlation is negative; if condition A was better than condition B).
- Report whether the null hypothesis was rejected (this may not be necessary, but some tutors require this). (Note: this is not to be confused with your experimental hypothesis. When performing a statistical test the null hypothesis assumes no difference between two conditions.)
- Detailed advice on figures and tables is available in chapter 6. Figures are useful for showing interactions or trends in data. Tables are more suitable for presenting numerical information that would be too cluttered if presented in the text.

The Results section should be able to stand alone so that the reader can understand what the findings were in the experiment. There should be no need for the reader to have to search for vital information in other parts of the report such as the discussion or in an appendix. This means that all the results necessary for the subsequent discussion should be in this Results section.

A useful tip when writing the Results section is to do some quick computer-generated figures of your main results to get a good visual idea of your results.

When I write Results sections I find that copying and pasting these figures into my document occasionally helps the writing; I obviously take these rough figures out later, perhaps to replace them with more professional looking versions.

Most psychologists would allow that a Results section presented on its own is going to treat the findings in the order of their importance. The writer will point out the direction of the findings and try to make clear exactly what was found. Preciseness is important so that one would not, for example, try out a 'belt and braces' approach by carrying out statistical tests that overlap each other on the same variables (e.g. by doing a correlation matrix, a multiple regression and then a factor analysis on the same variables) unless there was a good reason. Finally, remember there is more detail to come on the Results section in chapter 6.

'Results' or 'Results and Discussion'?

Psychologists put the writer in something of a straitjacket: writers are supposed to present only the results, not discuss them as well. (Because the Discussion part comes next you would not have anything to put in it, otherwise).

You could avoid this, assuming your instructor allows it, by simply merging the two and having a Results and Discussion section. If you opt to do this, present the most important findings first. This would mean addressing the hypotheses in their order of importance. Good experimenters are also aware of extraneous factors that could have affected the results. Therefore, pay attention to any variables that were introduced to serve as controls, to see if they have any bearing on the discussion. The latest APA manual suggests that you move to a Results and Discussion format if you have an experimental series.

Psychologists do not intend to make life difficult by suggesting separating Results and Discussion. It was originally motivated (I would guess) by a concern that the results should be presented neutrally to allow the reader to make up their own minds. This would then be followed by a discussion of the results in relation to the author's experimental hypotheses. There would also be a discussion of how other explanations might fit the same findings.

Introduction

The introduction gives the background research to the present study and then explains the contribution the present study is potentially going to make and why it is important. Finally, it (briefly) shows how this is going to be achieved. Box 4.4 is a list of the main points to note about writing an introduction.

Box 4.4 A Checklist of What Should Go in the Introduction

- Open with a statement of the problem or issue in general terms.
- Move from the general to the more specific by outlining the relevant background research findings and theories. Keep as close to the central issues as possible. Include analysis or commentary where relevant.
- Explain what your study is going to contribute to this research context and interest the reader in its relevance. Briefly describe how you tackled the question. Outline your results predicted by your hypothesis or hypotheses.

Thus you have moved from the general (discussion of past research) to the specific (introduction of your study).

One place to start writing the introduction might be at the end part of the introduction which is the part describing your own study. This should help the completion of the rest of this part knowing how the section is going to finish. This final section of introduction need only be one or two paragraphs. Within this you would briefly explain the problem your study examines and show in general terms how you have approached this. End by stating your hypotheses.

We looked at hypotheses in depth in the previous chapter. Do not mention these hypotheses at the very beginning of the introduction – they are only described at the very end. They need to have enough detail. For example, it is not enough for a hypothesis to suggest that a change in the independent variable will affect the dependent variable. Instead describe the nature of the expected change.

The circumstances of students writing the introduction will vary. For some, their instructors will have detailed everything that had to be covered in the experiment. For others, this is their piece of work. The enterprise may have started from a theoretical perspective and the experiment was designed to test the theory. A more likely beginning would be the student asking a question about a subject that interested them. Refer to the previous chapter to read about creating hypotheses.

Now we need to start writing the beginning part of the introduction knowing the objective (i.e. the hypotheses) that we are heading towards. As mentioned before, remember the important principle in writing: the beginning and the end are the most important parts in an enterprise. This applies to paragraphs, sections and whole papers.

The starting sentence is important on several counts: it is the beginning of a paragraph, the beginning of the Introduction section and the beginning of the paper. Thus this poor sentence has a lot resting on its shoulders. I would not recommend that you start in a low-key way with some trite off-topic remark. Instead, you could begin with a statement of the problem in general terms. For example, 'One's body image can be affected by low self-esteem. This in turn can be associated with high neuroticism...' This could be followed up with a brief statement as to why this might be so. However, you could continue with the observation that there is some doubt about whether the opening statement is true. So in the opening paragraph you could in general terms outline the problem, perhaps keeping to the theoretical level.

Having introduced the problem, there might be several ways to go; to an extent this is up to you. Beginners to writing reports at this stage can then get locked into descriptions of various experiments that are related to the topic without thinking too much about where they are going. Try not to do this. Instead think of your introduction as a means of leading your reader from the opening paragraph all the way to your specific hypotheses at the end of the introduction. Along the way you are going to explain the nature of the problem by outlining the work of others and then explaining how your particular study contributes to this work.

When reviewing other people's research you may discover that the findings of some studies are difficult to reconcile with one another. Sometimes you may come across two studies that are nearly the same in design, but (annoyingly for you) they contradict each other. But you will be able to sort out some pathway through the research literature and outline the important findings that are relevant to your research problem. Remember the importance of critical evaluation. Describe any problems with an experimental method used in the past: perhaps it needs extending in some way, or testing with a different kind of participant. There is usually something that could do with improvement.

Student: How much detail in my literature review should I cut out if I want to reduce its length?

John: It all depends on how much space you can spare and how many available studies have to be described. From the view of the reader, the best balance is to use just enough detail for the argument. A simple test is: If some detail of a piece of research could go and the thesis (or argument) is not affected, then remove that detail.

Student: A similar kind of problem when cutting back is that I have found there are a tremendous number of research papers that could be relevant to my lab report. How do I choose which studies to include?

John: Just include those that seem the most relevant to your thesis. If there are still too many, try selecting only the most recent ones. ”

You have now completed the Method, Results and Introduction. At this point you have a clear perspective, as you have described the hypotheses of the study. You are now all set for writing up the final major section.

Discussion

Assuming the Results section is separate from the Discussion, there is now a need to discuss the results in relation to the hypotheses. It obviously helps to have a good introduction that has already introduced the important findings of others that will be referred to in the discussion. So it is important in the discussion to draw direct connections with the findings that have been examined in the introduction in order to assimilate your findings with those. Here is a summary of the main aspects.

Box 4.5 What Should Go in the Discussion Section

The Discussion section is your opportunity to consider your hypotheses in conjunction with your results.

- The section begins with a summary of the extent of support for your hypotheses. Explain the way in which they are supported, or otherwise, in relation to the results.
- After this, link back to the reviewed studies of the introduction comparing the present findings with these. This needs analysis (i.e. interpretation) in which inferences are made arising from these comparisons.

Box 4.5 *(cont'd)*

- Discuss any problematic findings and future research directions.
- The conclusion in the final paragraph is a statement of the thesis, which may also include implications for further research.

In the beginning part give a summary of your hypotheses in the context of your findings. This need only be brief to provide the reader with an outline of the important parts. This is not the place to present further statistical analyses – all that should have been done in the Results section. For example, you might describe a significant difference between the experimental conditions and explain the direction. Then comment on whether this finding provided support for the hypothesis.

Discussion and interpretation of the hypothesis can be easier when a statistical difference is achieved. However, even in this case a significant difference may not be due to the manipulation of the independent variable. Can you be sure that this was not due to a confounding variable or an artifact? Furthermore, if you are in a situation in which previous research failed to find a difference compared to your finding of a difference, you should be cautious about discounting this other research. Your significant difference needs to be considered against the weight of previous evidence.

Suppose instead, there is no significant difference, not even one close to being significant. This does not necessarily mean that there is no difference, just that you have been unable to provide evidence of a difference. There is still scope for discussion. You have shown in this instance a lack of relationship between the independent and dependent variables and would draw out the implications.

Sometimes, like a wall on a demolition site that can sway and fall either way, one has a result that is teetering on the brink of being significant. This would be where the probability level lies somewhere between .05 and .10. This could be written as: '... the results approached significance' or '... were of marginal significance'. We could then go on to discuss, perhaps, how, if more participants had been tested, there might have been a greater chance of achieving statistical significance. Otherwise, flaws in the design could be pointed out. One reason for the lack of significance may have been because of the effects of outliers; however, such outliers should have been removed before analysis.

Some take the view that you should consider what comes out as statistically significant from the statistical analyses and no more. In other words, if you failed to get a significant difference between two conditions, there is not much more to discuss. My view is that if you are close to reaching statistical significance and an analysis of effect size shows that there is at least a modest effect, then this should be discussed. The experiment described in the sample report in Appendix 2 is a case in point.

> *Student:* To what extent should I be critical of my own experiment?
>
> *John:* If you get too critical the reader might wonder why you bothered doing the experiment in the first place! If you try the opposite tack and praise your experimental skill, this is going to backfire as well. One would hardly ever find writers who tear their results apart in a quality journal. When they are critical, there could be a few underlying reasons: (a) they want to deflect any critics, to show that they have also noticed these problems; (b) a reviewer or editor of the paper has insisted that they discuss certain awkward anomalies in the findings; or (c) they have genuine doubts about their own findings and want to bring it to everyone's attention. For your own write-up a combination of the first and third of these approaches is probably the best way forward. There is no use thinking that others won't see the problems with your results, so you might as well write about them and evaluate whether they seriously challenge your hypotheses. But don't let your report degenerate into a long list of woes.

The next part is concerned with relating your findings to the work of others and showing the wider implications of the findings. Do not simply state that someone's particular result does not agree with yours. Instead try to explain why this might be. Perhaps there was a difference in design or in the type of participant used, for instance. In this section also deal with unexpected outcomes in more detail.

You can end this part of the discussion by looking at the implications of the findings for further research. It would be even better if you could suggest a specific way forward. Perhaps there is an associated aspect of the hypothesis that needs to be explored, or perhaps a new variable needs to be introduced, or a different method explored? Additionally the research may have practical implications. An advantage of some discussion on the implications of the research at this point means that future directions can be mentioned briefly within the conclusion without introducing new information into the conclusion.

Conclusion

This is always the most satisfying part to write as the end is nearly in sight. Most reports do not have a Conclusion subheading. However, all should have a concluding section, which may be no more than a paragraph, as there is a need to summarise the findings and theoretical interpretations. In other words, it is a statement of your thesis. This is not an abstract. Nor does it introduce new information not previously discussed. The conclusion should not be just about the findings and their interpretation, but should look ahead to the implications.

In this final paragraph give a summary of your thesis, or central arguments. This needs to have evidence and reasoning. Leave out anything that could be just a minor distraction. There are several directions this could take; for instance, if the results were positive you would outline how support for your hypotheses was provided by the findings. You would also show how this supports and extends previous research. On the other hand, you might show how the findings did not support the hypothesis. From there you might want to argue that this was an unexpected outcome given the strength of previous research and offer an explanation as to why this happened. Alternatively, you may want to argue that these unexpected findings might be accounted for by offering an alternative hypothesis that will need to be further tested. As can be seen, there are many possibilities. The reader should be able to read this conclusion and come away with an understanding of the thesis of the paper.

At the tail-end of the conclusion the implications of the research might be outlined especially in relation to the questions the research raises for future investigations. Sometimes final statements in student reports are like this: '... more research is needed in the future'. This is vague, so try to be more specific.

Abstract

Although it comes at the beginning of the report, this is often the last section of the paper that is written. At this stage it should be easy to complete, but it does have certain conventions. It is also one of the most important parts of a paper, because when searching a research database, the only part of a paper that researchers can access initially is the abstract (or summary). All writers want their work to be read, so you would expect that these little windows into the bigger picture would be clear. How do you achieve this? Box 4.6 summarises the main parts of the abstract that need to be covered as concisely as possible:

Box 4.6 A Checklist of What Should Go in the Abstract

- Give the objectives of the research: What do you hope to achieve?
- What was the design of the study? This part may be optional.
- What methods did you use?
- What were the main results?
- What are the conclusions?

Start with a sentence or two that summarises the research problem. This can be a summary of the main hypothesis, but do not get bogged down if there are several; just go for the most important. Then describe the design and method employed. Sometimes researchers may give the number of participants (especially if they have tested more than usual) and may even mention gender if this is relevant to the orientation of the paper. The results are then described in general terms, but do not quote statistics (e.g. *t*-test values). Then give a brief conclusion based on the evidence and analysis. This would usually be giving emphasis to the theoretical implications.

Sometimes if the report has a complex structure and there is a lot to include, it might be useful to write an outline of the abstract from the beginning, to serve as a plan for the write-up. This may not be the final form of the abstract, but if it helps to integrate the writing during the write-up and help with the compiling of the eventual abstract, then it will have served its purpose well. This could be part of the 'headlights' approach to the writing mentioned earlier.

Your instructor may want you to write a structured abstract which breaks the abstract into main headings, similar to topics in Box 4.6, for example: Purpose, Design, Method, Results, and Conclusions. Hartley and Benjamin (1998) found that structured abstracts are easier to read than traditional ones. They seem like a good idea, but they appear to be catching on only slowly.

References and Appendices

How to do the layout of the References section is shown in detail in chapter 10. The appendices come at the end of the report and contain any additional information. This is normally raw data, printouts, any materials, such as text or word lists. Each section should have a clear subtitle and be referred to in the body of the report.

The Relative Length of the Different Sections

Once the Method and Results sections have been written, this should provide a good point at which to examine the word count. A rule of thumb would be that by this stage you should have used half or less than half of the total word allowance – that is, unless you have a particularly harsh word limit, in which case you may have rather less than 50 per cent available. If you have written over half of your total word count for your introduction, you probably have written far too much. Finally, your discussion is normally shorter than your introduction. If you prefer to have these guidelines in a much more concise, pseudo-code form, then see Box 4.7.

Box 4.7 Relative Lengths of Sections of a Report: A Rough Guideline

(Where '>' means more than, '<' means less than, and '>=' means equal to or more than)

(Introduction + Discussion) >= (Method + Results)
Introduction < (.5 * the rest)
Introduction > Discussion

There is not much room for adjusting the length of the Method section, so having written the method first, this gives a much better idea early on as to what flexibility you are going to have with your word length. It is always a good plan to write more than you need for the introduction, and then this gives you the luxury to be able to edit and cut back to make a better job of the final product.

The notion that the Method and Results sections should be about 50 percent of the report is arbitrary. The more complicated experiments are going to need more words in these sections, leaving less for the rest. On the other hand, a simple design would mean that you have much more available for the introduction and discussion. Table 4.2 is an example of how the report's sections could be allocated within a 2000-word limit. It is not an exact prescription.

Table 4.2 An example of the relative proportions of words allocated to the various sections of a quantitative lab report

Section	*Word count*	*Part of report*
Abstract	100	.05
Introduction	600	.30
Method	500	.25
Results	300	.15
Discussion	500	.25

Table 4.2 assumes the inclusion of the Design subsection word allocation within the Method allocation and similarly the inclusion of the Conclusion within the Discussion word allocation. It is also assumed that the References section is not included in the word count.

“*Student:* I have to write up a lab report with a tight word count. Surely in this situation the chances of getting an excellent mark are about as high as two blindfold people of very different heights winning a 3-legged race?

John: I thought *my* metaphors were bad... When there is a tight word count it can be difficult to get high marks. Suppose that you have described your Method section, included everything that is relevant and expressed yourself as succinctly as possible. Further suppose that after all you have much less than half of your word allowance to go. You have little space to show much evidence of outside reading and little space for critical evaluation of the work of others as well as of yourself. In these circumstances there are several things to do:

1. Give a crystal clear presentation of your results, especially by the use of professional-looking figures rather than tables (see chapter 6), which could cut down on words.
2. Be prepared to retain only the most important studies that are directly relevant to your report – and even here describe these only succinctly.
3. Still try to include as much critical evaluation as possible.
4. It is the editing part in particular that will help to reduce words.

If this had been your own project that you had designed you would have avoided this problem by designing a less complicated experiment.”

Exploratory Studies

We have so far covered studies that are based on either a body of experimental results that are going to be examined further or else ones testing an aspect of an established hypothesis. However, what about when there has been little or no previous research on the question you want to look at? We are referring here to the exploratory experiment. Students find them very attractive as they might uncover something new. For instance, you might construct a questionnaire looking at a new aspect to see what might happen. It is difficult to write up an introduction for such a study because you do not know what is going to happen, having not had the benefit of much previous research to guide your hypothesis. In this case try at least to find research in a related area that might suggest what to expect.

Chapter Summary

Instead of writing the report from beginning to end in the correct sequence, it might be easier to write it in the following order:

Method: (1) Participants (2) Apparatus and Materials (3) Design (4) Procedure
Results
Introduction
Discussion
Abstract

I should add that this is the order in which you would write the sections. The order they should be presented in the report is as follows:

Box 4.8 The Correct Order of the Sections of a Lab Report

Abstract
Introduction
Method: (1) Participants (2) Apparatus and Materials (3) Design (4) Procedure
Results

(cont'd)

Box 4.8 *(cont'd)*

Discussion
References
Appendices

The advantages of writing up in the order of the first list are: (1) you begin at the most straightforward part so it is easier to make a start; and (2) after the Method and Results sections are written this gives a better perspective on how much to write for the remaining sections. Remember the formula presented earlier:

(Introduction + Discussion) >= The Method + Results

This means that the sum of the introduction and the discussion are greater than or equal to the sum of the word allowance for the method and results. According to this, one should have reached less than 50 per cent of the report when the method and results are completed to allow a good quality write-up of the introduction and discussion. However, if the experimental design is too complex the Method and Results sections will consume a much higher proportion of available space, making the overall write-up difficult.

Continuing in the same order as recommended, the first section is the method, which is the story about what the experimenter did, but sometimes not in the order the writer would have wanted the story to be told. Make sure the components of this story are in the right subsection. In the Participants subsection, give just enough detail for the needs of the report. If a piece of apparatus is used, it obviously needs to be described in enough detail. Almost all Method sections have a Materials subsection. We elaborated the description that is needed.

The next part is the design and procedure. The subsection on design describes the independent and dependent variables involved in the study in detail. The Procedure subsection describes the instructions and the actions of the participants. This should show how carefully the experiment was conducted. The Results section is a straightforward stand-alone account of the analyses that were performed and the resulting findings. Special care needs to be taken at the appropriate stages to make the reader fully aware of how a particular test was undertaken (e.g. was it within or between participants? What particular variable was tested? Did it involve just a subset of participants?), and what the extent (effect size) and direction (e.g. describe what the negative correlation means) of the test showed. This is often accompanied by means and standard deviations, if not by a figure if the story is more complex. The description of the results would not include an interpretation of the results. It is enough to make it clear what was found.

The introduction sets the scene of the story and it ends by specifying the expectations of the writer in terms of the hypotheses. To get to this end point, apart from the elaboration of relevant theoretical ideas, studies and their findings from the existing research literature need to be described. This is the *general* part of the introduction. The *specific* part of the introduction follows in which you explain your own study within this context. Describe what you are going to do and describe the hypotheses. Such an introduction will form the basis for the later discussion where the major findings previously described will be mentioned once more, to compare with the current findings.

This brings us to the discussion which elaborates and interprets the findings described in the Results section in the wider frame of theoretical structure and past experimental results that were described in more detail in the introduction. The conclusion brings together the important elements of the discussion and draws a conclusion that reflects the thesis of the report. Finally the abstract takes the gist of the report and describes representative parts from all these sections in a brief and easy to understand manner. The reader of the abstract should understand why the study was done, how it was carried out, its findings and its implications for previous findings and theories.

5

WRITING THE QUALITATIVE RESEARCH REPORT

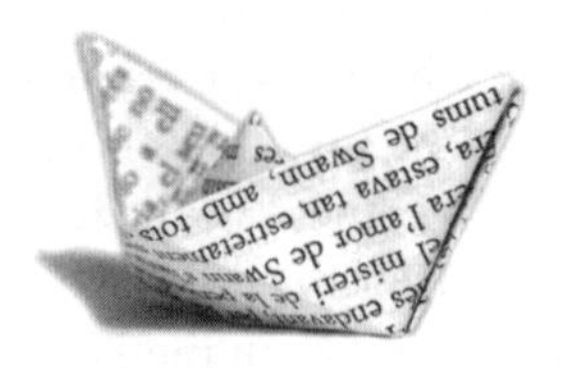

Qualitative analysis is a popular method of research with students, largely because it can often deal with personal experiences and settings that seem more relevant and useful. Qualitative analysis is different from quantitative research in several ways. Before examining qualitative analysis in detail, let us remind ourselves about what is meant by quantitative research. This involves taking measurements of variables and usually manipulating these to test hypotheses. We looked in detail at the scientific method in chapter 3. Those hypotheses that were discussed are tested by quantitative methods. I shall refer to such quantitative researchers here as 'mainstream'. This is meant to be a neutral descriptive label for the rationale and statistical methods employed by most researchers in psychology. This is in preference to using the term quantitative, which sounds and looks too similar to qualitative.

Turning to qualitative investigators, although they all have in common that they use a qualitative method, they have various philosophical (or, more accurately, epistemological) backgrounds. Such an investigator might be interested, for example, in analysing the content of a conversation between two people. In changing over to qualitative analysis, it might feel as if one is stepping out of a traditionalist world and moving into a conceptually different place. Willig (2001) felt that the mainstream approach was like following a recipe: selecting participants and statistical tests, running them in the right order, and then hoping the experiment worked. She likened the qualitative approach to an adventure, because in moving from the mechanical to the creative she had moved from recipes (that appeared to be of limited value) towards a method that was concerned with finding out more about the world.

Most qualitative researchers have a different perspective from mainstream researchers. Most notably, there are hardly any traditional statistical analyses as the analysis takes a different form. However, in case anyone thinks that this is an easy option, in some respects it can be just as difficult to conduct research, as even small projects need much painstaking work. There are computer programs available (e.g. NUD*IST; see Willig, 2001, for more information on this) that can help, but the creative, analytic side is still the responsibility of the researcher. The major theory behind qualitative analysis is grounded theory, which we shall look at briefly in the next section.

Grounded Theory

Grounded theory is essentially a method 'grounded' in the data from which new theories emerge. It was developed by the sociologists Barney Glaser and Anselm Strauss. The approach involves reading and analysing a database of text that can be derived from conversations or structured interviews. In reality, the database can be constructed from any number of possibilities, such as from observations of people interacting with one another. The analytic part involves discovering themes or categories and how they interrelate.

As part of this process each chunk of text is analysed for, among other things, its content, what is being referred to, and how the person is dealing with the situation. The investigator codes this information by labelling categories (i.e. themes) and properties (i.e. subcategories). Analysts can create code books that list the codes and their associated descriptions. They also write memos (to themselves) as the data are processed that might relate to coding, theory or to comparisons between entities. The objective is to produce from these data contextualised theories.

Since the arrival of grounded theory, there have been controversies of interpretation and there is a diversity of methods within qualitative research (e.g. see Reicher, 2000; Willig, 2001). Therefore, we are going to concentrate on just one study, by Veith, Sherman, Pellino and Yasui (2006; from now on referred to as the 'VSPY' paper). This interesting study will show how grounded theory can be used and we will examine it to show how qualitative research can be written up. You should be able to retrieve a PDF copy of this paper from the Web of Science or PsycInfo. In this way, you can refer to their paper in conjunction with reading this section of the chapter.

Just to give some background to the VSPY paper, the authors undertook a qualitative study of seven people who had left hospital after treatment for spinal cord injury (SCI), mostly caused by car accidents. The investigators examined the nature of peer-mentoring that these people had experienced in relation to other types of support that they had undergone. Peer-mentoring in this case is referring to mentoring by people who have also experienced SCI and who are now successfully living in the community. These seven people were not explicitly called participants in most of the paper, but instead referred to as 'mentees' as they had all received (and were receiving) mentoring. Now we can return to the practicalities of writing up a qualitative report.

Writing the Report Itself

An important aspect to consider if you are writing up a report employing qualitative analysis is the need to understand the epistemological perspective of your tutor. As already mentioned, there can be more variability in how people approach qualitative analysis, compared with the mainstream approach. No doubt, you will be given detailed instructions on this as well as information about the required layout for your particular report. This layout will probably be different in some respects from that shown in chapter 4 which is based on the mainstream perspective. We begin by examining the Introduction section to such a report.

Introduction

Here is a summary of a suggested format for your introduction:

Box 5.1 A Suggested Format for the Introduction

- Open with a statement of the problem or issue given in general terms.
- Outline the relevant research findings, theories and practical implications, and in the process move from the general to the specific area of investigation. This will include your interpretation of this research.
- In the final phase, explain how your particular study is going to contribute to the research context and show the reader its relevance.
- Discuss the method of analysis (e.g. grounded theory) and its appropriateness within the context of the study.
- End by providing the objectives of your investigation without giving your expectations of outcome.

The introduction to a study using the qualitative method can at first glance appear similar in construction to that described in chapter 4. There will be the transition from general descriptions and analyses towards the more specific aspects of your study in which the rationale is outlined. However, there are differences. For example, as we will shortly see, there will not be the construction of hypotheses towards the end of this section. In the VSPY study, they instead discuss objectives. A further change of emphasis, if one is using a grounded theory perspective, is that the introduction has an element of detachment from past theoretical work.

In the introduction to the VSPY study, the authors discuss, among other topics, the effectiveness of peer-mentoring in relation to the social comparison theory proposed by Thoits, Hohmann, Harvey and Fletcher (2000). This theory suggests that when people are in crisis they want to be with others who have been in a similar situation in their own lives. This is motivated by wanting to help themselves to cope better. An introduction to a qualitative report can discuss theories, empirical findings and practical implications, just like any other academic report. The difference is that this background is not normally used as the basis for bringing out expectations of outcome.

In the closing section of the introduction to the VSPY study, the authors write that they want to examine the experiences of mentees undergoing peer-mentoring using grounded theory, citing Glaser and Strauss (1967) and Strauss and Corbin (1990). This is followed by the description of three objectives which begin, respectively, with the words: 'to describe …', 'to identify …' and 'to understand …' There are no hypotheses predicting specific outcomes. (Some mainstream introductions do not do this either.)

Because the method in the VSPY study is based on grounded theory, this means that the authors are aiming to find out precisely what theory can explain this particular research environment. The theory emerges from the research, rather than the other way round. Hence, there is an element of detachment from previous research.

Method

In this section the experimenter describes exactly what was involved. Thus, it has a description of the participants, what they did, how the data were analysed and anything else that is relevant. This has three subheadings: Participants, Procedure and Data Analysis.

Participants

This subsection gives a detailed description of the participants, much like a mainstream report. The VSPY study is a useful illustration of the situation in which one might have not just participants but another relevant group as well.

In this study, the participants had mentors who were matched with them on a one-to-one basis. A table accordingly gives specific details for both mentees and mentors. This goes into more detail than would perhaps be normal in a mainstream report, but it is relevant to this particular situation. For example, marital status is important in this context as having a partner can be another form of support to compare with the experience of having a mentor. The VSPY study included information on age, gender, ethnicity, cause of injury, extent of injury, marital status, educational level, and so on. The circumstances of the selection of both mentees and mentors are outlined. This subsection also includes details of the training of the mentors by one of the investigators. It can be noted that there are relatively few participants compared with the numbers in mainstream research papers. However, this paper is close to the norm for qualitative work as there are so many data to process.

Procedure

One would normally state that grounded theory was used. You might also discuss what particular method was used. There is more than one type of application of grounded theory – but your tutor may be satisfied with you just reporting that you used grounded theory. You might possibly also be required to give a rationale for picking a particular method. Similarly, you may need to discuss issues of reflexivity. For instance, as an author you may have someone close to you who suffers from a similar condition to your participants (see Willig, 2001, for an elaboration of this point). The main part of the subsection on procedure will be providing details of how the study was carried out and providing any ethical considerations.

In the VSPY study, the mentees were given a structured interview by phone about 1 to 4 months after they had left hospital. This duration was mainly to allow time for them to adjust to their community. When they were interviewed, they had had between 1 and 4 sessions with their mentors. (Note that this particular information was not given in the Procedure subsection in the VSPY paper.) They were all asked the same open-ended questions, which are given in the appendix of the paper, and all the answers were recorded and transcribed.

Data analysis

This subsection gives a detailed description of how the data were analysed. In the VSPY study, two of the authors co-analysed the data. The recordings of the interviews had been transcribed and then each line of text studied, identifying categories and their contexts. They examined the consistency and frequency of the categories. After working separately, the coding of the two analysts was compared. There was found to be little disagreement and a consensus in these areas was easily reached.

“*Student:* I don’t quite understand how they did this analysis. Could you give an example of the identification of a category and its context in the VSPY study?

John: One of their categories, or themes, was ‘practical’. The context of this is that people with SCI during their time in hospital and soon after they leave, are trying to come to terms with the practicalities of their condition. In the paper, we read some touching descriptions related to this in the context of their mentor. These mentors had already had very similar experiences in this situation, and could provide advice and even inspiration. Thus, all instances in the transcriptions that were related to ‘practical’ within the context of mentoring and in other contexts were noted and analysed. Presumably, this particular category was developed on the basis of the analysis of the data, although it may have been considered a possibility before the analysis was begun.”

Results

Box 5.2 summarises the main aspects of this section:

Box 5.2 The Main Aspects of the Results Section

- This section is organised by categories or themes with the most important categories at the beginning. Each category is a subheading to clarify the structure.
- It is useful if the analysis can provide a flow chart of the categories and how they interrelate.
- The evidence is analysed, or interpreted, and at suitable points, samples of transcribed text are quoted to provide an illustration of a particular point.

There is a detailed figure in the VSPY paper showing a flow chart of the experience of being mentored. It shows the direct factors, namely: the mentees’

SCI, leading to their responses to their injury; from there the flow is to the mentoring strategies, and finally to their outcomes. Two indirect factors were input along the way: the mentees' context (e.g. coping style) and intervening conditions (e.g. the quality of the mentor-to-mentee match). This framework to an extent determined the structure of this section beginning with the direct factors followed by the indirect.

It is interesting to examine contrasts between the qualitative approach and the quantitative in this Results section, as this seems to be the section with the most differences. In the context of qualitative reports, quotations from transcriptions are expected and encouraged in order to illustrate your themes. Obviously, this has to be tempered by the requirements of a word limit. Therefore, try to be highly selective, choosing perhaps a couple or so per theme. After each quotation give the line number and paragraph number from the transcript, which should appear in your appendix.

Another contrast between the approaches is illustrated in the VSPY paper in that there are no statistical analyses to test any hypotheses. Of course, with only seven participants there is low statistical power in the paper, in the mainstream sense. On the other hand, on another level there is a large quantity of textual data.

One control in this qualitative analysis has been to have two people independently undertake their analyses. In this case, the paper reports that there has been little disagreement. It would have been useful to have had more transparency with a brief description of what these disagreements were. A final contrast is that in the qualitative paper an analysis or interpretation of the textual analysis in the Results section is important. The Results section of the mainstream approach does not have any such interpretation as this is given in the later Discussion section.

Discussion

The suggested key points of the Discussion section are similar to those for quantitative reports.

Box 5.3 The Main Aspects of the Discussion Section

- The Discussion section is the place to discuss the theoretical and practical ramifications of the study.
- The section begins with summarising at a general level the main theoretical findings of the study.

Box 5.3 (*cont'd*)

- In the process of doing this connect back with the research work reviewed in the introduction. There needs to be interpretation while making comparisons.
- Discuss anything problematic, any practical implications and future directions of research.
- The conclusion in the final paragraph is a statement of the thesis, which may also include implications for further research.

The VSPY study begins with a summarising paragraph that notes that the findings support in particular Thoits' (1986, 1995) theory about the substantial influence of the 'similar other' to help people cope with illness. In doing this, the paper is picking up on literature reviewed in the introduction. This is something we noted about the mainstream lab report in chapter 4 – the discussion relates back to literature that has been reviewed in the introduction. The rest of the discussion involves examining aspects that are problematic, exploring key theoretical findings and drawing out practical considerations. Their discussion has two final sections headed 'recommendations' and 'future directions'.

Student: What was the thesis of the VSPY study?

John: In a nutshell: peer-mentoring has a unique combination of supportive components that are not given by other relationships. Such programs are useful for helping adjustment after SCI.

Student: Two further questions please. First, you don't mention other aspects such as how to write the abstract and lay out the references. Second, you describe the sections here in the same order as they would appear in the report, unlike in chapter 4. Does this mean that they should be written in this order?

John: To answer the first question: The treatment in this chapter is briefer because many of the essentials of writing up a report have already been covered in chapter 4. For example, as far as the Abstract and Reference sections are concerned, the same advice applies as that given in chapter 4.

To answer the second part of your question, the order of the write-up of the sections can be the same as in the mainstream context. For example, begin with the Method and follow on with the Results section. This should give you a good idea of how much space is available to write the rest. I would further advise that regarding the relative sizes of the sections, you need to adjust these as I would expect that the Results section of a qualitative report is going to take up relatively much more space. I hope that your tutor can guide you on this. ”

Final Remarks

We have finished now with the different sections of the report, but let me make some additional closing observations about the qualitative approach. Such studies are not experimental in the sense of mainstream experiments. Therefore, do not refer to your investigation as an 'experiment'; refer to it as a 'study' instead. In the qualitative context, your tutor will probably allow you to use the personal pronoun 'I' within the text of your report, which is rarely acceptable in mainstream reports. This would be particularly appropriate if you have a reflexive section in which you reflect on your own position and viewpoint in the context of your study. In the Method part, try to give sufficiently accurate detail so that other people could do a similar type of study. Note the painstaking amount of detail given in the Method section of the VSPY study. This is despite it being a qualitative study. Unlike mainstream reports, there is not the same expectation that a study can be repeated in exactly the same way and the results accordingly replicated. This brings us to an aspect of the rationale of discussion of the results. In the qualitative approach, one does not normally make generalisations. Each study has a context with a different group of participants that is viewed as potentially not quite the same as what has been tested before. Instead, you need to deal with the specific results in the context of the setting of the study and the nature of the particular participants you studied.

Chapter Summary

Qualitative research reports are mostly based on examining textual information. For instance, this information can be transcribed from the conversations of participants during a structured interview. These data are not normally analysed by means of quantitative statistics.

We examined the rationale behind the qualitative report in terms of grounded theory. This is a method developed by sociologists Glaser and Strauss in which examination and analysis of the data generate new theories. One implication of this is that when introducing experiments, one does not propose hypotheses based on previous research. Instead, an analysis of the data produces new theories. This means that although the introduction of a qualitative report examines previous research, it does not use this research to generate expectations of outcomes as these outcomes will be determined by the data. Researchers will provide the objectives of their analyses in the final part of their introduction. This approach is in contrast to the mainstream one based on quantitative statistics, which generates hypotheses from previous research. The mainstream method then tests the experimental data against these hypotheses statistically.

The various sections (Introduction, Method, Results and Discussion) of the qualitative report were examined in relation to an example paper to illustrate the major aspects of qualitative research. Where appropriate, contrasts with the mainstream approach were made. We noted that the section with the greatest contrast to the mainstream approach was the Results section. This was because there are no statistical analyses. Instead, there is an analysis and interpretation in terms of the major categories or themes emerging from the data analysis. Quotations from transcriptions are used to back up the points being made. This can often be accompanied by a figure to illustrate the interrelationships between the categories. The final section, the Discussion, examines the major theories emerging from the data in relation to data and findings from the literature discussed in the introduction. The problems, practical implications and future research directions are also discussed in this final section.

6

PRESENTING NUMBERS, TABLES AND FIGURES

We have already covered the basics of how to write up the Results section for a quantitative analysis in chapter 4. This chapter is about the 'nuts and bolts' on how to present the statistical findings. It is about how to present numbers, construct a table and present a figure. To make this information easy to read sections of the text will be in bullet point form.

How to Present Numbers

The APA rules for writing numbers may seem to be complex at first, but close study will pay dividends. Many of these rules have developed through usage, so to protect your sanity please remember that sometimes logic does not come into some of these details! The first two subsections below are about deciding when to write a number (e.g. '2') versus when to write it in words (e.g. 'two'). The overarching rule, which unfortunately can be broken, is that for the numbers 10 and above, write the number (e.g. '12 or more errors'); but if the number is below 10 then write it in words (e.g. 'four groups').

When to express numbers in words

- **Use words for the numbers below 10** as long as they are not representing measurements:

  five of the words
  rotation of three-dimensional figure
  every three in nine cards
  numbers ending in zero were excluded

- **Avoid starting a sentence with a number**. However, if you can see no other way of writing your sentence, the number should be written (irrespective of whether the number is below 10 or higher). When the numbers 21 to 99 are written, use a hyphen where appropriate to connect the numbers. For example, you would write 'seventy-five'. When the number is over 99 do not use hyphens; for example, you would write 'one hundred and eight'.

  Twenty-four participants took part
  Thirty-nine per cent of the participants were better the second time
  Five participants were excluded

> *Student:* Writing out a number could get complicated with very large numbers.
>
> *John:* Yes it could, but trying to avoid beginning a sentence with a number by reconstructing the sentence can make matters seem even worse. The sentence might sound awkward if this is done – for instance: 'The percentage of participants taking part was 39%' sounds unnatural. Occasionally you might read: 'Of the 35 participants, 5 of them were excluded.' This particular attempt to avoid starting a sentence with a number would be regarded in some circles as awkward as the sentence is beginning with a prepositional phrase (see *prepositions* in chapter 11).

- **Use words for common fractions**. A rule of thumb would be to use words for fractions with low denominators up to five:

  half the errors
  two thirds of the females
  three fourths of the group (British equivalent: 'three quarters')

  The common fractions (i.e. fractions that occur often) for which this rule applies are as follows: a half, a third, two thirds, a quarter (or a fourth), three quarters (or three fourths), one fifth, two fifths, three fifths and four fifths. For other fractions we would probably be better using a decimal equivalent or percentage instead of a fraction (e.g. '0.17' instead of '1/6').
- **Hyphenation of common fractions**. In the examples in the previous section all the common fractions are not hyphenated because in these cases the common fraction is used as a noun. Refer to the entry *nouns* in chapter 11 where this point is elaborated.

- **Use words for numbers when describing an experiment** (and the number is below 10):

  Two thirds of the trials required a positive response
  rotation of a three-dimensional figure
  every nine trials
  five sessions

- **Use words when reporting tests:**

  two-tailed *t* test
  three-way interaction

- **Use words for ordinal numbers *first* to *ninth*.** Ordinal numbers show the relative position in a sequence. For these use words from first to ninth; however, above that use numbers.

  every third word
  ninth graders
  11th graders

When to express numbers as numbers

Unfortunately there are a few exceptions to the rule about numbers below 10 being written instead of expressed as a number. So the following rules for writing numbers as numbers cover the full range of numbers from 0 upwards.

- **Percentages, ratios, proportions, and percentiles:**

  5%, 56%
  2:3, 3:25
  4 times as many rewards (a proportion)
  .33 of the group (again a proportion)
  the 8th percentile

- **Mathematical function:**

  The resulting number was then divided by 8

- **Units of measurement**:

  each card measured 10.5 cm by 5.3 cm; 8 kg (*not* 3 cms or 8 kgs)
  the 25-ms prime
  a 2-second presentation

- **Numbers of participants** – this one seems to defy any logic, but here it is:

  5 participants (but you would write 'three raters', 'one observer')
  3 rats were placed together in the area
  6 children

- **Times and dates**:

  383 ms (Note: do not express milliseconds to one or more decimal places)
  The longest time was 1 hr 35 min
  The interview began at 3:34 p.m.
  over 6 minutes
  after 1 hour
  7 January 1978 (this is UK style; use the style of your country – e.g. 'January 7, 1978')

- **Ages** (the examples below also show the use of hyphening):

  The children were all 5 years old
  The 7- and 8-year-olds were …

- **Rating scales**:

  the first point on the 7-point scale
  the scale had 7 points
  any participant who scored 6 or more on the 10-point scale

- **Referring to pages, chapters, figures and tables**:

  page 3, chapter 5, Table 2, Figure 4, column 5, row 12

- **Straddling across the number 10 divide.** Two or more numbers that include one or more below 10 and one or more equal to or above 10 are written as numbers (e.g. '5 and 11') as long as they are in the same category (e.g. participants, stimuli). Thus the three examples below are about being within the same set of items, questions and words, respectively:

the 2nd and the 12th items
5 of the 28 questions
every 8th and 16th word

- **Straddling across the number 10 divide, but when the numbers are in different categories.** When the categories are *different* then numbers below 10 are written as words:

  there were 25 words in each of four conditions
  the second word in each of the 15 lists
  the fourth list for the 11th-grade students

- **Two numbers in juxtaposition** can be made clearer by being expressed in two contrasting forms (e.g. one as a number and the other in words):

  3 three-way interactions
  twenty-three 5-year-olds
  thirty 7-point scales

Other rules about numbers

- Use a zero before a decimal point if it is positive, but less than 1:
  0.35 s, 0.89 cm
- However, if the number cannot be greater than 1 (e.g. a correlation, level of statistical significance) then do not use a zero:
  $r(34) = -.34, p < .05$
- Roman numerals are not normally used except for specific cases:
  a Type II error
- Plurals of numbers are nearly always produced by adding –s:
  eights, the 10s (but note that 'sixes' has –es added), the 1980s
- For large numbers group every three digits (e.g. '1,345,746'); but there are exceptions:
  page 1038, 3000 Hz
  10011001 (these are binary digits)
- Report to two decimal places in the following cases: correlations, *t*, *F*, and chi-square. Significance probabilities are normally reported to two decimal places (e.g. '$p < .01$'), but some tests would be better reported to three

decimal places (e.g. Bonferroni tests). Units of measurement such as ms are sufficiently precise to be reported as integers (e.g. 'the mean was 425 ms').

Should I Use a Table, a Graph or Just Put the Data in the Text?

The APA guide gives the following rules of thumb in deciding whether to present a set of numbers in a text, as part of a table or to incorporate them into a figure.

Table 6.1
Rules for Where to Put Data According to Their Quantity

How many numbers?	What to do
<4	Present them in the text
4–20	Use a table
>20	Ideally use a graph, though this is not obligatory

Thus, if there are just a few data points (e.g. if you have only two or three means to report), you may as well just describe these in the text:

> The mean scores and standard deviations for Groups 1, 2, and 3 were 32.47 ($SD = 5.84$), 42.9 ($SD = 8.43$), and 72.22 ($SD = 12.34$), respectively.

However, do not apply the rules shown in this table too rigidly. The decision as to whether to use a table or a figure when you have more than three numbers to present may not strictly come down to quantity, but whether you have data that would look clearer shown graphically.

One advantage of using a table is that the reader is given the precise results, whereas if one were to put the same data within a figure, the exact numbers would be lost. The reader can only infer what the values are from a figure. Future researchers conducting meta-analyses of past research data obviously appreciate data that have been presented in tabular form; but this would only be a consideration if you were publishing a paper. Unfortunately the decision to produce either a table or a graph cannot be solved by simply producing both. Present either one or the other. For example, you may have a crossover interaction in an ANOVA. This would probably look good in a figure, as it can show the extent and nature of the interaction. Similarly, if there is a series of points showing an interesting trend (e.g. an inverted-U shape), this would be better presented in a figure, as in the case of a curvilinear relationship showing just five data points in Figure 6.1.

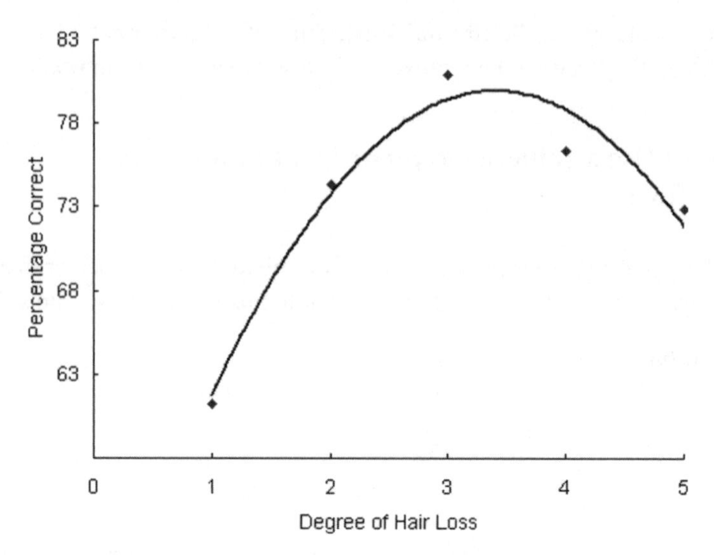

Figure 6.1 Percentage of correct mental rotations as a function of five different groups classified according to hair loss. (Source: based on data from J.R. Beech, 2001)

If on the other hand, you have a nested set of data with relatively few points in each subdivision that overall contains over 20 data points, the data might be better shown in a tabular rather than graphical form. Similarly, if the interaction in the ANOVA is not significant with perhaps weak main effects, one might be more inclined to just report the means and standard deviations in a table.

How to Present a Table

Tables are an excellent way of presenting data in an organised fashion. A simple example of this is Table 6.2. The next section has detailed instructions on how to construct this same table in Word.

Table 6.2

Means (and Standard Deviations) of Percentages Correct as a Function of Inner Versus Outer Word Parts and Word Frequency in Experiment 2

	Feature position	
Word frequency	Inner	Outer
High frequency	53.19 (26.06)	97.07 (8.10)
Low frequency	50.83 (28.43)	95.18 (10.10)

There are several aspects to note about constructing a table.

Box 6.1 Aspects to Note About a Table

- There are no vertical lines in the inner part.
- The title sits above the table.
- The title is in italics and the first letters of the main words are capitalised.
- The labels (e.g. 'High frequency') are in normal typeface and have a capitalised initial letter, but if there is a second word, it is normally in lower case.

In the text of the paper make sure that there is at least one reference to each table. Describe in this accompanying text what the results show. One does not necessarily need to go into every detail if there is a lot there. Allow the readers to hunt around for themselves. If the table is in a Results section rather than a 'Results and Discussion' section, only point out the highlights. By contrast, discuss the implications of these findings if writing within a Results and Discussion section.

If the analysis involves examining correlations, the obvious choice is to put these into a table to show a correlation matrix. Suppose there are six variables that are correlated with one another: The correlations would only be shown once. The diagonal in the matrix showing each variable correlating with itself would always be 1.00 in each cell. Because of this redundancy these values would also be excluded. We are left with just 15 correlations to show in the table (see Table 6.3).

If there were enough participants, all the correlations for the females could go in the top right above the diagonal and the corresponding correlations for the males in the matching lower left portion of the matrix. There would have to be horizontal rows at the bottom to give the means and standard deviations of the females, with the male means and standard deviations in the two right-most columns.

How to Construct a Table Using Word

Our aim here is to go through the steps needed to produce Table 6.2 using Word based on Word 2003. Note that this is available in Microsoft Office, which

Table 6.3
Intercorrelations Among the Principal Variables for all Participants (Source: based on Beech & Mackintosh, 2005)

Variable	Sex rating	Masc.	Fem.	LH	RH	Mean	SD
Sex	.667***	−.146	.406***	.655***	.634***	–	–
Sex rating of writing		−.039	.281**	.457***	.491***	3.02	.97
Masculine BSRI scale			.138	−.235*	−.197*	4.558	.701
Feminine BSRI scale				.437***	.381***	4.832	.518
Left-hand (LH) fingers					.855***	1.006	.021
Right-hand (RH) fingers						1.007	.020

$N = 120$ in all cells, *$p < 0.05$ **$p < 0.01$ ***$p < 0.001$

can be run on a Mac or a PC. (To check your version click 'Help', then access 'About Microsoft Office Word'.) Please note that there are several ways to make a table (and a graph for that matter) and I have just selected one of these.

When composing a table the items are arranged into a rectangular (or square) matrix so first we need to work out the number of rows and columns of this matrix. In Table 6.2 there are 3 columns and 4 rows. Note also that the body of the table containing the data is in the four cells in the bottom right. The rest of the table consists of labels and the top left corner is normally left blank. As an aside, the top left corner would not be left blank if there were only one variable; normally, however, one would write a description of such tables within the body of the text.

To continue with the current table, there is also a degree of nesting with 'Feature position' at the top and then 'Inner' and 'Outer' for the levels of the feature position variable. The same applies to the word frequency variable. This means that we need two rows to show these relationships. Now we are clear about what we want, we need to do the following:

- Select 'Table' from the top and select 'Insert' in the dropdown table and slide across to Table and click. To create the rows and columns choose '3' for the columns and '4' for the rows and keep the 'Fixed column width' set to 'Auto' and click 'OK'. This produces the beginning 3 by 4 matrix.
- Fill in the cells of the matrix with the information from Table 6.2 for the second to the final rows and in the top row in the rightmost cell type in

Table 6.4
An Almost Completed Table Based on Table 6.2

	Feature position	
Word frequency	Inner	Outer
High frequency	53.19 (26.06)	97.07 (8.10)
Low frequency	50.83 (28.43)	95.18 (10.10)

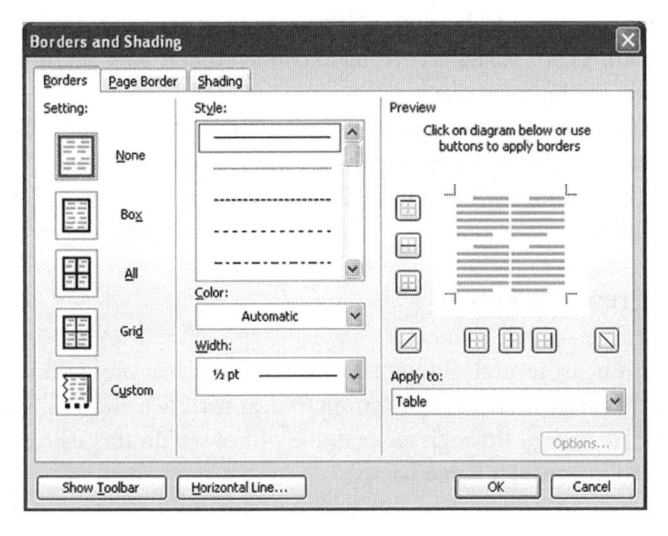

Figure 6.2 Dropdown box when Borders and Shading is selected

'Feature position'. Thus all the cells have something typed in apart from the first and second cells in the top row.

- To merge the cells in the two top right rows, highlight them by dragging the mouse cursor over them while holding down the left-hand key and then right click on the mouse. Then select 'Merge Cells' and click. This will merge the second and third cells on the top row. Centre the label 'Feature position'.
- Highlight the second and third columns including the merged cell and centre them using the centring icon on the tool bar above and your table at this stage should now look like that shown in Table 6.4.
- We now need to get rid of those vertical lines and build up the table with the required lines. First, make sure that all the cells are highlighted (i.e. scroll over them holding down the left button of the mouse). Select 'Format' from the top menu and the dropdown box looks something like Figure 6.2 when the 'Borders and Shading' tab is selected.

- Select the 'None' setting to the left to clear out all the lines. The lines on the table will be fainter and will not appear if the table is printed out at this point. We now have to put back the lines we need, starting with the outline box. So click the 'Box' setting in the dropdown box. This will produce an outline of the overall table. Then use the buttons on the right-hand side under the 'Preview' heading to add the required lines. For example, go back into the table and highlight the 'Feature position' cell and then go back into borders and shading box and click the preview box down on the right that has the dark line at the bottom and click OK. Then highlight the entire third row to put in the horizontal line on the top of that row. As the Borders and Shadings box varies according to context it may vary slightly from that shown in the figure above.
- As a final touch, put two spaces in front of the 'High frequency' and 'Low frequency' labels to indent them slightly. The final version of your table should be identical with Table 6.2.

How to Present a Figure

A figure can be in several different forms (e.g. line, bar, pie) and is normally computer-generated. We are only going to deal with two-dimensional graphs here. Later we will go through an example of how to do this using Excel, but first we need to consider some basics.

It is possible to present two-dimensional plots to look three-dimensional but APA guidelines suggest that we should avoid this. It is fairly rare for data to be in a three-dimensional format. One such example would be the representation of phonemes in a three-dimension space represented by pitch, duration and average amplitude. The construction of such a mapping would require a bit of prior experimentation.

Returning to two dimensions, the figure consists of the horizontal (or x) axis and the vertical (or y) axis. It is important to understand that the convention is that the x-axis has the *known* values whereas the y-axis depicts the *measured* values. Put another way, the x-axis represents the independent variable and the y-axis the dependent variable or variables. For example, the experimenter asks people to choose between 1, 2, 4 or 8 alternatives on each trial. These numbers of alternatives are the values known beforehand and would be shown on the x-axis. The reaction times of people to these stimuli would be measured during the experiment and the mean reaction times for each alternative would be shown in the figure. In cases like this always ensure the axes are the right way round. There will, however, be other times when the two variables represented by each axis are both measured values (otherwise known as dependent variables) so it would be a matter of judgement which way round they are plotted.

Different graphical forms

Line and bar graphs

These are the most common forms of graphical representation, and usually they are interchangeable. There was a time when the advice would have been not to use a line graph when the data are non-continuous (which is a position still held in other sciences). The figure in appendix 2 is an example of one depicting bar graphs. Each bar represents a *discrete* (or separate) category. This is in contrast to a *continuous* variable. Examples of a continuous variable might be the angle of mental rotation between two objects or the physical distance between two stimuli in a perceptual experiment. In this case it would be better to use line graphs to represent data that are moving continuously from one point to the next along the *x*-axis. If a line graph is used there are two sorts to choose from:

- **Dot-to-dot** is where the lines are drawn …

> *Student:* dot-to-dot?
> *John:* Yes. More specifically, the data points are connected with straight lines.

- **A line fitted between the points** as shown in Figure 6.1 which is a curved fitted line. This can be of any kind of function, but a linear one is the more usual.

The scatter plot

This usually does not have any line going through the data points and is a rarer form of graphical representation. It is used to show, for example, the closeness of the most concentrated part of the scatter plot to a linear function. Investigators like to plot them to see how the data look for themselves. Incidentally, you would not normally show a scatter plot of a correlation in your results section – the correlation *r* statistic will in itself be enough. However, as an exercise, your tutor may want one.

The pie (or circle) chart

These are circular representations of percentages or proportions in wedges within the circle with the sharp ends in the middle. The APA guideline is to keep to five parts or fewer, ordering the wedges by size with the largest at the 12 o'clock position. The guidelines also advise shading them systematically from light to dark corresponding to each of the large to small parts. The pie chart is rarely used in presentations.

Photographs

These should look professional and care should be taken to provide a background with suitable contrast.

Box 6.2 Aspects to Consider When Constructing a Figure

To make this clearer we will revert to bullet points again:

- As already shown, there are different ways to represent data graphically (line, bar, scatter). This may need some experimentation before choosing the most satisfactory form.
- When referring to the figure in the text only refer to 'Figure 1', 'Figure 2' and so on, and not 'Graph 1', or whatever. Notice the word 'Figure' always begins with an upper case F.
- The graph should be easy to read. This means the size of the font for the labels should be large enough. The APA manual suggests using a simple font such as a sans serif (e.g. the commonly used font Arial). Similarly, there should not be too many lines to clutter up the image. It may be better to break the data up into more than one figure.
- Experiment with the dimensions of the axes. If the vertical axis is too compressed it may look as if there is little effect. On the other hand, if indeed there is hardly any effect, do not try to bolster it by exaggerating the height of the vertical axis.
- Similarly, make sure the intervals on the vertical axis are not too crowded together. For instance, it may be better to put percentage changes into units of 10% rather than 5%.
- The figure should be easy to understand. This is helped by a good caption, which we will deal with next.

Caption writing

Every figure caption should have a neutral description of the variables. Here is a (fictional) example: 'Children's reaction times to high versus low frequency words as a function of age.' The caption might end with minor details such as: 'The bars represent the mean reaction times and the vertical lines show the standard errors of these means.'

How to Produce Figures in Excel

Starting with the Excel spreadsheet

We are about to go through an example of how to produce a good quality figure that is APA formatted from an Excel spreadsheet. Most of what we will be doing is mechanical, but there are aspects that need some judgement, such as deciding on the best position for the figure legend.

The first task is to put the data into an Excel spreadsheet. The sample of data we are using here is from a study by Beech and Harris (1997) comparing two groups of children. One group had no problems with hearing whereas the other group consisted of children who were born without the ability to hear and the two groups were matched in their reading age. Figure 6.3 shows what the spreadsheet looks like with these means entered. These numbers are the mean errors in performance in a task in which the children had to say if regularly spelled words (e.g. hand) or irregularly spelled words (e.g. choir) were words or not. Just in case you are curious about the rationale, the hypothesis was that these hearing impaired children were learning to read without being aware of the sounds represented in words. Thus, they were not affected by whether the words were regular or irregular in spelling. However, children with hearing found irregular words more difficult to read because the phonological codes created from the spellings were different from how these words actually sounded.

Notice how we have not just put in the error data (e.g. '8.87') for the conditions; the labels are included as well. We then highlight the whole table (by holding down the left button of the mouse) from the cell with the label comprising 'Group' in the top left-hand corner dragging the mouse across to

	A	B	C	D
1	Group	Regular	Irregular	
2	Hearing	8.87	12.2	
3	Hearing Impaired	8.92	9.72	
4				
5				

Figure 6.3 The table of data as entered in the top left-hand corner of an Excel sheet. It shows the mean errors for each group for regular and irregular words entered into the Excel spreadsheet

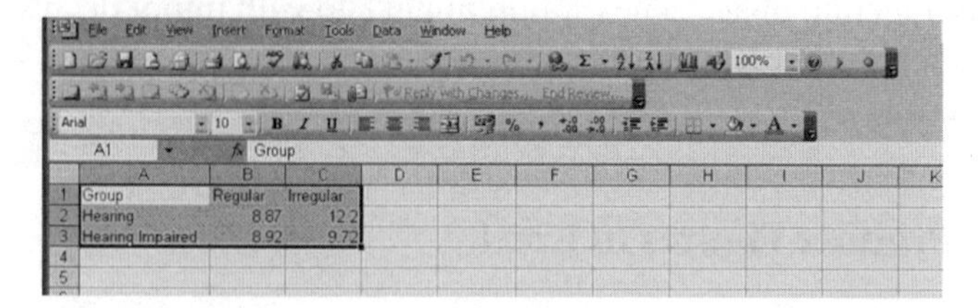

Figure 6.4 Highlighting the table of data on the Excel spreadsheet. The Chart Wizard icon looks like a bar chart

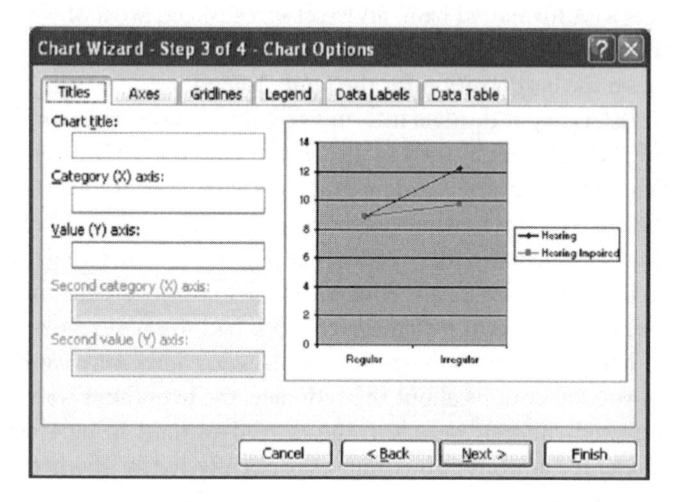

Figure 6.5 Screenshot of the third step of the Chart Wizard from which there are six tabs available to make changes to the chart. In this case the 'Titles' tab is active

the datum '9.72' in the bottom right. Then select the Chart Wizard, which is the icon that looks like a bar chart. Position the mouse cursor over this icon and a box with 'Chart Wizard' in it will appear underneath. You should then double click on the mouse. (Trust me, you won't disappear in a puff of smoke, or at least it doesn't happen often.)

Under the 'Chart type' window on the left select 'Line.' ('XY [Scatter]' will be the preferred choice if the data on the *x*-axis are not linearly scaled.) Then click the 'Next' button at the bottom twice and at this point we will have reached the 'Step 3 of 4' box as shown in Figure 6.5 (assuming the top tab 'Titles' has been activated).

At this point, it is a good idea to examine this beginning chart. Check that the top line in the figure is also the top line in the legend box. In our case, the lines in the legend box are aligned with those on the chart. If there are several lines, make sure that the order of the lines in the legend box is congruent with those in the main figure. As far as I can see, the only way to change this ordering is to change round the items in the beginning table in the spreadsheet and then start again building the chart. This ordering cannot be changed later, so if your lines are incongruent, change the order on the spreadsheet and start again.

To continue with composing the chart, leave the 'Chart title' box blank. Put in the *x*-axis box 'Type of Word' and in the *y*-axis box 'Mean Errors'. Within a few moments, those axis titles will appear in the right-hand chart. Then select the 'Gridlines' tab. The *y*-axis 'Major gridlines' box has a tick. Remove this with one click to remove the horizontal gridlines. Then click the Next button to get to 'Step 4 of 4' and click the bottom Finish button. This will produce the chart on the spreadsheet; but there are a few more tasks to do before the chart is ready. These changes are as follows:

- **Removing the shaded background.** Place the cursor in this shaded area and double click (left button). This produces the 'Format Plot Area' box. Click the 'None' option in the right-hand 'Area' section. Go to the next bullet point. This will remove the shading.
- **Removing the top and right-hand chart axes.** In the same Format Plot Area box, click the None choice in the left-hand 'Border' section. Then click the OK button at the bottom. The top and right-hand borders of the inner box will disappear.
- **Dealing with the legend.** This is the right-hand box representing what the two functions mean (i.e. Hearing versus Hearing Impaired). APA formatting requires that the surrounding box is removed and that the legend is integrated with the figure. To do this we put the mouse cursor over the legend box and holding down the left button drag it to the upper left-hand side. The box may not go willingly at first, but it should do after some experimentation. Then highlight the legend box once more and right click. Select the 'Format Legend' alternative and you should be within the 'Patterns' tab. Now change the left-hand Border choice to None, click OK and the legend's surrounding box will disappear.
- **Removing the outer rectangle.** Put the cursor inside the outer rectangle and it will be highlighted by small black squares. Right click and select 'Format Chart Area' and in the left-hand Border section choose the None option and click OK at the bottom. Figure 6.6 shows how the figure should look at this stage.
- **Truncating the *y*-axis.** From an aesthetic viewpoint, there is a very large gap between the *x*-axis and the data lines. In my view, the *y*-axis needs to be truncated at about the level of 8 errors on the vertical axis, which will also emphasise the interaction. A problem with Excel is that it is possible to show a broken vertical axis (by having two slanting parallel lines at the base of the axis showing a gap in the axis), but technically it is difficult. I take the practical view that it is still better to truncate the vertical axis (by taking

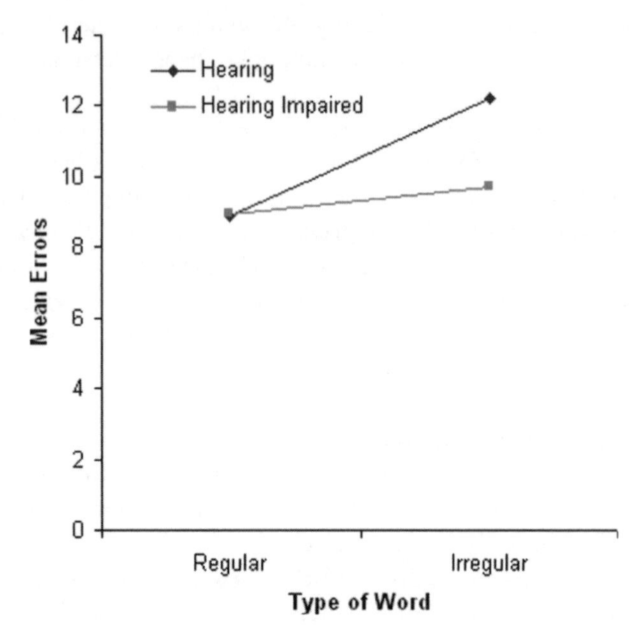

Figure 6.6 The figure so far as it reaches the closing stages

away its bottom section), even though the axis cannot be shown to be broken. Most authors go down this route.

> *Student:* If it ain't broken, don't fix it.
>
> *John:* Well, sort of. There is a quick workaround to this problem of showing a broken axis. You could draw in those parallel lines using a ruler and black pen and then white-out the gap between them. Then photocopy the sheet so the white-out fluid can't be seen. Alternatively, you may have a drawing package that would enable you to do this directly on to the image.

- To truncate the axis, left click on the *y*-axis to highlight it. This bit can be slightly tricky. Make sure that *only* two small black boxes appear at either end of the vertical axis. Right (or left) click on 'Format Axis' to produce the Format Axis box and choose the 'Scale' tab along the top. Change the '0' in the 'Minimum' slot to '8' and click OK. At this point I decided to move the legend box slightly to put it into a better position. (Oh what fun we're having.)
- **Changing the scale**. Now the vertical scale has been truncated it looks unnecessarily cluttered as the Excel software has also calibrated the half units. It would be better to get rid of these. Do the same as in the last point

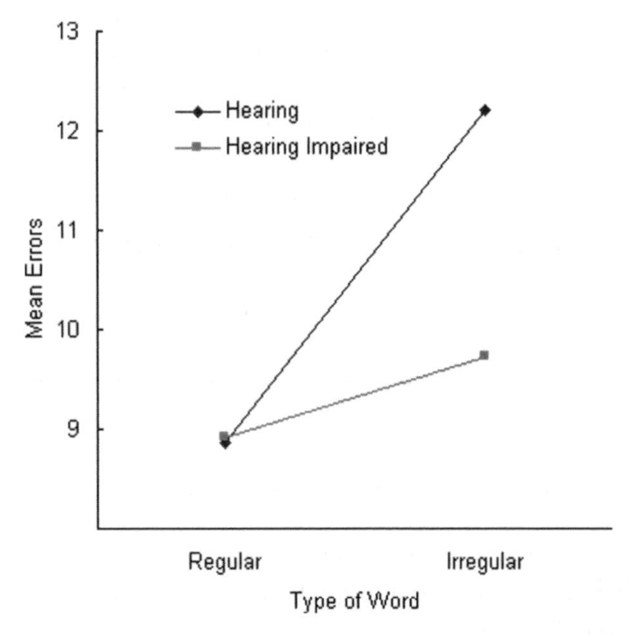

Figure 6.7 Mean errors in a lexical decision task made by children matched in reading age who are either hearing-impaired or who have unimpaired hearing as a function of spelling regularity. (Source: based on data in J.R. Beech & M. Harris, 1997)

to activate the Format Axis box and go to the Scale tab once more. This time change the 'Major Unit' from 0.5 to 1.

- **Dealing with ticks.** If you're a pet owner, you might be feeling a little itchy right now. However, in the current context the little ticks refer to the currently outer facing horizontal lines on the vertical axis and the little tick in the middle of the horizontal axis. We need to get these to face inwards on the vertical axis and delete the one on the horizontal. As in the last two points, highlight the vertical axis and go back to the Format Axis selection of tabs once more and this time choose Patterns. Currently in the section 'Major tick mark type' the 'Outside' alternative has been chosen; change this to the 'Inside' option. Then highlight the horizontal line and similarly access the Format Axis section and go to the Major tick mark type section. However, this time choose None as we do not want any tick marks.
- **Changing the bold font of the axis titles.** The fonts of these need to be changed. Highlight each label (e.g. 'Mean Errors') and select 'Format Axis Title'. Select the 'Font' tab and change from 'Bold' to 'Regular.' Do the same for the *x*-axis title. The completed figure and its accompanying caption are shown in Figure 6.7.

All that remains is to click the outer area of the chart to activate it. Right click on the mouse and select 'Copy' and then paste it on to your document. As a checklist and as a way of revising the procedures during the making of this figure and the construction of its caption, note the elements in Box 6.3:

Box 6.3 A Checklist of What is Needed for the Figure

- The caption is below the figure (unlike the table which has it at the top).
- The word *Figure* and its number are in italics but the rest of the caption is in regular font.
- The legend (the inner box explaining what the different lines mean) has the lines in the same relative position as the lines in the main graph.
- The box usually surrounding the legend is removed and the legend itself is placed as close into the lines as possible, without coming between the lines.
- The *y*-axis label ('mean errors') runs parallel with the axis.
- Try not to squeeze too many numbers on to the *y*-axis. Instead aim for reasonable spacing between the numbers.
- Make sure that tick marks point inwards.
- All the labels have the first letter in capitals and the rest in lower-case. This applies also whenever there are second or further words (e.g. 'Hearing Impaired').
- If there is a substantial gap between the lines and the *x*-axis it is usually advisable to cut the *y*-axis.
- If anything is in bold font it needs to be changed to regular font.

Chapter Summary

This chapter is a spillover from the Results section of the quantitative chapter (chapter 4) and deals with how to format numbers and how to construct tables and figures. As far as formatting numbers is concerned, if you can come away from this chapter remembering that numbers under 10 should be written (e.g. 'two') and those that are 10 or above should be in numerical form, then something will have been achieved. Instead of remembering rules most of us opt for 'what looks right'. That sense of familiarity is helped by reading many Results sections, so you gradually pick up the correct usage. If I could pick out the one rule that seems to get broken the most, it is the one about not starting a sentence with a number (instead of writing it out). This is particularly a problem for describing participants. We mostly want to start our sentence (wrongly) with, for instance, '84 participants were tested . . .' Unfortunately we either have to write out that wretched number with all the problems that entails (e.g. Do I hyphenate it? How is 'eighty' spelled?) or rephrase it in such a circumlocutious manner that the sentence reads oddly. It would be nice to produce some logical tree for the usage of numbers, but the guidelines arose from accepted practice, which does not appear (at least to me) to have developed in a particularly logical way. I hasten to add, of course, that I am sure psychologists are otherwise perfectly logical.

We then turned to the issue of whether to present summaries of data in tabular or graphical form. One simple method is to base one's decision on the number of data to be displayed, but sometimes this has to be overridden by other considerations. For example, there is nothing like a graph to show the linearity or curvilinearity of a relationship or the degree to which variables interact. Under no circumstances try to avoid this decision by both plotting the data and then tabulating the same data for good measure.

A good proportion of this chapter has been devoted to producing figures. This is not just because they look better than tables, but they are also more difficult to do, if they are to look good. The first issue is the form that your graph should take. The most common form is the line chart. Various considerations are given to the best way to achieve this, including some guidance on how to produce a good figure caption. The chapter ends by taking the reader through an example from the table in the spreadsheet to the final product. If you have never done a figure before in this way, it would probably be helpful to work through this example.

7

WRITING THE PROJECT

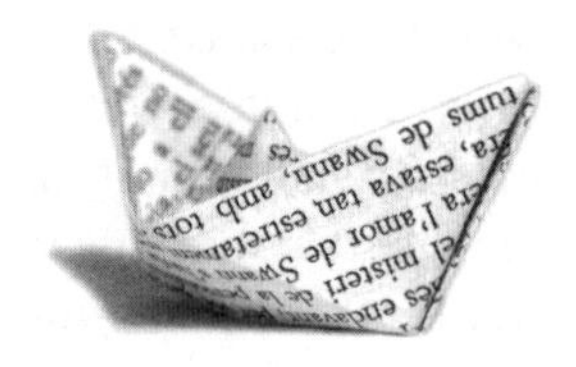

In this chapter we are going to consider more aspects to the writing process when dealing with a project. Such projects are pieces of work that mainly involve your own design and are typically longer than the average research report. They can be a prescribed project with a limited number of topics to choose from that may have a relatively short time limit. Alternatively a project can stretch over several months and can include more than one experimental study.

Planning the Study

Generating ideas

The process of writing in itself can even help to create ideas for the project. Write down the general topic that you might be interested in, such as memory for faces, attitudes to keeping fit, or development of spelling. Try to choose a topic that is going to be motivating enough to continue all the way through to a satisfactory conclusion.

The next stage is to start a brainstorming session writing down the kinds of research projects that you could do within this topic. After this, put the writing away and go for a walk, a swim, or at least do something that is different. This helps the incubation phase. Further ideas should emerge later. This can be an enjoyable creative process. Next, start searching out research papers that could be relevant and after reading these the possibilities should snowball. Keeping a daily diary or blog of ideas can be useful as a record to look back on and as an idea-generator in its own right. If notice has been given earlier about the kinds of topics that can be done for this project, then this can begin as soon as possible. The more ideas that are produced, the better for the eventual selected project; as you will have a better set of quality candidates from which to choose.

Getting the design right

Although this book is more concerned with the writing process, we are first going to examine the design stage of your project. If the final written product is kept in mind, it can help the planning stage, to realise that some ideas are just too vast to fit within the bounds of the word count. You may decide that you need two experiments, within the project. This may just be planned so that the design of Experiment 1 will not affect Experiment 2. For example, Experiment 1 may be on young children, but you may also want to try out the same materials on an older group in Experiment 2. On the other hand, the design of Experiment 2 may depend on Experiment 1; so one outcome might suggest one particular follow-up, whereas a different outcome would suggest a different direction. (This would be Impressive Science.)

A more likely situation would be that Experiment 1 did not work out well and it may have been because of a critical variable. Therefore, an adjustment is made and a second experiment is tried out. If you have a complex single experiment or one or two further experiments, you could again find yourself up against a word limit problem. This arrangement will have all the attendant frustrations of limited space to provide a good critical review. You need to weigh up what would be achieved by a more sophisticated project, gaining possibly better findings, against the cost of the more limited available space for the final write up.

Some may think that having many variables and participants, and a literature review packed with references, gives them a cast-iron insurance for success. Well, they certainly will not fail with all that hard work, especially if it comes in a well-written and well-presented package. It will surely get much credit. But they may not have spent a great deal of time thinking about the experimental design and what their expectations (hypotheses) were going to be beforehand. It could be particularly difficult to decide on the central thesis of such a project.

The best projects are going to be those that have been intelligently designed. (They will also, of course, have a good research review, a sensible number of participants, and other excellent qualities.) The writers of such models of virtue will have considered likely criticisms. They will have done their best to control for possible confounding variables. Thus they will have spent much time in reading and preparation. This will have been time well spent as it could make the resulting write-up much easier. They will also produce a finished project that might potentially end as a short publication in a quality journal. If you want to find examples of such good experimentation and professional presentations, look no further than at some of the shorter papers in the quality journals. In practice, research is not meticulously planned in many projects and the experimenters finish with a pattern of outcome that they did not expect. Nevertheless, it is surprising how an excellent write-up can help to bolster the findings. This brings us to the topic of how to avoid disasters.

Creating a safety net in the design

Consider introducing some kind of insurance against not finding anything. One misguided way of getting such insurance is to try to include too much. When there are too many variables, this is sometimes derisively called the 'blunderbuss' approach. It is much like the effect of the old blunderbuss gun that scattered lead shot in many directions in the hope of maiming the victim. Someone using this strategy might reason that by chance they are going to get lucky with a few variables and will at least have something to write about in their Results section. At the other extreme some, perhaps supremely confident, people have a minimalist approach and have just one or two manipulations, so their hopes may be pinned on just one or two outcomes.

Try to avoid both the blunderbuss and the minimalist approaches as they both have problems. Three main reasons for not using the blunderbuss approach are: (a) it will be difficult to write a good introduction – where is the focal idea? (b) statistical analysis could be complex; in an ANOVA analysis, for instance, it gets complicated trying to work out an interaction between more than three variables, and (c) you could be in danger of getting too many false statistically significant findings unless you make an adjustment to the (alpha) probability level. However, this particular problem is too technical for this book. The problem for the minimalist study is that there is the real risk of the expected outcome not being found, with an invariably low-quality Discussion section to follow.

This does not mean that there is a golden rule about the number of variables to be examined or about the type of design to be used. However, one thing that can be done is to include as part of the design a replication of something that is known to have worked consistently in the literature. In this way there will be at least one significant effect to write about in the discussion. Of course, there will also need to be other aspects of the design that integrate well with this particular finding. Otherwise it could look odd if everything else has no relation to the effect that is being reproduced.

Another aspect is to test enough participants for the design, already discussed in chapters 3 and 4. Finally, the type of design used can be important as well. The ANOVA design can be a good structure for a project with 2, 3, or 4 variables within it. Sometimes a multiple regression or a factor analysis might be more suitable. Be careful if you are using just *t* tests, as an adjustment needs to be made to the alpha probability level according to the number of tests used (e.g. the Bonferroni correction).

> *Student:* I was wondering about doing research involving a questionnaire for my project. You don't need any fancy equipment and it can be relatively easy to get large numbers of people to fill them in.
>
> *John:* Hi, I thought you'd gone to sleep. Questionnaire studies are easy and fun to construct. See chapter 9 for some advice on their construction. But they can rapidly get you into blunderbuss territory. They need to be planned fairly strictly so that they can be reduced to a limited number of variables. For example, you might be interested in attitudes to dieting. There could be many reasons why people do or don't diet. Try to break these down into major groupings and if necessary use something like factor analysis to cluster questions together. But a better approach would be to use as part of your study a standard questionnaire that is already in the literature and perhaps compute scores from its subscales, if it has them.

Pilot testing

This next section might sit oddly here, but it is relevant to planning the experiment already discussed above. Pilot testing means testing a few people on your experiment before running it properly, to iron out any possible difficulties. For example, instead of printing off many questionnaires, try initially going through your questionnaire with a few people, one person at a time. Ask them to point out any misunderstandings they might have as you sit alongside them while they complete it. When satisfied that the questionnaire has no problems, go ahead with printing them off. Similarly, if you have an experiment running on a computer try testing a few participants first. Then examine the data and do an early analysis to look at the direction of the responses.

Although there is a cost in time and effort, think of this as an insurance policy. The chances are that everything is fine. However, there is just a possibility that without such a pilot there is an important error somewhere that can affect the outcome of the experiment. The number of people you involve in the pilot

is going to depend on how long the experiment takes, how difficult it is to get participants and how much insurance you feel comfortable with. If you just test (say) 5 people, this may be enough to spot some obvious errors, but testing a few more would probably uncover most likely problems.

Writing Up the Project

Getting the motivation

Many students keep putting off writing up their project until the last moment. This delay in writing can seriously affect their overall work especially if it makes disastrous inroads into exam revision time. I mentioned a little earlier about writing up a diary of your reasons for doing the experiment and other ideas. This writing process needs to be continued throughout the time of your project. It helps to do lots of 'messy writing' in which everything to do with the project is put down without any editorial input. It does not matter how this is expressed. The important idea is that regularly you are writing about your project. There are two ways you can potentially do this: by time or by quantity. One could decide to spend 15–30 min every day, preferably at the same time each day to write on *anything* related to the project. Alternatively one could write 200–300 words every day employing the same process. Weighing up the two methods, the word count criterion is the better one. When sat down for a fixed time one does not have the same incentive to produce anything compared with having to produce a fixed number of words a day.

Student: I can see that would mean the project would be ready well in time for the deadline, but isn't that overkill? Time spent writing on my project, writing that way, would take up far too much time for my situation. It would be taking me away from other important things to do with my studies, such as meeting deadlines for other pieces of work.

John: Fair enough; but let me suggest that you embrace this idea and fit it to your own needs. If in the next two weeks you have to finish off an essay or do some other urgent piece of work, then of course, you have to direct your energies towards that. It is always a good principle to give priority to work according to its value in terms of the marks it is going to earn. However, your project is going to count proportionally much more than other pieces of work. Writing X number of words a day is not going to take up the whole day; it need normally only take less than an hour. The point is that a routine is being set up that will make this process easy, if not enjoyable. You will find that by doing this your thoughts will become clearer as you continue. By contrast, it is a much more painful process when, because of procrastination, writing is foisted on you at a time close to a deadline, when you need to be concentrating on other matters. Let's make a deal: You decide what the X is going to be for your daily word count, and if you have to interrupt that process occasionally, that's fine. But let me suggest that you write every day, come what may, allowing yourself only one day off a week. To find out more about this method have a look at Bolker (1998).

Comparing the Project and Short Report

An obvious difference between a project and report is that the project is longer. Because of the greater length it will be helpful to break longer sections down into subheadings; but consult any available guidelines on this. Usually a longer write-up has more complicated analyses of the data. This means that more decisions have to be made about layout. If the project as it develops appears to be too difficult and confusing, it may be necessary to experiment with different ways of presenting the data in tabular or graphical form to make it easier to understand.

One of the problems with the transition from a short research report to a project is that the writer can lose sight of that central thesis or conjecture in the project. The conjecture might be, for example, that there is a more important factor behind a commonly found interaction between word frequency and spelling regularity. So why is this particular piece of research being carried out? The writer must have been interested by a research question that they were trying to solve. If from beginning to end the writer does not lose sight of this, they will have produced a coherent piece of work and if other criteria are satisfied, a work of excellent quality.

A commonality between the project and the short report is that both should be critical about the research work that forms the basis of the study. Almost all research findings, including even our own, have their frailties. However, when it comes to our own research we are trying to lessen the problems by providing as many controls as possible. Care also needs to be taken in the use of language. All the time there is the need to write concisely. The grammar that you use should be correct. Finally, unlike this book there should be no humour in it whatever.

> *Student:* What humour?
>
> *John:* Very funny. But seriously, do not put in any jokes or puns (and especially puns followed by 'pun intended' to show the reader that the writer doesn't make accidental puns). By all means do this during your messy writing phase if you find it therapeutic, but take them out soon afterwards.

To conclude, both the research report and the project involve good quality writing. The major challenge for the project is to keep up that quality when the length increases substantially.

Revising Your Writing

The more you revise your writing the more you should improve the clarity and flow of your exposition. This is a necessary part of your work and I suspect that for some little time is spent on this.

“*Student:* I sometimes feel that I don’t want to alter what I’ve written because the first time I wrote it I expressed myself spontaneously – and besides, I liked the way that I had expressed myself. Changing around and fiddling with the text for me can seem to remove its good qualities, disjoint the text and make it sound awkward. So I sometimes feel that I have actually made it worse.

John: I have heard this view expressed before. I think this may just be a product of writing experience and especially to do with how much revising has been undertaken in the past. Obviously the more one writes and corrects, the easier it will become, so eventually one should find that the new text will almost always be an improvement on the original.”

A simple tip is whenever you change a sentence (e.g. by putting in a new piece of text), be sure to read through that sentence again. It seems to me that when people make corrections they sometimes make it worse because they have not read over what they have just corrected. This should include reading the wider passage to ensure the context is correct.

“*Student:* Also could you tell me how much time that you think I should spend on revising my project?

John: If you are an experienced writer you may be able to get away with spending the same amount of time on your revision as you spent writing the first draft to produce a good project. It is difficult to be too specific because even during the first messy writing stage you may also have spent some of your time going back and revising and correcting what you had written. This counts as a revision, but what we are referring to here is the considered and thorough revision that one undertakes perhaps at least a few days after writing the original text.”

Getting out the heavy diggers

We already briefly examined the revision process towards the end of chapter 2. An important distinction to make is between 'shallow' proofreading revisions, such as in the way ideas are expressed, checking spelling and grammar and so on, and deeper revisions that need structural changes. To give a little practice with the editing process at the shallow end, the final chapter of this book has examples of problems with student writing for you to work on.

What is the best way of revising the writing? Instead of hanging around in the shallows, it is better to begin by wading into the deep end. Forget for the moment about whether something was expressed in the best way, or checking if a word was spelled correctly. Instead, deep revision means being willing if necessary to get out the 'heavy diggers' to change around the order of the text to provide the best logical structure. There may be a need to create further sections of text to fill in gaps and above all there may be a need to be ruthless in taking out anything that is unnecessary. Incidentally, if you feel unhappy about just deleting text, create a dump file into which the dirt is dumped. It may be pulled out and put back in later, but that is unlikely.

When structural changes are made to text it is important to reexamine the flow within and between paragraphs. A useful but perhaps painstaking way of looking at the flow between paragraphs is to examine each paragraph's theme and judge how well this particular sequence of themes produces a coherent story. This is not going to work in all sections, particularly in the Method and Results sections. However, it can help you to find out whether you have the best arrangement in terms of your central theme or conception of your project.

Another aspect to consider during the deep revision is to make sure that any interpretations have not been misjudged. Could you have distorted the reality of the results? Do not try to talk up your results. In particular do not try to praise what you have found. This is not to say that you should not be enthusiastic about your project in your own mind. If you have good results, this will be plain to the reader, especially if their theoretical implications and importance are pointed out. You might find after a reappraisal that a different interpretation could be viable and you may want to do some further analyses to follow this through.

You may be wondering why we should start at the deep end. This is because if you started the other way you could potentially waste your valuable time tinkering around with text that you decide to discard later when making structural changes. You might also become too attached to what you had written. There is nothing to stop you starting at the shallow end, as it would at least give you practice in your proofreading skills. However, efficiency is a major consideration and your time is precious.

Wading towards the shallows

When we refer to the shallow end of the revision this is by no means lessening the importance of this aspect. As mentioned in chapter 2, you will of course be checking all spelling and grammar. You will also have checked out that your format is correct and checked that you conform to APA style as outlined in this book. Your instructors will also have their own ideas on style, which of course must take priority.

Use your eyes and ears when revising. Use your eyes to spot over-long paragraphs and transgressions in formatting and layout. Use your ears to decide if sentences are so long that you turn blue with lack of breath before the end is reached – as you might well do when you reach the end of this marathon sentence. A problem for projects is that word repetitions can become more obvious. Use a thesaurus to produce different versions. (I had a student who was fond of using the word 'whilst'. It is an unusual word, so its continual repetition began to grate.)

Types of revisers

Perhaps with tongue in cheek, I will describe different types of revisers. See if you can spot elements of your own revising style. Some people may be Deluded Revisers. When faced with doing a revision they cannot see much wrong with what they have written. Perhaps there is nothing wrong with it. However, using the analogy of a song contest auditioning members of the public, there will always be singers who are infuriated with the panel of judges because they think their own singing is pitch-perfect. To everyone else they are clearly singing out of tune. Similarly, some writers who think that they are perfect writers may be deluding themselves. One obvious sign is if they keep getting feedback from markers who say that their writing is poor.

The Vague Reviser may suffer from lapses of concentration and lose their line of thought. They are prone to making repetitions, both in vocabulary and with ideas. The Timid Reviser may have some emotional block about wanting to read the text too deeply. They prefer to skim the text and play around in the shallows with the more obvious aspects of the text because they are not confident enough to make more substantial changes.

Then there is the Thorough Reviser who works diligently at reading through successive drafts, ensuring that the quality is improved with each one. They are not afraid, if they find a knotty problem, to unpick any tangled logic and they painstakingly work at arranging their writing into a better form. Without hesitation they will run a different statistical analysis if a new approach suggests itself, or will go back to the literature to find further experimental work if it were to help cover a new idea. They probably could go on almost to infinity, but eventually they have to stop. Guess which type of reviser is going to get the highest marks?

The final version of the project should be such that the reader would be completely clear what it was about. If you have put enough effort into your revision, this aim should have been achieved.

Chapter Summary

We started this chapter by considering the idea generation phase of the project and considered why it was a good idea to write such ideas down regularly. We then spent a little time examining how the design of the project could impact on the quality of the writing. A complex ambitious design may well be oozing quality through its pores, but that is not going to be much use if at the same time it makes everything a tight squeeze to fit within the word allowance. That is not to say that the other extreme should be chosen by taking on a design that is so simple that it would be difficult to produce a good quality write-up.

Discussing further the Results and Discussion sections we considered what could be done at the design stage that would improve the chances of finding significant effects. We then turned to a method of improving motivation and heightening enjoyment that could be done daily. No, we were not talking about that! Instead we were considering something much better – writing a little bit each day on the project as a means of clarifying ideas on your project.

In a long piece of work such as a project it is important to spend time and much care on the revision. We considered this in terms of the division between deep and shallow revising. By 'deep' we meant altering and deleting text where necessary, to improve the transitions between major ideas and to give the text a coherence unified by the central thesis. We suggested that this would be the first approach to the revision. This would then be followed, in no particular order, by checking spelling, editing grammar, and attending to format, sentence, and paragraph length. We looked at different styles of revision and decided that the Thorough Reviser was the model to be copied. You are well on your way to excellence if you have perfectionist inclinations. However, I do not suppose that if you keep a shipshape room or home it follows that this will have any bearing on your mark for your project. On the other hand it might.

8

WRITING FOR EXAMS AND ANSWERING MCQs

The subject matter of this chapter may not be directly related to writing, but it is surprising how important the writing process is to examination performance, particularly if the examination involves writing essays under time pressure. When writing an essay from memory with limited time it is obviously important to have good skills in writing.

Preparation for Essay Exams

Revising for examinations can be time-consuming and, to an extent, both stress inducing and stress reducing. Stress can be brought on when revising because it is a reminder that there is an examination in the future. However, it can be reduced (on a longer timescale) because as it progresses it gradually dawns on you that you have the skills to cope with this situation. For some who are well prepared there may even be an eager anticipation for examination day so that they can display their knowledge.

As a starting point, consider how to approach exam revision strategically. Most students consider their goal to be trying to learn the least amount of information that is reasonably likely to be examined. In other words, to consider what areas of the exam are more likely to be questioned and to select the minimum amount that needs to be covered.

However, this comes at a cost. The narrower the focus of the revision, the greater will be the likelihood that there will not be enough available material at the appointed hour to cover the questions being asked. Thus, it is important to consider strategy. It is not necessarily the best strategic option to learn the whole syllabus. Although covering the whole syllabus is altruistic and enables you to learn much more about the subject, it is not likely to achieve the goal of earning maximum marks, unless you have a remarkably good memory. There are many factors that work against the perfectionist approach, such as energy, motivation, concentration, and the need to revise for other exams. In addition, there are the competing demands of coursework. It is far better to concentrate energy into a narrower focus.

> *Student:* So what specifically are you suggesting?
>
> *John:* At one extreme, you don't want to be in a position in the exam where you can't answer anything for one of your exam questions. Therefore, you need to think about what you can select from the syllabus to revise for a particular exam in such a way that you are almost 100 per cent certain that you can answer all the required questions.
>
> *Student:* Sorry, I still don't get this. Surely, that means revising the whole syllabus?
>
> *John:* It depends on your situation and the system you are in, as I'm about to explain.

In the British system, students at university can typically have a 2-hour exam with two questions to answer of equal weighting, which means 1 hour to answer each. This module, sometimes called a *course*, involves a series of lectures and the examination is a culmination of that module. The students *may* have been told how many questions each lecturer is setting. In this situation, one method of selection would be to decide to answer only the questions set by one particular lecturer. Another method might be to look at past papers and note what potential topics are going to be presented. There is a reasonable chance that certain topics come up regularly. It would be good insurance to revise for these regularly occurring topics. Another aspect might be that the paper is in two sections with each section covering roughly half the syllabus. This can help in further selection of what is likely to come up.

Unfortunately for students many, if not all, lecturers will refuse to give any hints about what is going to be included, but obviously any hints would be useful. In some places, it is difficult to predict examination questions from year to year. Here a two-pronged approach is called for: first, prepare so that excellent answers can be given for a limited number of highly probable topics. Second, perhaps revise to the level of being able to give reasonably adequate answers for anything else. With good organisation during the revision period, you may even be able to get up to a high level on everything.

At the other extreme, an institution may tell their students what the questions are going to be earlier. These places reason that the examination system can be very stressful for some, so to level the playing field the questions are made available beforehand to allow for more focused preparation. It also removes the problem of potentially being caught out with not having revised the right topics.

Active recall of material should be a part of exam revision. This can take the form of just talking through an answer to a question, or typing it up. However, it would be better to simulate examination conditions as much as possible and write down the answers with a pen. Try to get good pens. Felt tip or rollerball pens need hardly any pressure on the paper and anything that reduces the need for grip strength is preferable. Even better would be to use a pen that has ink that can be erased easily.

The advantages to writing out answers to exam questions are shown in Box 8.1:

Box 8.1 Advantages of Writing Out Exam Answers

- It develops muscular stamina (in the arm, wrist, hand, and fingers) for continuous writing in the exam room.
- The process highlights areas of weakness in understanding that require further attention.
- It is reassuring to be confident about recalling information about a particular area.
- Increasing confidence reduces stress. This in turn makes one feel better so that sleep is longer and deeper and this can help to maintain a strong immune system. Thus, a useful byproduct could be less likelihood of being troubled by the usual infections and other afflictions that are reported by students around exam time.

A final aspect of revision preparation should be learning to relax. Some people are able to go into the exam room feeling relaxed; but most of us feel nervous. We are dealing with the uncertainty of not knowing what the questions are going to be. Many feel more relaxed when this uncertainty transforms into certainty once the exam questions are read. Few people find that they get so worked up that it undermines their performance. A little stress probably helps performance by improving clarity of thinking and giving the impetus to impart information quickly. However, for those for whom the stress is too high, learning to relax and meditate perhaps months earlier would motivate them to revise well in time, instead of postponing it. This will also help later performance. There are plenty of books and websites on how to do this.

The Essay Exam – In the Exam Room

Which questions on the paper should be answered and in which order?

Answer the easiest first to allow time to contemplate subconsciously the more difficult remaining question or questions. However, there can be exceptions to answering the easiest question first.

Asha decides to go for questions that are slightly more difficult because she thinks this will produce from her an answer of better quality. She wants to avoid the simpler, undemanding questions, such as one that asks for a description of X's theory of memory. Instead, she wants to go for a 'compare and contrast' question. She may even have anticipated such a question before going into the exam. She is well prepared to give a first-rate answer. Thus, Asha tries to go for the difficult answer first, but only because she is well prepared.

Bob, by contrast, needs to start with the easiest question first. In reality, this is his only choice because he realises quickly at the beginning of the exam that he is slightly stuck for his second question. My advice to him would be first, not to panic; and second, to give this problem of the second question a little thought, but only perhaps for 2–3 minutes. In this period, he should choose which question to answer second and think about the subtopics he will cover. Then he should return to the first question. There is little or no scientific basis for this idea, but it could allow him subconsciously to mull over the second question while he is thinking about and writing about the first question.

The nature of the question

So now the first question is chosen, and Bob is rereading it. It is important to read carefully the question and during the course of answering the question, to refer to it again occasionally. As a marker, it is clear to me that some do not read the question carefully enough and do not fully understand what it means. All questions should have a precise meaning. We examined in chapter 2 the major kinds of questions that can be asked and the ways these kinds of questions need to be tackled.

Should I devise a plan?

I sometimes find that students have written on the first page a long list of subtopics and even further details that are going to be in the answer. A detailed plan could waste valuable time if the question is straightforward, but a brief plan consisting of broad topics may be helpful. However, if answering a complicated question such as a 'compare and contrast' question, a more detailed plan could be indispensable. Perhaps those who write detailed plans do not trust their memories enough and if they had revised by writing practice exam answers they would have developed more confidence in their abilities to retrieve information? Occasionally only the note form is offered as a response to the question, and a comment left at the end by the unorganised writer when time has run out informing the examiner (rather obviously): 'I've run out of time!'

Timing

This brings us to the problem of timing. One way of thinking about time while answering the exam question is that for each unit of time spent the return in marks steadily dwindles. After (say) a page or so, the point will have passed where the answer has reached the pass mark – if you were to stop at that point. So already, perhaps half the potential marks have been earned if you are aiming high. However, continuing on, the rate at which one will get more marks decreases. To get a first-rate mark you will need to have covered much ground. However, there is a catch. Suppose there are two questions to answer in 2 hours. If one strays over the first hour while still answering the first question, one is earning few extra marks; whereas, if the next question is started on the hour, the potential return will be maximised.

I can't answer any of the questions!

I could respond robustly in terms of bulls and what they deposit to the effect that this is simply not true. There would be a few points to make here:

1. Although it is difficult in these circumstances, breathing deeply and getting into a more relaxed frame of mind can help one to assess the situation more rationally.

2. Could it be possible that there are questions here asking about something you know, but for the moment, you do not recognise this? If necessary, ask for a dictionary to explain any terms that you may be unsure about in the question. If you are desperate, you could always ask an invigilator to explain a question.
3. It rarely happens, but there could have been a proofreading error. These occur occasionally in my experience when I am an invigilator in the exam room.
4. It is important not to give up. When invigilating I see students walk out of the exam room early and wonder if they would have been better just sitting there and trying to recover more information from memory. It can be surprising what can be written that could at least get a pass mark. Try to give an answer that directly answers the question and bring in any psychological knowledge from your revision to back yourself up. Remember that under these circumstances you need to be creative.

I can only answer two questions, but I need to answer three!

We can consider the same course of action for this one. At the beginning of the exam concentrate as thoroughly as you can on one of the questions that could be the third candidate. Do not immediately put your head in the sand and avoid thinking about the problem until the first two questions are finished. During the time that you are answering the first two questions, your subconscious should have time to work on that third question.

I can answer four or five questions, but only need to answer three: Which do I choose?

Lucky you! Choose those that are going to give you the highest marks. Do not spend much time agonising on which ones to answer. Here are factors to consider:

1. Choose those that you are most confident about answering. (This is the most important factor.)
2. Choose those questions that fellow students avoid because they think that they are conceptually too hard. However, do not overdo it. Some questions may be beyond the powers of even you. As long as you have the self-confidence to go for the more conceptually difficult questions, then go for these.

3. Avoid those that are pitched at too general a level. One problem with these can be that you will have far too much material to answer them in the time available and will therefore get too frustrated in trying to compress your information. For various reasons they are questions for which it is difficult to achieve a good result.

What about a question that is too specific and for which I haven't got enough material?

Mike has revised a topic that has many details and is prepared for a question set at a more general level. However, he is not prepared for the actual exam question that covers very specific ground within this wider area. The simple course of action is to go on to another exam question. However, let us assume there is no alternative. This is a difficult situation. Mike is in danger of answering the question directly but in so doing providing such a short answer that it is likely only to get a pass. A better solution, in my view, would be to try to introduce some of the other more general information as part of the background to the answer. With luck, it might be possible to bring in much of this material by trying to make it as relevant to the question as possible. In addition, the core material may promote ideas that could contribute to more critical evaluation during the act of writing. Before Mike knows it, he has written a decent essay of reasonable length after all. That can be part of the magic of writing.

Revising the finished draft

In contrast to the coursework essay, there will be little time to look over and correct exam answers. Valuable time might be better spent just continuing to write. However, from your own experience of rereading your practice exam questions during your revision period, you may be the kind of person who makes many minor errors. These are not going to bother markers and correcting them may only bring these little problems to their attention. It is up to you.

To finish this part on exam essays it is clear to me that some students do not think of the exam essay as having the same qualities as a coursework essay. They do not realise that this exam essay should answer the question – this is perhaps the most important aspect of all. It should also have an introduction and a logically organised internal main body with an underlying theme. Wherever possible back this up with evidence and this means learning the names of the authors of the relevant studies and their dates. Do not be too pedantic about this; if, for example, there are more than two authors I would just put 'et al.'. Finally, it should have a full conclusion bringing concepts together with a concluding theme. However, in contrast to (say) the 2,000-word coursework essay, the limit is not in terms of words, but in the time to write as many words as possible on that topic. This means that one does not need to be too careful about expressing oneself concisely. However, if one can write quickly and legibly, preferably in such a relaxed way that rapid writing is not an effort, then more ground can be covered and probably there will be more marks for the taking. The excellent exam essays are written by students who understand the question, martial their material together appropriately with a decent amount of critical analysis, and who express themselves well.

" *Student:* Sounds to me like the markers are marking exam essays just by measuring their length!

John: No, you've got it all wrong – we throw them down the stairs and give the highest grades to those that reach the bottom! But seriously, there is an element of truth in what you say as there's probably a correlation between how much students write in their answers and the final marks they get for those answers. However, the closing remarks I make above still apply. The overwhelming reason for getting good marks lies in the quality of the answer. Quality shines through and wins every time. "

Tim always carefully filed his lecture notes after each exam

Ten Points to Consider for a Multiple-choice Exam

Instructors consider the Multiple-choice Questionnaire (MCQ) exam to be useful for testing knowledge of all the areas covered in the module or course. Another advantage is that if it is used skilfully it can test different kinds of information. This means that during revision you have to consider whether you can remember the detail, and whether the material is understood. We examine here 10 points about the MCQ. The first two are about your preparations and the next six are about what to do within the exam itself. The final two are about afterwards.

1. Try to invent questions.

When revising, try to imagining yourself in the position of the lecturer and think of the kinds of questions that could be asked. When reading over the handouts and lecture notes in this way, learning becomes more active and it makes one realise that the task is manageable.

This is the same advice as for revising for essay-writing exams. However, revising for a multiple-choice exam may need a slightly different approach than just writing everything down from memory. In one revision session, mock questions could be devised and the answers written down – and then the answers put somewhere else. To do this properly set both factual questions and conceptual questions. Written responses could be given (e.g. 'The difference between the /t/ and /d/ sounds is in terms of what?' – answer: 'duration'). Then in another session a week or so later test again. Be determined and do not try to look at the answers too soon if the information cannot be retrieved immediately. Practice in this way should increase confidence coming into the examination, if testing is done regularly. It could also show the value of making educated guesses and showing that some of the time you will be correct. When testing is over, try to devise some further questions to add to the question pool so that the next testing session has some new material in the following week. Obviously allowing enough revision time helps and there is no reason why this process should not go on while the course is proceeding.

2. Look at example questions.

If sample questions are available it will give you an idea of the type that will be set. If these are not available do not be reticent in asking the instructor for a set of examples to study.

3. Use ALL the time allocated in the exam intensively.

When it comes to the examination itself, normally there will be plenty of time to answer all the questions. (Perhaps the exception is a statistics exam with calculations to do.) Do not just work through the questions and then leave as soon as you can. Instead work intensively through the questions for the duration of the whole exam.

4. Read each question carefully.

Read each question carefully and understand fully what the questioner is asking. This cannot be stressed enough.

5. First work through the questions, discounting the least likely alternatives.

First try to discount the least likely answers by putting a mark next to each. If possible, try to trim down the alternatives to two likely answers. Then leave the question temporarily.

6. Spend much more time on the difficult questions.

Having gone through and hopefully answered with a fair degree of confidence the simplest questions, return to examine again the more difficult questions. For each one, try to run through everything you know that may be relevant to this question and go for the most likely answer. (Think how the better contestants go through this process with a good outcome on the quiz show *Who Wants To Be a Millionaire?*) If it seems impossible to decide, opt for what you think is more likely, even if this is actually just a guess.

If a question has been trimmed down to two alternatives, this gives good odds with a 50-50 chance of being correct. A win means getting 1 point, and a loss incurs the loss of one third of a point. Try running this game by tossing a coin, giving yourself 3 units of money when you get a head and taking away 1 unit when you get a tail to see how quickly you get rich!

7. Don't leave any question unanswered.

An excellent strategy is to answer all the questions to maximise marks, even though if you get a question wrong, a third of a mark is lost for that question. (To explain, usually these exams are corrected for chance so that a correct answer gets one point and a wrong response loses one third of a point, if there are four alternatives.) It can be difficult to answer all the questions if you are a naturally cautious person. This course of action can force you to give answers when you are underconfident about your response. But it is worth making the guess because on a few occasions such as this the answer is likely to be correct.

8. Don't get distracted by trivial aspects.

Do not distract yourself by looking at more trivial aspects of the MCQ. For example, do not reason that because you have selected a lot of first choices

Mike solving his multiple-choice problems

across the paper, that you must be going wrong. Some setters do try to distribute the correct answers evenly across the alternatives, while others do not. Similarly, if you are asked to choose between one of four ranges (e.g. between 1–4, 2–5, 3–6, or 4–7 years), do not reason to yourself that the correct answer cannot be at the extreme ends (i.e. in the example 1–4 or 4–7 years).

9. If it went badly, try to write down questions after the exam.

If afterwards you feel that you have done badly in the exam, the first step should be to try to write down as many questions that you can remember from the exam, and the alternatives that were offered. This is so that if you have to do the exam once more later in the year you have something to help you with your revision.

10. But you may not have done as badly as you think.

The situation may not be as bleak as you think. For simplicity, let us suppose there were 100 questions and there were 25 questions that you thought you had answered correctly. So that is 25 marks out of 100 for a start. Let us further suppose there were another 25 questions that you had whittled down to two alternatives. According to chance, you would have answered these correctly half the time, so that could be a further 12 or 13 marks. Already you might have 37 or 38 marks out of 100 for half the paper, bringing you close to the pass mark. If the other 50 per cent have all been guessed, by chance the rest would be worth zero. On the other hand, you may have had enough underlying knowledge to make some guesses in the right direction to get you to the pass level.

Contrasts Between the Two Kinds of Exams

There are three slight contrasts between the two types of exams. First, in the written examination it is important to divide time to questions in proportion to their overall worth for getting marks (e.g. three equally weighted questions need 60 minutes on each in a 3-hour exam); whereas in the multiple-choice examination, one would spend far less time on the easiest questions and much more on the difficult ones. Second, in revising for the written exam it is normally an efficient strategy to concentrate on some parts of the syllabus over others, whereas in the multiple-choice exam it is necessary to revise the whole syllabus. Third, testing oneself during revision should replicate as closely as possible the type of exam to be taken, so that written recall would suit a written exam whereas recognition testing (having to choose between alternatives) would be better for a multiple-choice exam.

Multiple-choice examinations are considered to be easier by many, but in practice weaker students do less well on them than they would expect in comparison to the examination essay. This is because it seems to be easier to do a multiple-choice as the correct answer is already sitting there 'staring you in the

face' among its alternatives – you just have to recognise it. However, when the alternatives are close it is a bit like trying to spot a bearded culprit in an identification parade of identically bearded gentlemen. This is why the revision needs to be careful with attention to detail and unfortunately it has to be on the whole syllabus. Perhaps one consolation is that if you are not very good at expressing yourself in words, this is not going to be apparent in a multiple-choice exam.

Chapter Summary

In preparing for a written examination, it is usually possible to be selective and concentrate mainly on particular parts of the syllabus. It is also helpful to be proactive in thinking about the kinds of topics that could come up, especially with a view to trying to answer these under timed conditions. There is no need to feel worried about needing to learn thoroughly the whole syllabus, as long as you are satisfied that you will be able to answer the required number of questions. The advantages of answering exam questions for practice were outlined. In particular, the knowledge that you can do this should inspire confidence when going into the exam room.

Within the context of the exam room, we discussed the strategies that can be used to improve performance. One of these for the essay type of exam was to tackle first the easiest of the questions. While answering this it will help one to get into a calm frame of mind. We examined how returns in marks decrease (probably exponentially) with time. It is not a good idea to go over the allotted time on any particular question when you could increase those mark returns per unit of time by going on to the next question. A corollary of answering the easiest question first is that you save those questions you know least about until last. I hope that a mix of your subconscious and perhaps a little magic can conjure up enough information for you to provide a decent response.

We noted that the examination answers that were going to get the best marks answered the question in a thorough, critical manner with appropriate organisation, and were 'topped and tailed' by a good introduction and conclusion. It is not impossible for most students to achieve this standard: It needs good preparation, cool-headedness, self-belief in difficult circumstances, and willingness to think carefully about the research covered in the syllabus.

Although not strictly relevant to a book on writing, we also examined how to prepare for and take multiple-choice exams. As in written examinations, devising mock questions and answering them a week or so later is useful revision.

In the examination room a sensible course of action, providing there is enough time available, is to answer the easy questions first. When tackling the more difficult questions try to remove as many alternatives as possible. Finally try to make an educated guess on the more difficult ones that are left. An important strategy is to end by answering all the questions because this will probably improve the overall mark. The advice here is similar to that for the written examinations: Start the revision early and revise by testing yourself. We ended by comparing the two kinds of examinations and decided that the multiple-choice exam was not necessarily easier than the written exam if one wants to earn excellent marks.

9

WRITING FOR OTHER PURPOSES

This chapter covers writing for purposes other than those considered so far. For example, we look at how to write to recruit participants (including how to write letters), giving the instructions for an experiment and how to give a debriefing after an experiment. We shall then look in the final part at how you can devise questions for questionnaires. I think that should just about cover everything else to do with writing, and no, I am not covering writing love letters and writing to the bank manager. Although I recognise that psychology would have a role to play in these as well.

Writing to Recruit Participants and Writing Letters to Organisations

There are two aspects of this section: The first is how to compile the preliminary description that you write to recruit people to undertake your experiments; the second is how to write to an organisation in order to access potential participants.

Recruiting participants

Writing a piece to recruit participants is a balance between trying to get readers motivated to do your experiment and giving them an accurate picture of what the experiment is about. On the one hand, you want to get as many as possible to sign up; but on the other, there is the ethical consideration that they should not be misled. For example, do not exaggerate the shortness of the duration of your study. This could backfire if word gets around about such a deception and recruitment could subsequently become much more difficult.

Some experimental designs are going to attract recruitment more easily as they are intrinsically more interesting. Therefore, if you think that your study might not be so interesting, try to think of aspects that might appeal to people.

What to include in your advertisement for participants (whether within or outside the department) will depend on the policy of your department. Here is a checklist.

Box 9.1 What to Include When Recruiting Participants

- You will need a title (e.g. 'A study examining effects of disguise on face recognition').
- Give your name, e-mail address, and the name of your supervisor.
- Describe briefly the purpose of the research.
- Give any eligibility criteria (e.g. 'between 18 and 25 years old').
- The description should also give the time commitment (e.g. 'usually 20 minutes, but can be up to 30 minutes').
- State if there is any payment involved or what credits will be available.
- If this is an advert outside your department then you will need to give the department's name and address.

There are other aspects to consider; for example, the language used in the description should be tasteful and plain, avoiding any abbreviations. Be clear about what type of participant you need in order to avoid having to turn people away later.

Your institution may have further stipulations. You may be required to outline any possible risks. The participants should know what they will be asked to do, although they would not be told about any deception until the experiment was over. The participants should also be told the intended destination of the research write-up, for example, if it is intended to be written up as a project. You may need to tell them the arrangements about confidentiality and access to information collected from the experiment. Finally, you may have to give a contact they can get in touch with in case they are concerned about a particular aspect of the way the research was conducted.

Writing letters

You may occasionally have to write a letter to an organisation to begin the process of recruiting participants. For example, you may need to write to an organisation such as a school or college to get permission to test students and to make suitable arrangements. When I first started writing 'thank you' letters as a child, my mother told me always to begin with 'Dear Aunty X and Uncle Y, I hope you are both well . . .' However, as you are not so familiar with the recipient, an enquiry into their state of health might be considered odd. In this case, you would begin by introducing yourself. You would write that you were (for instance) a third-year psychology student who is beginning her psychology project as part of her degree course. You would follow this with the name of your supervisor, probably with a contact e-mail address and a phone number, or both. You would then describe briefly the nature of your project and end the letter by asking if you could make an appointment to discuss the project further.

The format of the letter needs careful consideration. You are probably familiar with how letters are laid out. The top left of the letter would have your full correspondence address, followed by the date. It would be even better if you were allowed to use the department's official headed notepaper; as long as you are assured that a return letter will get to you. You will also need to give a contact telephone number and your e-mail address. Each of these would be on a separate line to the left. Then leave a blank line.

When addressing the recipient (i.e. the 'Dear X' line of the letter) it is always better to use someone's name rather than his or her position (e.g. 'Dear Ms Hamilton' rather than 'Dear Head Teacher'). If necessary, phone the organisation and ask the secretary for this information, or else their name may be available on the web. Do not write 'Dear Emma Hamilton' – always use a title in this formal situation. This 'Dear X' line is followed by a new line, which is the beginning of the letter. You could end the letter with 'Yours sincerely' followed by at least three blank lines for your signature and underneath that your name in print. You would not normally need to enclose a stamped-addressed envelope.

Instead of writing to gain access to a group of participants, you may need to write letters to individual participants to get them to take part in your research, presumably to complete a questionnaire. If this involves using an address list or a list of e-mails that you have obtained, it is important to do this in consultation with your supervisor. Your department probably has a policy against sending out mass mailings without adequate supervision. The letter itself, if it is being sent by ordinary mail, would follow similar lines to that previously described. It is important to stress in this case that the participant should know enough about the person with whom he or she is going to be dealing. Further, avoid any deception if the sole contact throughout will be only by correspondence. This would be because a deception needs to be explained in person after an experiment is completed. Obviously, it would not be possible to do so if you only have contact by e-mail.

Giving Instructions About Your Experiment

This part deals with the way to instruct people so that they understand what they have to do before beginning the experiment. We are focusing specifically on instructions for those undertaking a quantitative experiment. Here is a checklist of the primary aspects that you need to consider:

Box 9.2 How to Instruct Participants

- Use standard instructions. In other words, each participant should get the same instructions. There should be no deviation in the way they are informed and in the content.
- The best way to achieve this is to give written instructions and then follow these up after they have been read with a brief oral recap of the main points.
- If the instructions have to be issued orally, consider recording these, so that everyone's experience of how they are delivered is the same. (If you are in an interview situation for a qualitative study, giving a recording of instructions at any point would normally be unnecessary.)
- Use plain language in the written instructions so that it is easy to understand what to do and be friendly in tone. Diagrams or pictures may also be useful.
- After your oral recap, ask them if they have any questions, but confine your answers to details of the task rather than tackling wider aspects, such as the purpose of the study.
- Do not discuss or even mention the hypothesis of the experiment. This can be done after the experiment is completed.
- In some designs, there can be different groups with different instructions. There would be standard instructions within each group and wherever possible use similar instructions across the groups for those aspects that are similar.
- During the experiment, participants may communicate with you. For example, they may ask for reassurance about their performance. Although it is difficult, try to be non-committal, otherwise this could affect their performance.

One aspect of this instruction phase is whether you want to 'prime' them. For instance, in a reaction time experiment should they respond as quickly as possible, or as accurately as possible, or should they respond both as quickly and as accurately as possible? Another kind of design is one in which there are two different groups who are going to view the same stimuli, but each group is given a subtly different orientation. The instructions would be crucial in providing the appropriate mental set.

Finally, if your experiment requires deception, you will have obtained ethical permission to do this before the experiment. Obviously, you will not tell the participants at the beginning that you are going to deceive them! Deception is not to be confused with withholding the hypothesis before doing the experiment. In this case, you are simply postponing disclosing the nature of the hypothesis until the end of the experiment. By contrast, when using deception participants might be led to believe that the purpose of the study is different from the true intention, or that the conditions of the study are 'genuine'. For example, they might presume (mistakenly) that another participant is as naïve as themselves.

Debriefing After an Experiment

In the section on ethics in chapter 3, we discussed the debriefing session and noted that when the experiment is over the participants should be told the reasons for doing the experiment. The major ethical consideration of this debriefing phase is that there might be a particular intervention in the experiment that induces some negative state. For instance, one might have been trying (for whatever reason) to convince the participant that they had a below average IQ. The nature of this deception should be made clear afterwards.

Experimenters who find themselves under time restraint find it more convenient to give a written description of the purpose of the experiment immediately afterwards. Alternatively, they take the participants' e-mail addresses and send them a fuller description once the results are analyzed. It is perhaps a better idea to send the purpose of the experiment after analysis to provide a more complete idea of the study. Of course, this would not apply if there has been any deception or anything slightly problematic about the experiment from an ethical point of view. In this case participants need a personal debriefing at the end of the experiment.

A more satisfactory debriefing than sending it by e-mail is to give a short interview about the purpose of your experiment and indeed your own department might require it. A brief interview involving questions and answers in both directions will probably make the whole experience more satisfying for participants and make them more willing to take part in further experiments. The interview would be used in particular for social psychology experiments in which deception had been used. The interview has other uses such as being able to explore the participants' own evaluation of the effectiveness of a particular intervention. In addition, did they guess correctly the purpose of the experiment?

If you are worried about participants telling later ones about the experiment, obviously you will need to ask them to keep the details of the study confidential. As a precaution, you could ask all participants what they thought the experiment was about and see whether responses change in a qualitative way for later participants. Similarly, they could be asked directly if anyone had told them anything about the experiment. This would be more important in an incidental memory experiment when the experimenter wanted to test memory for incidental stimuli that were presented earlier without telling the participant at that time to attend to them.

The Wording and Other Aspects of Questionnaire Construction

There are many aspects to devising a good questionnaire, but as this is a book on writing, we will only deal with the basics of constructing questions. If you want to construct a specialised test to measure psychological attributes or attitudes, you will need to consult elsewhere to go into aspects such as selecting items and the issues of reliability and validity (e.g. Beech & Harding, 1990; Kline, 2000).

We do not specifically deal here with the structured questionnaire with open-ended questions, such as those used in qualitative research studies. For example, in a qualitative study of people suffering from severe headaches one might ask in such a setting: 'Could you describe how your headaches affect the quality of your sleep?' However, some of the final section on the wording used in questionnaires would be relevant.

Types of questions

Rating or Likert scales

This is the most commonly used type of question in psychology in which a statement is made and the respondent has to give a rating, usually on a 5-point scale. The Likert scale is bipolar, meaning that the rater can rate the entity either positively or negatively. For example, the question might be:

Dogs tend to look like their owners.

1. Strongly disagree ☐
2. Disagree ☐
3. Neither agree nor disagree ☐
4. Agree ☐
5. Strongly agree ☐

To save valuable space a code for each outcome can be given near the top, so that the ratings can be arranged left to right, as shown in this example:

Please rate each statement below according to the following rating scale: SD = Strongly Disagree, D = Disagree, N = Neither disagree nor disagree, A = Agree, and SA = Strongly agree. Please circle only ONE choice for each question.

	SD	D	N	A	SA
1. Dogs tend to look like their owners.	SD	D	N	A	SA
2. Dog owners tend to walk like their dogs.	SD	D	N	A	SA

A more professional appearance might be as follows:

	SD	D	N	A	SA
1. Dogs tend to look like their owners.	☐	☐	☐	☐	☐
2. Dog owners tend to walk like their dogs.	☐	☐	☐	☐	☐

Student: How did you produce this last layout?

John: Using Word, create a 6-column table and in the first column put in the questions. In the rest of the columns to insert the boxes, go to 'Insert', select 'Symbol', and within *Wingdings* select the symbol you wish to use. Obviously, you then need to do some adjusting of the formatting to produce something that is acceptable. However, the layout previous to this that has no boxes is also an acceptable one to use.

(Perhaps in the interests of reflexivity I should disclose in relation to the above examples that I own two cats, so incline toward their view.) It is important to put a reminder of what the scale means on the top of each new page of the questionnaire. This need only be 'SD D N A SA' in the top right-hand part. Similarly, if the questionnaire is being presented on computer, as each question appears the description of the rating scale should remain available on the screen. The rating each respondent gives is treated as a score for a variable representing that particular question. So on Question 1 if SD is assigned 1, D = 2, N = 3, A = 4, and SA = 5, a mean score of 4.2 on this variable shows a consensus to agree with the statement that dogs look like their owners.

Multiple responses

This is the kind of question in which the respondent is offered several choices. For example:

Which of the following do you prefer to drink in the morning before lunchtime?

1. Coffee ☐
2. Tea ☐
3. Orange juice ☐
4. Water ☐
5. Other (please specify) ☐

In this form, there is the problem that people do not have a particular preference for one drink, but instead like to imbibe more than one type. The question would have been better as: 'Which of the following do you drink in the morning before lunchtime? Tick all the boxes that apply.' Treat the analysis of such questions differently from Likert scales because these are nominal scales. This means that each choice (e.g. for coffee) has to be treated as a separate variable coded '0', if the box is unchecked, and '1' if it is checked. Clearly, if you had treated the question as one variable with a score potentially ranging from 1 to 5, that score would be meaningless. We can learn from this sort of question that 45 per cent of respondents drink coffee in the morning and of these, 40 per cent drink other beverages as well. (I'm just making this up.)

This kind of question is used to find out more about participants (e.g. to check that eyesight is normal) and it can be useful as a basis for further analysis. For example, we may want to do further analyses of males versus females or divide those who drink coffee from those who do not drink it at all to compare them on the rest of our measures. As we are dealing with nominal scales here, we use non-parametric statistics such as Chi-square for analysis. For example, we can use Chi-square to find out whether significantly more males drink coffee than females, as long as we have enough people.

All investigators ask for the age of the respondent, but occasionally an investigator uses a choice of boxes (e.g. 16–20, 21–25, etc.). It would be better simply to ask the participant for their age in years. Then the ages can be divided into groups by computer analysis, if necessary, later. This would probably produce a better classification of the sample by age rather than by relying on divisions composed before running the experiment. In addition, the mean and standard deviation of the ages can be calculated and reported.

An advantage of running a pilot questionnaire earlier for the multiple-choice question is that it can help in the generation of categories. One can try out open-ended questions such as: 'Give a list of all the types of drink (e.g. coffee) that you drink in the morning before lunchtime.' You can then use these responses as the basis for the categories in your final questionnaire.

Ranked responses

This is where you ask respondents to place the items in order of importance (e.g. put a '1' for first choice, etc.). This is a more difficult operation and if the respondent has too many of these kinds of questions it can be off-putting. There is the complication of ties in which, for example, someone may want to choose two options as joint first. Some participants may have a problem with understanding that if there are two joint firsts the next rank after these two would be third, instead of second. However, the experimenter can sort this problem out later. Another difficulty is when there are too many items to be ranked. Despite these problems, getting people to rank items can be more informative than just the multiple-choice form. Like the multiple-choice, this question type involves nominal variables, so each category would be coded 0 or 1. As in the multiple-choice situation, this means we can use non-parametric testing for analysis. Finally, it is a good idea to instruct people to rank all the categories. Suppose despite this there are six categories in a question and the last two are left blank by a participant. You could either leave these as blanks (i.e. as missing data) or assign each of them the tied rank of fifth. You would note this in your report.

The wording used in a questionnaire

Care has to be taken so that the language is concise, unambiguous, and as neutral as possible. It is too vague to ask 'Do you exercise often?' Instead, you could use the multiple-category type of question and ask them to choose if they exercise every day, every 2 days, and so on. Also, try to avoid leading questions. People have a tendency to want to agree with the questioner so the way questions are phrased can influence their responses. For example, avoid asking a question such as: 'Would you agree that it is better to show your children the value of giving by being financially generous to your children?' This could lead to a contrasting view to the one expressed in the following question: 'Would you agree that it is better to show your children the value of money management by restricting their pocket money?'

If you are devising a particular psychological test, it is a good idea to examine both positive and negative aspects as a way of countering the problem of having leading questions. For example, if you are looking at attitudes to hygiene, you might ask on the one hand: 'Do you believe that it feels good to have clean hair?' At some later point in the questionnaire you could ask: 'Do you think that it doesn't matter to have unclean hair?' However, in doing this avoid the participant having to deal with more than one negative. For example, it would be a little more difficult to respond 'disagree' to the question: 'Do you disagree that it doesn't matter to have unclean hair?'

The structure of the questionnaire deserves some consideration. You would begin by thanking the participants for agreeing to complete the questionnaire. You probably want to give a context to the questionnaire to explain what you are trying to explore (but at such a level of generality that the results would not be biased in any way).

A questionnaire always has a section asking some personal questions, even if it is only about age and gender. The constructors of questionnaires vary in where they put such questions. Some put these at the back and others use the front. I prefer to put them at the front so that if one or two questions get left off the end, at least I have the important information at the beginning. You might start this bit with something like this: 'Please could you begin this part of the questionnaire by answering some personal questions? This is so we can assess the rest of your responses within a suitable context.'

In the rest of the questionnaire, you might want to block the questions according to their category. Thus, all responses that need a Likert scale would be in one place and those needing multiple responses in another section. Avoid a complicated branching structure in which participants have to go to different sections according to the responses they have given. Above all, try not to have too many questions. This is the worst temptation of the questionnaire constructor: to try to squeeze in too much. This can lead to a great decrease in the number of participants who are willing to respond to the questions all the way through and can result in a substantial loss of statistical power. We have already discussed the problems of having too many variables (refer to the 'safety net' section in chapter 7).

At the end of the questionnaire, it is a good idea to have a brief section outlining the treatment of the confidentiality of the information. For instance, you might state that the respondents' identities cannot be connected with the published data, if these identities are available to you. Finally, thank them for completing the questionnaire and if you are not going to be physically with them at the completion point, give instructions about where to post the completed product.

Chapter Summary

The main part of this chapter was concerned with recruiting participants, giving them instructions and then debriefing them at the end of their experiment. Although the recruitment and debriefing of participants applies to any type of study, the part about giving instructions was aimed more specifically at the experimenter running an experiment for quantitative analysis. One theme running through this part of the chapter was ethical considerations. From an ethical perspective, care has to be taken not to give a false impression of the nature of the experiment when recruiting participants. This would contravene the principle of informed consent. However, obviously no deception could be disclosed at the recruitment stage, or during the course of the experiment. In the debriefing part, researchers should let the participant know of any deception and the participant should be informed of the purpose of the experiment, either at the end of the session or at a later point when the results are available. If this is your own study, you will need to apply to an ethical committee in order to get approval if there are any elements of deception in the design.

The final part concentrated on the types of questions asked in questionnaires and how to code them. There was also a consideration of the main ways to make it easier for respondents to understand questions. It was noted that investigators were more likely to get their questionnaires completed when the length was modest and furthermore statistical power would be enhanced as more people would be willing to complete it.

10

ATTENTION TO DETAIL: MORE ON APA FORMATTING, ESPECIALLY REFERENCES

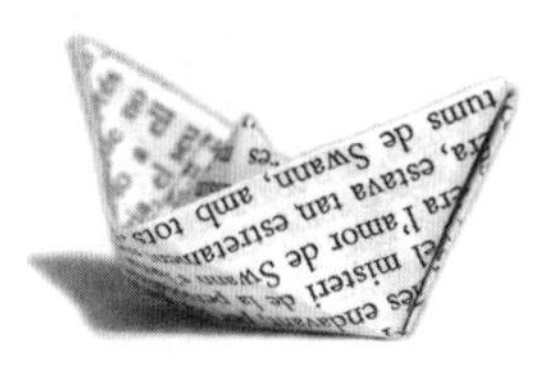

The American Psychological Association (APA) guidelines have already been referred to as a set of rules for writing in psychology. The description of these guidelines is contained in the 5th edition (American Psychological Association, 2001). These guidelines have evolved over the years by successive committees deciding on the best format for publishing papers in APA journals and they have become a benchmark for psychologists. In practice, most psychology journals have adopted a format style based on the APA guidelines. This is not to say that there are many variations even comparing psychological journals published in the United States. Other countries have also produced their own guidelines, but over time these have tended to become closer to the APA standard. We have already examined some of these guidelines in detail, especially in chapter 6 which looked at how numbers, figures, and tables should be configured, and in this chapter we are going to examine the rest of the formatting issues. Most of this chapter will concentrate on how to write references correctly in the reference listing and how to cite them correctly in the body of the text. The APA manual itself is comprehensive so inevitably not all the fine detail has been included here and it would be advisable to consult this if you have something that seems to be tricky. However, for most purposes there should be enough information within the present book.

Writing the List of References

The list of references and the three main types

The list of references given at the end of a report or essay allows readers to retrieve, if necessary, any particular publication. This is a list of all the references

Table 10.1 A checklist of the essential elements within three main types of publication

	The main types of publication					
	Journal paper		*Chapter or paper in an edited book*		*Books (authored rather than edited in this case)*	
1	Surname and initials of each author in sequence. As in: 'Sahdev, M. D., & Shaheen, M. A.'	✓	Surname and initials of each author in sequence. As in: 'Simpson, Y. A., & Brown, J. M.'	✓	Surname and initials of each author in sequence. As in: 'Smith, K. L., & Keeley, B. T.'	✓ ✓
2	Year. As in '(2003).'	✓	Year. As in '(2007).'	✓	Year. As in '(2001).'	✓
3	Title of paper. As in: 'Effective training in phonics.'	✓	Title of chapter/paper. As in: 'Flatulence and its psychological consequences.'	✓	Book title (in italics). As in '*Personality disorders: Their assessment.*'	✓
4	Title of journal (in italics). As in '*Journal of Psychology*,'	✓	'In' then initials and surname of each editor in sequence followed by '(Eds.),' As in: 'In F. T. Beltch & W. T. J. Wind (Eds.),'	✓	Place (and normally the abbreviation of the state if in USA). As in: 'New York:'	✓
5	Journal volume number (in italics). As in '*103*,'	✓	Book title (in italics). As in: '*Eating disorders: Vol. 2.*'	✓	Publisher. As in 'Oxford University Press.'	✓
6	Pages of paper. As in '325–334.'	✓	Pages of chapter/paper. As in '(pp. 231–254).'	✓		
7			Place (and normally the abbreviation of the state if in USA). As in: 'Newbury Park, CA:'	✓		
8			Publisher. As in 'Sage.'	✓		

Do not include any of the quotation marks shown in the table used in the piece of work and it is therefore necessary to check these through when it has been completed. Go through all the citations of sources in the text and tick off each reference listed at the end to see if anything is missing.

Ensure the citation to a reference in the text and the reference in the reference list is the same. It is easy to miss out an author in a list of authors, to misspell a name or to have a mismatch in dates. This is the stage when you will appreciate using a system in which you have noted the full source of all relevant references during the earlier writing phase.

The references themselves need to be complete, as one missing element, such as a volume number, can mean that the source is going to be more difficult to access. It helps to think of the distinct parts that are needed for each reference. There are several elements required for journal papers, book chapters, and whole books. If these are treated as tick boxes to check through each time, it will be unlikely that any element will be missed out. Table 10.1 is a checklist of the elements that are needed for each reference.

Here are these three (fictitious) references in Table 10.1 written out as if appearing in a references section:

Sahdev, M. D., & Shaheen, M. A. (2003). Effective training in phonics. *Journal of Psychology, 103*, 325–334.

Simpson, Y. A., & Brown, J. M. (2007). Flatulence and its psychological consequences. In F. T. Beltch & W. T. J. Wind (Eds.), *Eating disorders: Vol. 2.* (pp. 231–254). Newbury Park, CA: Sage.

Smith, K. L., & Keeley, B. T. (2001). *Personality disorders: Their assessment.* New York: Oxford University Press.

There are a few extra points to note. Journals normally have several issues within each volume. These issue numbers should not be cited; only the volume numbers should appear. However, just to muddy the waters there are some journals, not in mainstream psychology, that need the issue numbers. For edited books with only one editor, then it would obviously be '(Ed.)' in the bracketed part. Make a careful note when to use italics. Also, be aware of your country's use of punctuation, which will largely depend on the local adaptation of your instructors.

Journals: The major form of publication

Most research in psychology appears in journals (or 'periodicals' as the APA manual likes to call them). As already mentioned, journals publish several issues each year (e.g. one issue every quarter) which collectively come under a volume number. A journal that handles many papers can have more than one volume in a year. Almost all journals are publications to which authors send their papers for consideration for publication, rather than being invited to submit. In most cases, these go out for peer review (to academics with similar research interests). The editing process involves the papers eventually either being rejected or accepted after revision. The term 'citations' refers to the number of times a particular paper occurs in reference lists in other research papers. Journals vary in importance and the best ones attract on average a high number of citations for each of their research papers. Over time, important papers can be cited hundreds of times by other researchers.

Special issues in a journal

Journals sometimes invite one or more people to edit a collection of papers that will come out as a 'special issue' with a collective theme, in place of a normal issue. Usually issues in journals are an assortment of papers that are not themed in this manner. Sometimes a special issue is not large enough to fill the entire issue, so other papers are added to the end part to make up the space. In this case, the front themed part is sometimes known as a 'special section'. The special issue usually has named editors. If no editors are given, the title of the issue is the starting point of the reference in the References section and in the text use a short title, such as 'Assessing autism (2006)'. Here is an example of a reference to a special issue that was the entire issue of the journal:

> Nation, K., & Coltheart, M. (Eds.). (2006). Reading and genetics [Special Issue]. *Journal of Research in Reading, 29*(1).

Note here that the issue number, (1), was given. If it had been just a special section (in which other papers were included in the issue) then just the page range of the section would have been given. The volume number is in italics, as usual, but the issue number is not. If this reference had had no editors given, it would have appeared as follows:

> Reading and genetics. (2006). [Special Issue]. *Journal of Research in Reading, 29*(1), 1–132.

In the text, the citation might, for example, then appear as '... this controversy is also covered in "Reading and Genetics" (2006)'.

Edited books

A far less frequent type of publication is the chapter or paper appearing in an edited book. This can be a paper that reviews an area of research or presents an author's theoretical view of an area. We have already seen in Table 10.1 how to reference chapters in edited books. Let us turn to citing the whole volume. This type of reference is formatted in a similar way to the authored book. Two non-fictitious examples are as follows:

Manstead, A., Hewstone, M., Fiske, S. T., Hogg, M. A., Reis, H. T., & Semin, G. R. (Eds.). (1996). *The Blackwell encyclopedia of social psychology*. Oxford, England: Blackwell.

Nadel, L. (Ed.). (2003). *Encyclopedia of cognitive science, Vol. 3*. London: Nature Publishing Group.

Note that this last reference has six authors. If there had been a seventh author then 'et al.' would have been used, as in 'Manstead et al.' This is dealt with in more detail later in this chapter.

“ *Student:* You can imagine that in this situation the second to the sixth authors would be displeased if a seventh author jumped on board as it would reduce them all to an 'et al.'

John: An interesting point – I wonder if there's any connection with choosing this seventh position as the point where six authors magically disappear and Miller's (1956) paper about the magical number seven? Anyway, this thought might help you to remember it. ”

Sometimes a reference work, such as a dictionary, has no listing of editors or authors. Therefore in the references miss out the author part and start with the book title. In the text part just refer to the title followed by the date.

Potential difficulties referencing books

Publishers and their locations occasionally present one kind of problem. The principle is that if the book is published within the USA, the state is given as well. If the book has been published outside the USA, give the city and the country of publication. (These rules are drawn up by an American organisation after all – but would it have been more suitable to have taken a more international perspective?) As far as seven major American cities are concerned, their state does not need to be given: Baltimore, Boston, Chicago, Los Angeles, New York, Philadelphia, and San Francisco. The US states are referred to by two-letter abbreviations; for instance, Idaho is ID – very Freudian. These two-letter abbreviations are used for postal purposes and at the time of writing were easily found on Google – just put in 'abbreviations for states'. Ten major cities outside the USA are listed as not requiring their countries to be listed: Amsterdam, Jerusalem, London, Milan, Moscow, Paris, Rome, Stockholm, Tokyo, Vienna (American Psychological Association, 2001).

Other problems with books are that sometimes when you have a book that needs to be referenced it can be difficult to work out just how to reference the publisher, the location, and even the date. One, taken randomly from my shelf, has at the bottom of the title page 'THOMSON' followed by 'WADSWORTH' directly underneath. It then lists alphabetically eight different countries to the right of this! In my own copy of the APA manual itself, there are two dates, 2001 and 2002, with 2001 as the date of first printing and August 2002 as the 'fourth printing'. So which publisher, which location, and which date do we choose?

“ *Student:* Choose another book?
John: I'm sure a few people do just that! ”

In the Thomson Wadsworth book on the page following the title page there is: '© 2006 Thomson Wadsworth'; so it looks like they want to be referred to as 'Thomson Wadsworth'. Further down it states 'Printed in the United States of America' and a US address is given which includes 'Belmont, CA', so this can be used as the location. As far as the date is concerned, turning to the APA book, 2001 is the date to use because that is the date next to the copyright sign. Below this is just a listing of the months and dates of the different printings. However, if there is a revision to a book, then the date of the revision ought to be given, especially if quoting from this source. Publishers could help us by putting somewhere at the front of their books (that are likely to be used by psychologists) a heading such as 'our preferred reference to this book for APA formatting would be as follows:'

Uncommon types of reference sources in the reference list

The following are examples of other sorts of references.

Translated book

Piaget, J. (1995). *The child's construction of reality.* (M. Cook, Trans.). London: Routledge & Kegan Paul. (Original work published 1954)

When this is cited in the text, in this case it would be 'Piaget (1954/1995) argued that ...' The name in brackets followed by 'Trans.' refers to the name of the translator.

Conference proceedings

Conferences papers may be available in some published form after their presentation. Some regular conferences have later proceedings, which more often have abstracts of paper rather than full papers. Much less often, the presented paper could have been part of a symposium in which several speakers gave a presentation, followed by a discussant who tried to draw some conclusion. Sometimes these symposia can become part of a chapter in an edited book. In a typical essay or laboratory report it is unlikely there would be a need for a student to cite conference papers or posters (see the next heading). However, an example of an unpublished conference paper would be:

Vollm B., Stirling J., & Richardson, P. (2003, June). *The neurobiology of impulse control and sympathy in normal, anti-social and anxious individuals.* Paper presented at the annual conference of the British & Irish Group for the Study of Personality Disorders, Dublin: Ireland.

Poster session

A poster is a description of research presented on a large board that attendees at conferences can visit. The author or authors of the poster may occasionally be present to explain their work to anyone interested. As in the conference paper, it is normal to include the month as well as the year in the reference listing.

Engelhardt, P. E., & Ferreira, F. (2006, November). *Processing coordination ambiguity in the visual world: Frequency and context do not override the preference for syntactic simplicity*. Poster session presented at the 47th annual meeting of the Psychonomics Society, Houston, Tx.

Doctoral dissertations and other types of thesis

A reference to a full unpublished dissertation or thesis would be as follows:

Almeida, D. M. (1990). *Fathers' participation in family work: Consequences for fathers' stress and father–child relations.* Unpublished masters thesis, University of Victoria, British Columbia, Canada.

Chera, P. D. K. (2000). *Multimedia CAL and early reading: Iterative design, development and evaluation*. Unpublished doctoral dissertation, University of Bristol, UK.

Online references

References from the Web can be problematic especially if the URL is a long one. The URL should be given exactly as it appears and it should not be underlined. This might be tricky for beginners because as soon as the return button is pressed, the URL becomes activated simultaneously turning blue and becoming underlined. To correct this, place the mouse over the URL and right click and choose 'remove hyperlink'. Do not follow the URL by a full stop. There are now journals that are only available online and occasionally they do not have page numbers available. To reference such a paper, give the author or authors, date and title of the paper, and volume number, as normal. Then follow it as in this example: '... Article 35. Retrieved 3 June 2007, from http://fictitious.org/madeup.html'.

Deciding the order of the list of references

Obviously, the list of references should be organised in alphabetical order, but occasionally it can get a little more complicated, as can be seen in Box 10.1:

Box 10.1 Getting the Order of Authors Right

- **When authors have two or more papers with others or by themselves.** For instance, how would the following be arranged in a reference list: Smith, 2007; Smith, 2002; Smith & Brown, 1993; Smith & Brown, 1986? The answer is that these papers would be arranged so that the single-authored papers come first, followed by the multiauthored papers, and then date ordering would come into operation. Thus the final order would be: Smith, 2002; Smith, 2007; Smith & Brown, 1986; Smith & Brown, 1993, if Smith and Brown are the same people within these references and not different people.
- **If an author appears first in the list of authors for more than one paper** (e.g. Smith & Mitchell, 1982; Smith & Hanson, 1987; Smith & Brown, 1992) then the listing is arranged in alphabetical order by the second author, or by the third author, if the first two authors are the same for two papers. In this example, the order would be: Smith & Brown (1992); Smith & Hanson (1987); Smith & Mitchell (1982).

Box 10.1 *(cont'd)*

- **Identical authorship in the same year.** It can happen that not only does the same author or combination of authors occur in two different papers, but the papers come out in the same year. The two (or more) papers are labelled 'a' and 'b' (and 'c' and so on) after the date; for instance: '(1999a)'. The ordering of 'a' and 'b' will depend on the alphabetical order of the title, ignoring *A* or *The*. However, if the papers are in a series (Part 1, Part 2, etc.), place them within the series order.
- **Getting authors' actual names in the correct order.** There are a few points to note here:

1. Beech or Beeching: Which goes first? Nothing goes before something, so it's Beech then Beeching.
2. Is Mc treated as Mc or Mac? Treat literally, so the order is MacX, McX, where X stands for Donald or whomever.
3. Some surnames come in two or more parts (e.g. Danny La Rue). There is no rule here out of respect for a person's language of origin.
4. When two authors have the same surname in different publications (e.g. J. T. Brown, 1976; R. L. Brown, 2005) they are arranged alphabetically by their initials in the reference list. Although not directly relevant here, their initials should be given when citing in the text (e.g. 'R. L. Brown found that …').

" *Student:* Reading the bit about 'identical authorship in the same year', why can't these people wait until the following year before publishing their next paper and make life easier for the rest of us?
John: Yes, it's very inconsiderate. "

How to do a hanging indent

Just to finish off this section on constructing the reference list, here is some advice about how to do a hanging indent, which is a paragraph for each reference that has all lines apart from the first one indented. To get this in Word, highlight all the references and then click 'Format' on the top menu and then 'Paragraph'. The dropdown box has a section entitled 'Indentation' and within that 'Special'. Click the down arrow and click the 'Hanging' item in the dropdown box and then click OK.

How to Reference Citations in the Body of the Text

We should always back up a description of a piece of research with a reference to at least one study that has been written about this research. This reference that is given in the text (e.g. '... as found by Jones (1974) ...') is referred to as a 'reference citation' as opposed to the 'reference listing' which is the listing of the references.

When the source is a single author

The simplest form of citation would be: 'Smith (2007) proposed that ...' Here the author's last name comes first followed by the date of publication in brackets. However, writers understandably like to add variety, so it is also permissible to put the citation entirely in parentheses or to use no parentheses: 'This hypothesis has been criticized for its vagueness (Smith, 2000) ...' or 'in 2005 Smith criticized the hypothesis for its vagueness ...' However, this latter example ('in 2005 Smith ...') should be used rarely, if at all.

If the same author of the same study is referred to again in the same paragraph, there is no need to cite the year for further citations within this paragraph. Obviously, if a new paragraph is started, then the date needs to accompany the author's name once more.

Sources by multiple authors

There are conventions for citing more than one author in the text.

Reference by two authors

Both the names need to be cited every time in the text; for instance: 'Smith and Brown (2003) showed ...' This would change to 'Smith and Brown also showed ...' (no date) if the citation is still within the same paragraph.

Reference by three, four, or five authors

In this case all the authors and the date of the publication are cited the first time, but subsequently the citation is only to the first author followed by 'et al.' (Note the lack of italics and the presence of the full stop.) Here are the rules in more detail, with A, B, C, and D representing the authors' names:

Box 10.2 Rules for Citing Three or More Authors

- Is it the first time ever cited? If yes: 'A, B, C, and D (2000) showed ...'
- Is it cited again in that same paragraph? If yes: 'A et al. showed ...'
- Is it a first citation in a following new paragraph? If yes: 'A et al. (2000) showed ...'
- Is it a following citation in this same new paragraph? If yes: 'A et al. showed ...'

Thus the second, third and fourth authors represented here as B, C and D only appear in the first paragraph in which the first citation of the study appears. The date is given only when it is the first citation within any paragraph.

Reference by six or more authors

In all citations in the text refer to the first author followed by 'et al.' and the year (e.g. 'Smith et al. (2005) showed ...'). In the reference list if there are just six authors, give the surnames and initials of the six authors. When there are more than six, the seventh and subsequent authors lose their identity and become just 'et al.'

Occasionally one can have two references with six or more authors that have the same first author. As would be the case with works by three to five authors, cite just enough early authors to be able to distinguish the two papers.

How to use 'and' with two or more authors

The rule is that *and* is used in normal text, as in 'Adams and Brown (2000) showed ...' and 'Adams, Brown, and Cherry (2000) showed ...' When the reference is in parentheses, tables, captions and the reference list then an ampersand (&) is used, as in: '... shown by two studies (Adams & Brown, 2000; Adams, Brown, & Cherry, 2000)'.

How to deal with more than one citation in parentheses

The previous section has shown how to arrange two references in brackets. The dates do not need to be further embedded in parentheses; instead, each reference is separated by a semicolon (;). The order of these citations should be the same as for the ordering in the reference list. (See the section 'Deciding the order of the list of references' for more detail.) Here is an example:

> Previous research (Forklift, 2006, in press-a, in press-b; Witherspoon & Hardknife, 1982, 1983a, 1983b) ...

Note that the authors within parentheses are ordered alphabetically by the first author's surname. There can be an exception to this if there is a separation between the authors within the parentheses by a phrase such as 'see also':

> ... has led to some support for this position (Blandness, 1995; McAgree, 2002; see Adamson, 2003, for a review).

Authors with the same surname

When two sole or first authors are cited in the text who have the same surname in single-authored papers, their initials need to be used to distinguish them:

> J. K. Smith (1978) and P. M. Smith (1987) have demonstrated ...
> H. Braine and Granger (1997) and J. T. Braine and Stringle (2000) showed that ...

These initials would also be used on later occasions and within parentheses. Note that this only applies with *primary* authors, defined as a first author or the first of two or more authors. Thus had the second reference been Stringle and Braine, then the initials of Braine would not have been given.

References in the text with no authorship

Give the title of the work, surrounded by quotation marks, and the year:

> ... has been shown to be highly effective ("Ways to Cope with Stress," 1997).

An authorship that is explicitly anonymous can be cited as such in the text:

> ... as shown by Anonymous (2007).

Such a work would be referenced as by *Anonymous* in the reference list.

Personal communication

This is a collective term for any form of communication to you. For example, you may have written to an author asking about an experimental detail. In your text, this might appear as:

> '... however, only five females were tested in this study (J. T. Smith, personal communication, February 20, 2002) ...'

Alternatively, the name of the communicator can be outside the brackets. Note that the initials of the author or authors are given in personal communications. This communication can be by e-mail, letter, telephone, or text message, but it must be relevant in the context of your writing. A key aspect is that you personally received this information. This would not include something posted to a newsgroup, for instance. A personal communication does not appear in the reference list.

The next section moves away from referencing and is a brief summary on how to punctuate.

Punctuation (including Hyphens, Quotes and Quotation Marks)

Imagine text without any punctuation. What would you make of 'Eats shoots and leaves?' which happens to be the title of a 2003 book by Lynne Truss on punctuation?

> *Student:* How do you know it's not about a gun-toting panda?
> *John:* You've been reading too much sci-fi.

If a writer does not know the distinction, for example, between the colon and the semicolon or between the comma and the full stop this can lead to problems of understanding. The prosody in speech (intonation, rhythm, etc.) normally disambiguates meaning. When we change over to writing to communicate, all we have available is punctuation. Therefore, it needs to be correct.

The basic role of punctuation is to signal when we have a pause, or want to take a detour, or simply when we want to stop and move on to the next complete thought. Let us begin at the end of the sentence which has the full stop, the question mark or the exclamation mark.

Sentence endings

A *full stop* is used to at the end of a complete sentence. So how do you know when a sentence is complete? Here is an example of an error that is occasionally made:

> The first participant in each pair had to describe the picture, the other had to draw it only on the basis of the description.

It can be seen that these are two complete sentences that should have been separated by a full stop instead of the comma. One can appreciate why the error has been made in the first example, as the two statements seem to be too short in themselves, making the construction appear clumsy. The writer of the first example may have considered that the second statement is a kind of continuation of the first. Perhaps a better construction would be to use *and* as a connection between the two:

> The first participant in each pair had to describe the picture and the other had to draw it only on the basis of the description.

There is an alternative way of correcting our first example and that is to use a *semicolon*:

> The first participant in each pair had to describe the picture; the other had to draw it only on the basis of the description.

As can be seen, the semicolon can be used to join two complete sentences together. This would be when the relationship between the two sentences is considered by the writer as too close for the use of a full stop. However, it would be better to use the semicolon in cases where it is difficult to use a connecting word such as *and*. Here is an example of the *incorrect* use of the semicolon:

> The first participant had to describe the picture; but only briefly.

When a semicolon is used, both sides of the semicolon have to be complete sentences. Therefore, this example is incorrect because the second part 'but only briefly' is not a complete sentence. Read the beginning of chapter 11, which explains how sentences are constructed, if you are still unsure about this. In psychology, the semicolon is also used for components of a series that are already separated by commas:

> Each participant experienced the order picture, word, sound; word, picture, sound; or sound, word, picture.

The *question mark* is used at the end of sentences that are direct questions:

> How does this hypothesis explain the orientation reflex?
> What is the outcome of an authoritative parenting style?

The question mark is not used, however, for the indirect question:

> The participants were asked if they had smoked within the past 24 hours.

Punctuation within sentences

The colon (and semicolons)

We have just examined the semicolon in the last section. A close relative is the colon, which seems a bit too enigmatic for some. There are several things to note. First, two fairly trivial errors connected with the colon are (1) to have a space before it – it should only ever have a single space after it – and (2) to have a hyphen after it. Second, the sentence construction is typically a general statement ending with the colon and followed by a more specific aspect. The part that is before the colon should be a complete sentence, but what follows need not be. Third, in the USA the colon is followed by a capital letter only if what follows is a complete sentence. However, this is rarely the case in British usage in which there is normally no capitalisation after the colon, although there are signs of this rule relaxing in Britain. The following examples illustrate when a colon is used or not used in the USA:

> His bread always failed to rise: It was as dead as a dough-dough.
> The difference between the groups disappeared with the inclusion of the covariate: $F(1, 76) = 4.11, p = .05, d = .06$.
> The participants were either (1) unaware of the context or (2) primed beforehand. (In this example, there is not a colon after *either* because at this point there is not a complete sentence in this first part.)
> The first category of irregular word, the "mildly inconsistent" (MI), is composed of two types of word: (1) Those that possess a minor correspondence…

The colon has a few minor uses. It is used in ratios:

> The ratio of words to nonwords was 2:1.

The colon is also used in references between the place of publication and publisher (e.g. Oxford: Blackwell); and when a title of a book or paper has a title and subtitle. Here is an example of such a title in the journal *Science*:

> Sex and the single hemisphere: Specialization of the right hemisphere for spatial processing.

Unhelpfully the colon and semicolon not only have similar labels but also look similar. It is not surprising that they can get confused in their use. However, there can be subtle differences in their use. If we consider two juxtaposed statements (see the examples 1–3 below), the extent of the connection between them can be shown by punctuation. If there is no connection to speak of, then a full stop is used. If there is a slight connection then use a semicolon. Finally, if there is a more definite relationship between the two, use a colon:

1. The difference between the two conditions failed to reach significance. The hypothesis may not seem to be supported.
2. The difference between the two conditions was not significant; the hypothesis is not supported.
3. The difference between the two conditions was not significant: The hypothesis is therefore falsified.

Interruptions

Interruptions in sentences occur when the writer wants to provide extra information that is not completely relevant to the main idea (e.g. by putting such material in parentheses like this). Parentheses, known also as round brackets, are used more often than bracketing commas by writers:

> Outliers in the reaction times (2 or more SDs from the mean) were removed before the analysis.

Occasionally parentheses may surround a sentence, but remember to capitalise the first letter of the first word and put the full stop signalling the end of the sentence inside the end bracket, rather than after it. Parentheses are rarely used as 'asides' in scientific writing, but just to show this kind of use, here is an example outside the scientific context:

Our city transport doesn't always run on time (as rumour would have it).

It is advisable not to use asides by the writer to the reader in psychological writing. If the parentheses are too long, consider rewriting the whole sentence to break it into two parts without the need for brackets.

Another problem that can arise with brackets is when there is yet more information that initially the writer thinks needs to be embedded within further brackets. If this is unavoidable then use square brackets for the inner brackets; but often there can be a work-around using commas, as shown in these two examples:

(See Pleabody, 2007, for an elaboration.)

(This example surrounds the date 2007 by commas instead of embedded square brackets.)

... this showed a significant effect for parenting, $F(1, 83) = 41.96$, $p < .001$, and...

(This example shows how bracketing commas are used to give the statistical details of the *F* test to avoid having to put the degrees of freedom within square brackets, if round brackets had been used instead of these commas.)

Dashes and hyphens

There are a number of functional differences between the hyphen, the *en dash* and the *em dash*. The hyphen is typed using the key next to the zero on your keyboard. This same key is also used to create the en dash (type as one hyphen) and em dash (type as two hyphens). In all three cases no space should be put either before or afterwards. The exception to this 'no-spaces' rule is the hanging hyphen (e.g. 5- or 6-year-olds – see below). A pair of em dashes can serve an identical role to brackets and give a strong interruption to a sentence to provide added information:

Outliers in the reaction times—2 or more SDs from the mean—were removed before the analysis.

A program such as Word will normally convert this into the uninterrupted line shown in this last example—as long as a word is typed subsequently. It might also be noted that the em dash has been preferred in US English, but not widely in UK English. However, that might be changing now. A further use of the em dash is illustrated earlier in this paragraph, in which extra information is added to the end of the sentence. As with brackets, try not to overuse these dashes.

> *Student:* In this case are pairs of brackets and pairs of dashes interchangeable?
>
> *John:* Yes they are; but there are subtle distinctions. First, using dashes this way is perhaps giving rather more emphasis to the extra information. Second, in the 'etiquette' of writing people generally prefer brackets over dashes, so try to minimise their use. In any case, try to reduce the use of brackets as well. Too many interruptions in this form can disrupt the flow of the writing.

The en dash is used with words within a compound adjective where the words have equal value (e.g. Yerkes-Dodson law). Of course, in practice you are typing the same key as you would for a hyphen.

The hyphen is used in compound words. In the English language there is a tendency to start new compound words with hyphens (e.g. felt-tipped) and then to combine them into a new compound word with use. Because the application of hyphens in this context is based on usage, there are no clear guidelines about when to use them. Perhaps in time the hyphen in compound words will die out altogether. Meanwhile the dictionary needs to be consulted on current use.

A hyphen should be used if it is necessary to clarify the meaning:

2-year-old rats were tested.

(As opposed to two rats that were a year old; this would have been expressed as 'Two year-old rats were tested.')

Sex role difference

(This is unambiguous and therefore does not need a hyphen.)

In the case of ages, hyphens are used as follows:

An 18-year-old female who has epilepsy was shown …
The groups of 8-, 9-, and 10-year-olds were all given instructions on …

Note the hanging hyphens after the 8 and 9, respectively. The same principle shown in this last example applies to other series:

The pictures were shown successively for 100-, 200-, and then 300-ms durations with 500-ms intervals between each presentation.

Finally, when expressing the numbers 21 to 99 in words use hyphens where necessary (e.g. thirty-two), as we saw in the 'numbers' section of chapter 6.

Commas

Everyone knows how to use the comma, don't they? Commas occur so often in print that it is rare to see people making errors with them in cases of common usage. However, there are some rarer occasions when mistakes can occur. Sometimes the use of commas is down to personal taste, particularly in long complex sentences in which the pauses can be assigned somewhat arbitrarily. Commas have several functions, as shown in Box 10.3:

Box 10.3 The Various Functions of Commas

The comma is used:

1. in lists to separate the items (e.g. '... green, red, and yellow'). In UK punctuation the comma would be missing before the 'and'.
2. to separate sections of complex sentences to make the sentence more readable.
3. around a non-defining relative clause (i.e., a clause that is not essential to the sentence's meaning – see the entry for *that/which/who(m)* in chapter 11 for further explanation). Such a clause might be considered as a section of a sentence and it is similarly surrounded by commas (e.g. 'This theory, which was introduced by Bland (1946), is deficient in three respects ...'). By contrast, a defining clause is not set off by commas. A useful clue that you are dealing with a defining clause is that it often begins with 'that' (e.g. 'The witness identified the knife *that was shorter than the rest* as the murder weapon').
4. to serve the purpose of brackets. We have already referred to 'bracketing commas' whereby commas may be used in place of brackets.
5. in numbers, if there are four or more numbers (e.g. 1,844; 210,455). However, there are exceptions, such as for years (e.g. 1976) and page numbers (e.g. page 1189).
6. after certain abbreviations. APA requires that the following three abbreviations are followed by commas: (1) 'e.g.,' as in '(e.g., Granger, 1987)' (2) 'i.e.,' (3) 'viz.,'

(cont'd)

Box 10.3 *(cont'd)*

Finally, here are some examples of miscellaneous uses (or lack of use) of the comma:

Each tall male participant was asked... (Thus it is *not* 'Each tall, male participant...')
There was one problem, however, that had to be corrected.
Clearly, this was an important variable in the study.
Jencks et al. (2004) found... (Thus there is no comma before *et al.*).
Jencks, Hind, et al. (2006) proposed... (This time there is a comma before *et al.* because there is more than one author cited here.)

"*Student:* In this last example, why are two authors cited before the *et al.*?

John: Because in this case the piece of work with this particular citation has two references with multiple authors that can only be distinguished by citing the first two authors."

Using quotations

Before quoting something that an author has written, think carefully about whether you need to make a quotation. Occasionally a beginning student will hand in an essay that is full of quotations, perhaps showing an underconfidence in being able to express the ideas of others in their own words. By contrast, for a quantitative research report quotations have an important role (see chapter 5). Here is some advice about when to use quotations:

Box 10.4 Guidelines for Using Quotations

1. Use double quotes ("...") for short quotations in the text; for instance:

Sydney Smith (1771–1845) proposed that "Prejudice is opinion without judgement."

Box 10.4 *(cont'd)*

2. Use the exact words of the author. This means that anything else must be outside the quotations. For example, authors might be tempted to adjust the quotation slightly to fit within context:

> Sydney Smith stated that "prejudice was opinion without judgement."

However, this temptation must be resisted.

3. One would hope that your quotation is below 40 words, but if it is 40 words long or over, the quotation instead needs to be within an indented block of text. This text should *not* have quotation marks surrounding it and it should not be in italics. It should begin on a new line.

4. All quotations, no matter what length, should have (a) the author, (b) the year, and (c) the specific page or pages. The convention is for the page number or numbers (e.g. 'p. 302') to appear at the end of the quotation (outside the quotes, if there are quotation marks) as shown in these two examples:

According to Frith (2007):

> We have no direct contact with the world or even with our own bodies. Our brain creates this illusion by hiding from us all the complex processes that are involved in discovering about the world. We are simply not aware of all the inferences and choices our brain constantly has to make. (p. 81)

Rutter (2007) in discussing the effects of genetics on different aspects of personality considers these "to be of importance in relation to risks for mental disorder but the findings to date remain rather uncertain" (p. 171).

5. Occasionally, the source of the quotation could be from the Web and there may be no page number available. In this case, cite the heading of the section containing the quote and the paragraph number, as in: (Effingham, 1999, Introduction section, para. 9).

(cont'd)

Box 10.4 *(cont'd)*

6. The complete reference to the source of the quotation needs to be in the reference list.
7. Use square brackets to clarify anything within the quotation. For instance, if you choose to italicise some of the words to give them emphasis, it should be noted within square brackets immediately afterwards that italics have been added.
8. If the quotation has within itself a further quotation, or some speech, then this part should be surrounding by single quotes.
9. Use a suspension, also known as ellipses (…), if parts of the quotation have been missed out. It may be necessary to insert your own words within square brackets to provide some minor joining of a section. Care must be taken not to distort the original meaning when doing this.

The apostrophe

I am not a member of the Apostrophe Protection Society (yes, there really is one – see Truss, 2003), but I can see why people of a more perfectionist persuasion flock to join. The apostrophe is much misused, but its correct use will only be treated briefly here. The apostrophe should be used as follows:

- To indicate a missing letter (e.g. 'he can't' instead of 'he cannot'). However, in academic writing a *contraction* such as this is not permitted.
- To show possession (e.g. 'the participant's right hand'). This changes according to whether it is singular or plural. If we referred to all the participants we would write 'the participants' right hands' and the apostrophe would come after the *s*, as shown.

The following cases do not use an apostrophe:

- Possessive pronouns do not have an apostrophe: *hers*, *his*, *its*, *whose*, *ours*, and *yours*.
- Do not use the apostrophe for plurals: *DVDs*, *1980s*, and *bees*.

Jim tried out Maslow's peak experience for himself

Font Style (Bold, Italics and Capitalisation)

Bold

For student work, it is advisable to use bold font for all titles, heading, and subheadings (unless advised otherwise). As mentioned before, do not use bold to emphasise a point that you are making.

Italics

Box 10.5 When to Use Italics

Italics are used

1. for linguistic examples, such as letters or words: 'The word *big* had accidentally been included in the list…'
2. for the first occurrence of a key term; for example: 'We will be examining the technique of *priming* in the context of…' Note that after this first occasion, the word is no longer placed in italics.
3. for statistical symbols or variables in an algebraic expression:

   $t(34) = 4.67$
   $F(2, 43) = 4.53$
   On the $(n - 1)$th trial

This is something that students sometimes forget to do.

(cont'd)

Box 10.5 *(cont'd)*

4. for probability level (e.g. '$p < .001$').
5. for the titles of tables (but not for figure captions). The figure *labels* (e.g. *Figure 1.*) are in italics, but not the table labels (e.g. Table 1). Italics are not used within tables or figures. (The word *note* alone is in italics for notes under tables.)
6. for book titles.
7. for volume numbers of journals.
8. occasionally to show emphasis (see the last line of this box). However, use italics with moderation.

Do *not* use italics for Greek letters or for foreign phrases (e.g. et al.).

Capitalisation

Box 10.6 When to Use Capital (Upper-case) Letters

Use capital letters for

1. the initial letter of the first word in sentences and after a colon (:), if what follows is a sentence. The UK English rule is not to capitalise after a colon.
2. all proper nouns that are the names of people or places: Stroop effect, Paivio (1978), Manchester, the Irish Sea, the Golden Gate Bridge, Prime Minister Harper, University of Sydney.
3. trade names: Raven's Coloured Matrices, a Leica Camera.
4. nouns followed by numbers or letters: Trial 1, Figure 3, Table 5, Experiment 2, Week 3, Factor C. (There are APA exceptions: (a) when referring to part of a table: 'row 5'; and (b) referencing part of a book: chapter 3, page 6.)
5. names of variables in ANOVAs if with a multiplication sign or signs: 'A significant Dominance × Frequency interaction …' (However, when there is no multiplication sign do not capitalise: 'A significant dominance by frequency interaction …')

Box 10.6 (*cont'd*)

6. names of day, weeks, and months: 'Participants were tested on every Monday, Wednesday, and Friday during January and February 2005.' However, note the seasons (spring, summer, autumn and winter) are not written with a capital.
7. names of languages, nationalities, and ethnic groups: 'The bilingual participants spoke English with either Hindi or Gujarati.'
8. all main words in headings and subheadings: Method, Results.
9. book titles quoted in the text: 'In Broadbent's 1971 book, *Decision and Stress*, he argued ...' However, given that word counts are normally tight it would be better just to put 'Broadbent (1971) argued ...' It should also be noted that in the reference list only the first letter of the first word of a book title is capitalised. If there is a colon in the title, the word following also has its first letter capitalised. To complicate matters, British book titles usually are not capitalised after the colon.
10. the major words in the title of a journal.
11. the major words in table titles: '*Mean Percentages of Correct Spellings* ...' But use capitals for only the first word for figure captions: 'Mean reaction times in the priming ...'

Box 10.7 When NOT to Capitalise

Do not capitalise

1. names of hypotheses, models, and laws: 'the dual route hypothesis'. However, if a person's name is included, the name should be capitalised: 'Emmert's law'.
2. conditions or experimental groups within an experiment: 'The introvert group was found to have ...'
3. when not referring to a specific kind of test: a recognition test.

Abbreviations

Abbreviations can sometimes be helpful in cutting down the number of words in text. They can also be especially useful, for example, with an abbreviation such as MMPI-A, which is much easier to use than the cumbersome 'Minnesota Multiphasic Personality Inventory-Adolescent'. However, if abbreviations are used too much they can make the meaning of a passage difficult to understand. In a long project write-up, where an abbreviation is occasionally used, it can be frustrating for readers to have to track back to remind themselves what this abbreviation stood for. The APA manual advises us to use abbreviations only when the abbreviation is conventionally used (e.g. RT for Reaction Time) and when it saves a substantial amount of space (as with MMPI-A). It is fairly easy to invent many new abbreviations during the writing and become familiar with them; but the writer can fail to understand that the reader will not necessarily have the same background. This can impede communication. One further aspect is to avoid beginning sentences with abbreviations, in the same way that it is advisable not to start sentences with numbers.

Standard abbreviations

Many standard abbreviations such as 'etc.' do not need to be explained. To these can be added well-known psychologically related abbreviations such as IQ, ESP, and REM. Do not use abbreviations such as P, S, E, or O for participant, subject, experimenter, or observer, respectively.

Non-standard abbreviations

These are abbreviations of less commonly known terms. They first need to be elaborated in the text. For example: 'The effect of being exposed to Cued Speech (CS) on children with impaired hearing…'

Abbreviations and punctuation

Box 10.8 When to Use Full Stops

Use a full stop for

1. initials of authors: 'P. R. Wandelt'.
2. pseudonyms for particular participants: 'G.K.M.'

Box 10.8 (*cont'd*)

3. Latin abbreviations: 'vs., i.e., etc., and e.g.' (Note that these would *only* appear as abbreviations within parentheses, but within the text would be written out, and they are *not* in italics. The abbreviation *etc.* is best avoided altogether as it gives a somewhat vague impression.)
4. several abbreviations in the reference list: 'Ed., Vol., and pp.' (Note that pp. is used for 'pages'.)

Box 10.9 When NOT to Use Full Stops

Do not use a full stop for

1. capital letter abbreviations such as IQ, MIT, NATO, BPS.
2. abbreviations of measurements, either metric or non-metric, such as ft, cm, hr, min, lb.)
3. abbreviations of US state names: 'NY'.

Plurals of abbreviations

Simply add an 's' on the end, but do not italicise it or add an apostrophe: 'vols.'

11

SOME BASICS OF GRAMMAR AND COMMON CONFUSIONS

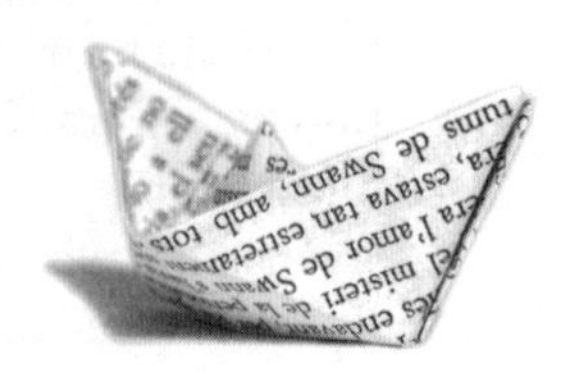

Apart from this brief introduction, the components of this chapter are organised in A–Z order to enable easy access. This has the advantage that a particular problem can be quickly accessed.

Let us begin with an elementary introduction to grammar. Consider this simple sentence: 'John saw Bill.' This sentence has only three words consisting of two nouns (*John, Bill*) and one verb (*saw*). Nouns and verbs are classes of words. Some words (and *saw* is one of these) serve as both nouns and verbs, depending on their context. When you look up a word in a good dictionary it will give the word class (or classes) of that entry and the different meanings of those words. Many words have more than one meaning (e.g. *bay*).

It is worth understanding the properties of a sentence. For example, the following should be two separate sentences: 'Jack climbed down from the horse, he then tied it up and walked down to the house.' The period should come directly after *the horse*. The sentence is a grammatical unit that according to the rules of grammar is self-sufficient. It has a subject (e.g. *John* in *John saw Bill*) that is explicit or is at least understood and it contains at least one verb. This is different from speech, when we can say sentences that do not appear to have a verb. For instance, 'Yes, please' or 'Tired?' but even in the latter example there is an implied verb: '*Are* you tired?'

The following is an A–Z of grammar; but it is not an exhaustive one. The rules of English grammar are mostly clear cut, although there are areas in which usage shifts slightly over time. Occasionally I will refer to the view of purists or traditionalists who lag behind these developments and who have a stricter view of these rules (e.g. see the entry for **absolute term**). You may wish to ignore the purists, but be wary that there is the risk that your marker may be a purist ('and a sadist' you might add). However, it is unlikely that minor transgressions will translate into lost marks, as long as the overall quality of the writing is good. Please note that information on punctuation and abbreviations is available in the final parts of chapter 10 and is not annotated here. Also note that if a term is written in bold (e.g. as in **absolute term** above), this indicates that it has an entry in this chapter.

A–Z Guide to Grammar and Common Confusions

A/an. It can occasionally be difficult to decide if some words beginning with *h* should be preceded by *a* or *an*. If the *h* is aspirated, then begin with *a* (e.g. *a hat, a hypothesis*), but if not, precede with *an* (e.g. *an honest person*).

Absolute term (e.g. *unique*). There are some words that are absolute terms, in that they cannot be modified. A fur coat is made of fur; it cannot be made of fur to an extent. One would not say: 'She's wearing a *very* fur coat' because a coat is either fur or it is not. However, there are terms that are more debatable. Purists would regard adjectives such as *unique, closed*, and *perfect* as not modifiable. An example of correct usage would be: 'Her particular type of training gave her a *unique* advantage over her fellow students.' While everyone would agree that *very unique* does not make sense, *almost unique* could be tolerated by most, but not all readers. 'Almost unique' is the equivalent of saying that something occurs rarely. (Refer also to the discussion of the absolute term **none**.)

Active versus passive voice. Here are two sentences; the first is active and the second passive:

Active: The overweight ballerina wore a three-three.
Passive: The three-three was worn by the overweight ballerina.

The active sentence has *the overweight ballerina* as the **subject** of the sentence who is performing the action of *wearing* as indicated by the **verb** *wore*. The **object** of the sentence is *three-three* (sorry, if you hadn't realised that this is wordplay on *tutu*). In the passive construction, the subject and object switch positions. In order to accommodate this, the preposition *by* is put in front of the agent *the overweight ballerina*. Note that the verb *wore* here is a transitive verb, which means the verb can take an object and therefore can be used for both active and passive constructions such as this.

It can be useful to be able to transform a sentence from active to passive or vice versa. Writers are often advised to use the active voice. However, in psychological writing it can be difficult to avoid the passive. An author may have written something that sounds remote such as: 'Participants were sought by the experimenter from various sources.' This is the passive form that would read more directly if were transformed into the active form: 'The experimenter sought participants from various sources.' This is an improvement, but it is not ideal. If the passive form continues with further clauses, it can sound even more complicated than when the whole sentence is transformed into the active voice.

Adjective. This is a part of speech that describes (or modifies) **nouns** (e.g. *huge* tree, *green* door, *clever* person). The adjective does not need to be directly before the noun:

Her ideas appeared *strange*.
That's fair *enough*.

Adjectives can often be modified by **adverbs** such as *very*, *extremely*, *mildly*, and so on to produce the adjective phrase: 'The actor was *mildly amusing*.' When a number or fraction is used as an adjective it is hyphenated (e.g. 2-second interval, one-third majority). See the entry for **nouns** for further details.

Adjunct. An adjunct is a **clause**, **phrase**, or word that is not an essential component to a sentences structure, but amplifies its meaning. Because they are inessential, adjuncts can be stripped away to leave a grammatical sentence. Adjuncts have many different functions indicating such aspects as time, place, cause, and modification.

An adjunct is one of the four types of **adverbial** (the other three are **adverbial complements**, **conjuncts**, and **disjuncts**). It provides the setting of the sentence, such as when or where the action took place, or as a conditional adjunct (as in the second example below):

In the afternoon, she left the palace.
Should it prove workable, the hypothesis will seriously challenge current opinion.

Adverb. This is a part of speech that has the function of a **modifier**. Adverbs are best known as modifiers of **verbs** ('She swam *powerfully*'), considering that the word *verb* is a constituent of the word. However, adverbs can modify a wide range of other parts of speech, but not **nouns**; thus, they can modify **adjectives**, **clauses, sentences**, and other adverbs:

The young president delivered his speech *brilliantly*. (*Brilliantly* is an adverb that modifies the verb *delivered*.)

In the present era, the English language is changing *rapidly*. (The first part shown in italics is an adverbial phrase indicating time and the final word is an adverb modifying *changing*.)

Adverbial. There are four types of adverbial: **adjuncts, adverbial complement, conjuncts**, and **disjuncts**. An adverbial (as a noun) has the function of telling us something about the verb or the sentence and consists of one or more words. Consult the individual entries of the four types (e.g. **adjuncts**) for further information. (Incidentally, the word *adverbial* when used as an adjective means that something is being used as an adverb, as in **adverbial clause**.)

Adverbial clauses. As we can work out from the label, this is a **clause** that acts like an **adverb** in that it is a clause that modifies the main verb of the sentence. To illustrate: 'He acted strangely *while I drove him to the airport*.' The italics show an adverbial clause in which the **subject** (*I*) is explicit. If this clause were to be replaced with *during the journey*, the implied subject would be *he*.

Adverbial complement. This is an **adverbial** that plays a similar role to the **adjunct**, but with a subtle difference. Both the adverbial complement and the adjunct provide the setting of the sentence. However, whereas the adjunct can be removed and the sentence left behind is still a grammatical sentence, for the adverbial complement, what is left behind would be ungrammatical:

She is *at the bottom of the garden*.

Affect/effect. These two words are so commonly confused. Perhaps one way to remember the distinction is to think of the phrase *cause and effect*. This phrase means that a particular cause produces a result. The word *cause* ends in the letter *e*; this relates to the version of *effect* that begins with *e*. *Affect*, by contrast, refers to the participant's mood, which is used far less often. So far we have dealt with the **noun** forms of these two words.

As verbs, *affect* and *effect* have different connotations. As a **verb**, the word *affect* is used more often as in: 'The participant was not *affected* by the distracting stimulus.' The less frequent use of *effect* as a verb would be as in this example: 'The stooge tried to *effect* some changes in the group's attitude.'

After/afterwards. Use *afterwards* (not *after*) as an adverb showing time: 'The participants were given a debriefing *afterwards*.' However, when following a word or phrase with a time measurement, then *after* is acceptable: 'He saw her several weeks after.'

Agreement – see also **collective nouns** and **either/or**. In English there has to be agreement between different parts of the sentence, such as between subject and verb. For example in 'They *sings* all the time', the verb *sings* is not in agreement with the plural **subject**. This occurs when the writer does not realise that words such as *media*, *dice*, and *data* are plural words. For instance, 'The data was analyzed' would not be correct. See also the entry for **none**.

The word **or** can present a problem: In the construction 'A or B' should the following verb be singular or plural? The rule is that if both entities are singular use singular and if they are both plural then use plural. For example, 'When the red or blue light *is* showing then proceed' and 'When red lights or blue lights *are* showing then proceed.' There does not seem to be a consensus about what to do if one is singular and the other is plural, so try to avoid this.

Among/between. For some purists *between* is used for only two entities (e.g. 'She had to choose *between* the red and the blue'). One should use *among* for more than two (e.g. 'He had to choose among the red, blue, yellow, and green buttons'). There is more universal agreement that when there are two choices *between* should be used. However, one may also use *between*, for instance, for the endpoints in a range, as in: 'They had to choose all the red objects in the array that were *between* the cross, circle, and diamond.' The use of *among* would be used in the context of within a mass: '*Among* the survivors were three Egyptians.' It would be different if we were discussing a boundary, in which case *between* would be used: 'They had to draw the boundary between the red and green objects.' In this case *between* is used to show that the entities are determining the boundaries; whereas *among* would have been used if, for instance, they had to throw something *among* the green objects.

Amount of, number of. These two terms are used in the context of whether something is an aggregate (or whole mass) or whether it consists of units or individuals, in other words whether it is countable. One can have *an amount of* sand, but *a number of* pencils. An *amount* is the sum or aggregate of two or more quantities: 'It took a certain amount of time.'

And. This is a **coordinating conjunction** joining two words ('fish and chips'), **phrases** (e.g. 'three French hens *and* two turtle-doves'), or **clauses** (e.g. 'She at last sat down *and* then slept for an hour'). Purists dislike sentences beginning with *and* (or **but** for that matter – see the discussion at that entry).

And/or. This is shorthand for *and* or *or*. This construction needs to be avoided in text, although it would be acceptable in tables. Often the substitution of just *and* or *or* will be enough. It is not often that the author means literally 'X or Y or both X and Y'. If this is the case, then the text can be written in precisely these terms, or else using **ellipsis** as: 'X or Y or both'.

Apposition. This occurs when two **nouns** or **noun phrases** are placed next to each other as an explanatory equivalent, as in: '*Mr Routley the butcher* arrived for his lunch as usual.' In this case, the noun phrases 'Mr Routley' and 'the butcher' work in parallel with each other and jointly are the **subject** of the sentence. Note, there is no need for brackets or bracketing commas to set off *the butcher.*

As. The two most common uses of this word are to indicate time or reason:

> The stimulus changed *as* the participant pressed the button. (time)
> She ate the pie voraciously, *as* she hadn't eaten for two days. (reason or cause)

Thus, *as* can be used in place of *because* or *while.* However, care needs to be taken so that *as* cannot be construed to suggest both time and reason: '*As* he was leaving, she stood up.' Note that in the two sentences above, the first does not have a comma, but when *as* is used in the sense of reason, there is a comma. (See also the entry for **since.**)

But. Purists dislike sentences that begin with *but*; and this issue can create a surprising amount of heat and dogma. *But* you should make your own choice, as this usage has become more commonplace. (The conjunction *and* is similarly placed at the beginning of sentences more often now.) Avoid using *but* in the same sentence as *however*: '*But* in practice, *however*, do not do this.' Remove either *but* or *however.* Do not follow *but* with a comma even though in speech we have a tendency to pause after saying 'but'. The most frequent use of *but* is as a **coordinating conjunction**.

Clause. This grammatical unit consists of a **subject** and a **predicate**, although the subject of the clause need not be explicit. The following sentence consists of two clauses separated by a comma: 'The book is too long, although it has been interesting to read.' An independent clause, as its name suggests, can stand alone as a sentence, but a dependent clause cannot. For example, 'He combed his hair' is an independent clause, but the addition 'to make it look neater' is a dependent or subordinate clause, as it is subordinate to the main clause 'He combed his hair'. Note also that the subject (*hair*) in this dependent clause is implicit.

Cohesion. Grammar can be used to provide cohesion in text and there are separate entries in this A–Z guide for such devices: **conjunction**, **ellipsis**,

reference, **sentence adverbials**, and **substitutions**. Much of the conceptual work on cohesion is based on the seminal work of Halliday and Hasan (1976).

Collective nouns and agreement of the verb – see also **agreement**. Confusion can sometimes arise when a singular noun is used to represent a collection of individuals: Is the verb that follows singular or plural? Here are some examples:

> The sheep were herded into the enclosure.
> The government is determined to clamp down on any avoidance of this tax.
> The committee was chaired dedicatedly by the senator.
> The committee were deeply moved by the witnesses' testimonies.

The sheep example is straightforward: If there had been just one sheep it would have been 'was herded' and for more than one 'were herded'. The next three examples consist of collective nouns that can be used either as singular or plural according to the context. However, it is important to employ the collective noun consistently in that particular context. For example, it would be confusing to treat *government* as singular in one sentence, plural in the next, and then back to singular further on.

Common noun – see **proper/common nouns**.

Comparative (e.g. *better*) – see also **superlative**. This is the adjectival form when a comparison is being made between two (and only two) entities: 'Sam was faster than him.' If the base (e.g. *fast*) is three or more syllables in length, then instead of *-er* at the end, it is preceded by the word *more*: '... *more* beautiful'. If it is a two-syllable adjective then it can take either the *-est* form or the *more* form. In conversational use to give extra emphasis two comparatives (known as *double markings*) might be used (e.g. "There's none *more crazier* than Sam"), which is a practice that extends back to Shakespeare and even earlier. However, this is to be avoided in academic writing.

Compound sentence. When two or more clauses are connected by a coordinating conjunction, the result is a compound sentence. See **coordinating conjunction** for an elaboration.

Concession (e.g. *although*). During an argument, we may need to make an **adverbial clause** of concession; in other words, we admit the truth about something: 'Although this theory can account for most previous findings, there are some anomalies.' The first part up to the comma is the subordinate clause and then the main clause follows. A different type of concession is when the main clause is true, even though the truth of the subordinate clause is conceded: 'Peter's played the best in the group, even though his measured verbal IQ was the lowest.' In this last construction, the main clause is before the comma and the subordinate afterwards. Here is a list of the main conjunctions that can introduce these clauses of concession: *although, despite, even if, even though, except that, not that, though, whereas, while, whilst* (this last form is not often used now).

Condition (e.g. *if*). This is sometimes known as the *conditional* and refers to sentences in which one statement depends on the other. Usually *if* is used, but *unless, were, should,* and *had* can be used as well. For example, 'Had he been alive today, he would have made a great contribution.' In this case, the subordinate clause is before the comma and the main clause comes afterwards.

Conjunction (e.g. *therefore*) – see also **coordinating conjunction** and **cohesion**. Conjunctions are a type of **adverbial** that serve to join words, **phrases**, **clauses**, and sentences. Examples are: *also, consequently, furthermore, however, in contrast, therefore, though,* and so on. If the conjunct *however* comes midsentence, it should be surrounded by commas, as in: 'It seems, however, that this turned out not to be the case.' Conjunctions can work causally (e.g. *because*), temporally (e.g. *during, after*), additively (e.g. *also*), and they can show something to the contrary (e.g. *however*). The word *and* is a conjunction that can be used as additive or equivalent to the preceding phrase or clause. The conjunction **either** needs special attention and has a separate entry.

Continuous, continual. *Continuous* refers to actions that are not interrupted: 'Throughout the experiment there was *continuous* white noise.' Whereas interruption would be feasible here: 'She was continually telling him that he was lazy.' It would be unlikely that the man was being told this message in an unending loop as presumably she would at least have to pause for breath!

Coordinating conjunction. This serves the function of joining two main **clauses** and the main examples are: *and*, ***but***, *or*, and *so*.

> Would you like to go out in the garden, or stay here indoors?
> He wanted a bubble bath, so he ate beans for dinner.

Other conjunctions are *for* (used in the context of *because*), *nor* (when joining two negatives – 'He neither wished to see Mrs Bennett, nor was he inclined to go out.' – and *yet* (like *for*, when used in the sense of *because*). A **compound**

sentence is constructed when there are two or more clauses joined by such coordinating conjunctions. Each of these clauses must be a 'complete thought' and they are normally separated by a comma unless short.

Countable/uncountable – see also **amount of.** Nouns can be either countable, as they refer to things that can be counted (e.g. cars), or they do not normally have a plural form and are uncountable (e.g. *flour*). There are even a few that can be both (e.g. *hair*). The question of whether something is countable raises problems for particular words; for example, see **fewer or less?**

Disinterested – see **uninterested/disinterested.**

Disjunct (e.g. *obviously*). Disjuncts are another type of **adverbial.** They provide an opportunity for the writer to provide a comment on the content of the sentence. They occur most often at the beginning of the sentence. Here are some common disjuncts: *admittedly*, *briefly*, *clearly*, *obviously*, *personally*, *possibly*, *presumably*, *fortunately*.

Either/or – see also **conjunction** and **agreement.** Traditionalists consider that when referring to only two entities, one should use *either*, and for more than two use *any*: 'The participant was allowed to press any of the three buttons.' However, when *either* is used as a conjunction (i.e. in the 'either-or' context) it is admissible to write the following, if what follows the conjunction has parallel elements: 'They advised that *either* the case should be closed *or* that the charges should go ahead *or* that the case should be postponed pending further enquiry.' There is also the problem of whether the verb following *either-or* should be singular or plural, if the two entities are singular nouns. In this case the verb should be singular; here is an example: 'She says that either Jane or Tom sings the solo right now.' Avoid mixing plural and singular nouns in the *either-or* construction as whichever form of the verb is chosen (singular or plural), it will seem to be incorrect.

Ellipsis (or omission). This is one of the devices to produce **cohesion.** *Ellipsis* means the omission of a word or phrase and its function is to avoid repetition. For example, if someone is asked 'Would you have rather have had the cod than the salmon?' the response might be 'Yes, I would rather have had the cod than the salmon.' But this would be better as: 'Yes, I would rather have had the cod.' Another example would be 'She has managed to learn to swim faster than me' instead of 'She has managed to learn faster than I have been able to.' The cohesion is achieved (perhaps only moderately) as it is acknowledged that the removed material was unnecessary padding that readers could have inferred for themselves.

Fewer or less? – see also **countable/uncountable**. Traditionally, *fewer* is used in the context of separate entities (e.g. *fewer* studies, *fewer* participants), whereas *less* is used in the context of quantity (e.g. *less* research, *less* water). However, the traditional rule can break down when using *less than* before a plural (countable) noun indicating time, amount, or distance: *less than* 5 minutes, *less than* $3, *less than* 30 miles. Here is another situation in which the traditional rule goes out of the window: 'You must write this essay in 2,000 words or less.'

Former, latter. These terms are for the first and second items, respectively, as in: 'The red clown and the blue clown came into the spotlight one after the other. The former was on a unicycle and the latter on stilts.' However, if there were more than two clowns, these terms should not be used, as *former* and *latter* only apply to two entities.

Imply/infer. These two words can get confused. *Imply* means that something is suggested implicitly, as in: 'Her glance *implied* that he did not meet her approval.' *Infer* means that one, or someone, has made a deduction: 'The judge *inferred* from her testimony that the accused could not have been at that location at the time stated.'

Intensifier. Intensifiers are adverbs that **modify** an **adjective**, such as *incredibly* fast. Overall, it would be preferable to keep these to the minimum in your writing in psychology as often intensifiers such as *rather* and *fairly* can be superfluous, if not meaningless.

Its/it's. These two forms can be confused. *It's* means *it is* or *it has*, whereas *its* is the possessive form of *it* and is equivalent to *belongs to it*. The following examples illustrate these two forms: 'It's been a long time since I've seen you' and 'The top had become detached from its base.' In formal writing in psychology, if you ever feel the urge to write *it's*, you should curb this overwhelming desire and write *it is* in its place. **Whose/who's** is a similar confusion.

Modify/modifier. The meaning of another word can be changed or enhanced by a modifier. **Adjectives** modify nouns (e.g. *dirty* hat) and **adverbs** usually modify verbs (e.g. swam *strongly*).

None are/none is. *None* is widely accepted as a singular word, as in: '*None* of the participants *has* consumed caffeine in the past 24 hours.' However, it becomes more difficult if *none* is preceded by *almost* or *virtually*. Here the plural is more acceptable: 'Almost *none* of the participants *were* able distinguish between the two stimuli.' Some purists would be uncomfortable with this last sentence as they would think that *none* is an absolute term. Refer to the discussion of **absolute term**.

Noun phrase. This phrase has as its headword a **noun** or a **pronoun**. This phrase may also include a **modifier** (e.g. a *pink* elephant).

Noun. This hardly needs an entry. Nouns are a class of words that identify things, places, people, and ideas. They can be **modified** by an **adjective** (e.g. *purple* lips). They can be either singular or plural (e.g. *hat*, *hats*, respectively). Nouns have other subdivisions that have entries elsewhere in this guide: **Countable/uncountable** and **proper/common**. Note that only common nouns subdivide into countable or uncountable nouns. **Proper nouns**, of course, do not have a corresponding subdivision.

You may have come to this entry on nouns because of a reference in chapter 6 to common fractions in which it was stated that if a common fraction is employed as a noun it should not be hyphenated. Before you give up the will to live, let me explain: In the sentence 'Two thirds of them were female' *two thirds* is a noun representing the concept of two thirds. However, in the sentence 'They won by a two-thirds majority' this time *two thirds* is an **adjective** modifying the noun *majority* and is therefore hyphenated. Wherever a number is employed as an adjective, then it is hyphenated; for example: '5-point rating scale' and 'a 4-year-old child'.

Number – see **agreement**. English grammar has either singular or plural (e.g. *book/books, he shouts/they shout*).

Object. In the active (see **active voice**) form of a sentence, the object comes after the **verb** (e.g. 'She pressed the *button*'). The object has often been acted upon by a person (as in the last example), a thing, a place, or even an idea or experience. For instance in 'The nightmare woke her up in a cold sweat' the **pronoun** *her* is the object. The object can be a **noun** or a pronoun, or a **phrase** or **clause** containing at least one noun. For instance, in the sentence 'Her treasure hunting produced *what turned out to be worth a considerable amount of money*' the part in italics is a noun **clause** that is the object of the sentence. An example of a noun phrase (in italics) that is the object of the sentence is: 'William picked up *his father's kitbag*.'

Object complement. The object complement follows the object referring to that same object. In the following two examples, the first illustrates noun object complements and the second adjective complements: (1) He crowned him *king*; (2) His actions made her *queasy*.

One. If using *one* in a sentence more than once, keep using the word rather changing to another pronoun (e.g. *you*): '*One* should always remember that *one* should not use this device without the safety catch on.'

Only. Be careful when using this word as it needs to be placed directly in front of the word or clause that it is intended to modify. Notice, for example, how its placement changes the meaning in these two examples: '*Only* I know where the key is' and 'I know *only* where the key is.'

Or – see **agreement**.

Paragraph. The paragraph has been dealt with in detail in chapter 2. Continuous prose is divided into paragraphs by starting a new line. The new paragraph is usually signalled by a blank line or an indentation at the start of the next. If there is not such a marking, the reader can miss the start of a fresh paragraph if the last line of the previous paragraph is close to the right margin. As described in chapter 2, the paragraph is supposed to comprise a complete topic.

Passive – see **active (vs. passive) voice**.

Phrase. A phrase is a group of words (usually without a finite verb) and it is a constituent of a **clause**. It has a headword that can be a **noun**, **verb**, **adjective**, **adverb**, or **preposition**. This headword determines the type of phrase; for instance, a verb phrase has a verb as the headword (e.g. *had witnessed*). Other examples are *a detailed questionnaire* (noun phrase) and *at the top* (prepositional phrase).

Plural – see **agreement**.

Predicate. Sentences consist of a subject and the predicate. Put another way, the predicate includes the verb and everything else apart from the subject. Thus, 'The book was placed on the desk' has *the book* as the subject and the rest of the sentence is the predicate.

Preposition (e.g. *by, to*). Prepositions typically come before a noun (or a group of words functioning as a noun – known as substantives) and their purpose is to show the relation of that noun to a verb, adjective, or noun. They are usually short single words (e.g. *above, after, as, at, but, by, of, on*), but they can also be more than one word (e.g. *as well as*). Most people know that they are not supposed to end a sentence with a preposition. This can be achieved by the use of *in which*. Thus 'This is the bag it was found *in*' would become 'This is the bag *in which* it was found'. The argument against this traditional view is that it can make the sentence appear too formal or awkward. My advice would be to try to keep to the traditional approach of avoiding prepositions at the sentence end (even though this view has no justification); but relax this rule if the rewrite does not sound right.

Prepositions have a rough time, as it can be problematic using them at the beginning of a sentence as well. Although using a preposition at the beginning of a sentence is not grammatically incorrect, some writing stylists consider that starting a sentence with a prepositional phrase (e.g. 'Of the 29 participants, 20 were male') is to be avoided. It would be better to use more direct sentences (e.g. 'Twenty of the 29 participants were male').

Pronoun (e.g. *her*). The pronoun is a word that helps writers avoid having to repeat themselves, as in: 'Polly put *her* hat down.' Thus the writer in this case does not have to write 'Polly' a second time (see also **reference**). The main kinds of pronouns are personal (e.g. *I/me, we/us*), possessive (e.g. *mine, ours*), relative (e.g. *who, whom*), demonstrative (e.g. *this, that*), and indefinite (e.g. *some, none, all*). This last group is large. The writer needs to be unambiguous about what is being referenced by the pronoun.

Proper/common noun. Proper nouns refer mostly to people (e.g. *Liz*), places (e.g. *Melbourne, Blackpool*), and things (e.g. *the Empire State Building*). They always have a first capital letter. Proper names include languages, names of products, company names, and anything geographical (e.g. *countries, states, counties, bodies of water*). Common nouns, by contrast, describe a class of entities such as people or things (e.g. *participant, lever*).

Reference – see also **cohesion.** This device used by writers to refer to someone or something has already been mentioned. One form of this is shown in this sentence: 'The child reached out for the candy and ate *it*.' Here the pronoun *it* is substituted for *candy*. The pronoun *it* is also referred to as an *anaphor*.

Relative clause. The relative clause is a **clause** that serves the same role as an **adjective** describing the noun or pronoun. For example:

> She is a *kind* woman. (Adjective)
> During the meal, Christine *who had a charitable nature* defended the woman criticized by the host. (Relative clause)

Relative clauses can be defining or non-defining. A defining relative clause has information within that is essential to the meaning of the rest of the sentence (e.g. 'The principle *that everyone is born equal* was dear to his heart').

This sentence does not make sense without this defining relative clause. A non-defining relative clause is surrounded by commas (in contrast to the defining relative clause). Because it could be removed and the sentence would still make sense (e.g. 'The jazz singer, who had deep blue eyes, came to the mike and began her song'). Relative clauses usually begin with these relative pronouns: *that*, *which*, *who*, *whom*, *whose*.

Relative pronoun – see **that/which/who(m)**.

Sentence adverbial – see also **cohesion**. The sentence adverbial is another device to help contextual cohesion. It consists of a word or phrase that helps to link text. It can achieve this by listing, as in 'First, break two eggs and, second, beat them together', or by giving examples, as in 'I think he's horrible: *for example, the other day I saw him push an old woman out of the way in his rush to get on the bus*.'

S/he. – Avoid this representation of *he or she*. Occasionally we may need to use phrases such as *he or she*, because referring to everything in the plural might be tedious. But many (including me) dislike the contraction *s/he* because in English there is normally a correspondence between letters and sounds. This particular construction destroys this correspondence as it literally reads 's, slash, hee', which sounds a bit S & M. Also avoid *she/he* and *he/she*; in fact, avoid the slash altogether, except for mathematical expressions, for fractions, or within brackets.

Since. This conjunction can be used in the sense of time or reason. Here are two examples: 'Since he had returned home he began to feel hungry' and 'She left him, since she couldn't stand his philandering any longer.' A word of caution: Some traditionalists think that *since* should not be used as equivalent to *because*, but I think the floodgates are open on this one. However, one should avoid using *since* in a way that creates ambiguity whereby either sense (time or reason) could operate.

Slang. These are expressions that are not Standard English. Slang develops within social groups. Sometimes this slang becomes incorporated into Standard English. In academic writing there ain't no slang.

Split infinitive. This refers to when the infinitive (e.g. *to dance*, *to desire*) has an adverb placed after *to* (e.g. *to frantically dance*). There has been controversy on this topic with traditionalists opposed to the split infinite. Many experts would advise that split infinitives are acceptable unless they sound strange. Sometimes splitting an infinitive can be difficult to avoid without altering the meaning or making the sentence sound awkward.

Subject. The subject of a sentence is the 'doer' of the action that is being described by the **predicate**. Thus in the sentence 'Jack kissed Jill' *Jack* is the subject and *kissed Jill* is the predicate. The subject can be a **noun**, a **noun phrase**, a **pronoun**, or a **clause**.

Subordinate clause – see **clause**.

Substitution – see also **cohesion**. Substitution helps cohesion and is different from **ellipsis** in that instead of omission, a word or phrase is put in the place of the first occurrence of the word. This can be important as the reader can soon tire of repetition of the same word. For example, in the sentence 'The police followed the car closely, but as the *vehicle* speeded up, they found it extremely difficult to keep up', *vehicle* is a generic term that includes *cars* that can act as a satisfactory substitute.

Superlative (e.g. *biggest*) – see also **comparative**. Adjectives often have three forms, for example: *pretty*, *prettier*, *prettiest*. These forms in the examples are known as the absolute, comparative, and superlative forms, respectively. The comparative form is employed when there are only two items (e.g. 'He was the *stronger* of the two brothers'), whereas the superlative form is used for more than two (e.g. 'She was the cleverest in the class'). Like the comparative, superlatives that consist of one syllable are in the *-est* form (e.g. *lowest*, *biggest*) and those of three or more syllables are preceded by *most*, as in *the most manageable*. Two-syllable adjectives (e.g. *happiest*) vary as to whether they are like their one- or three-syllable counterparts, but most are like the one-syllable and have *-est* added.

Tag question. As the label implies, this is when a question is tagged on to the end of a sentence, as in 'We're going over to the farm and could leave the gear there, *couldn't we*?' Usually in this construction, the writer or speaker is expecting a positive response.

That/which/who(m). These relative pronouns introduce **relative clauses**. The correct choice between *that* and *which* requires a little understanding of their respective functions. They can occasionally get confused. *That* can refer to people or things, whereas *which* is restricted just to things. Thus one would not write: 'This is the man, *which* the police are looking for.' However, this would be permissible: 'This is the book, which is easy to read.' This last construction is an introduction, so if a person was involved we would write: 'This is the woman who saved my life.'

The most noteworthy aspect of the distinction between *that* and *which* is that only *which* may be used in a non-defining relative clause (also known as a non-restrictive clause); for example: 'This book, which has a beautiful green cover, must unfortunately be returned to the library tomorrow.' The relative clause starting with *which* is non-defining because it can be lifted out of the sentence and the sense of the sentence remains intact. (Incidentally, note that it has commas surrounding it.) If we change the sentence slightly to 'The book that has a beautiful green cover must unfortunately be returned to the library tomorrow' the meaning of the sentence changes by making the clause a defining one. We are now saying that among the available books, the one that has a beautiful green cover needs to be returned to the library.

Who or *whom* refer to people. *Who* is used for the **subject** and *whom* for the **object** in a sentence. The sentence 'Jamie Oliver, *who* is a chef, changed the way that many children eat food' shows how *who* performs as a substitute for the subject (*Jamie Oliver*) of this sentence. In the sentence 'He's the one whom I saw earlier' *whom* is the object of the verb *saw*. (Try putting *him* in place of *whom* to understand why it is the object.) Unfortunately, it gets tricky deciding whether to use *who* or *whom* with sentences that are more complicated.

Uncountable noun – see **noun** and **countable**.

Uninterested/disinterested. A *disinterested* person is impartial or unbiased. An *uninterested* person is just not interested: 'She was uninterested in what her friend had to say by way of apology.' Currently speakers and writers often interchange *uninterested* and *disinterested* to represent lacking in interest, but to be on the safe side use each of these words in the right context.

Unique – see **absolute term**.

Utilise/utilisation. Wherever possible use plain English and in this case, *use* serves the purpose just as well, if not better. Similarly, try to use the following words instead of the ones in brackets: *finish* (not *finalise*), *first*, (not *firstly*), *rank* (not *prioritise*), *needed* (not *requisite*), and so on.

Verb. In grammar the verb expresses an action (e.g. *deliver*, *swim*), an occurrence (e.g. *radiate*, *freeze*), or a state of being (e.g. *think*, *slept*, *is*).

Verb phrase. This is the verb part of a clause. The verb phrase always has at least a main **verb**, which consists of only one word. If there is more than the main verb, then these are the auxiliary verbs in the phrase; for instance, *have been closed* begins with two auxiliary verbs, while *closed* is the main verb. The verb phrase is often seen as equivalent to the **predicate**.

Voice – see **active (vs. passive) voice**.

What/which. These two words can be used as interrogative **adjectives**, but when the choice is restricted (not necessarily just to two choices), then *which* is used: '*Which* of these cakes would you like?' When we are referring to an uncountable number, *what* is applicable: '*What* explanation would be most appropriate for these results?' Occasionally a student's vernacular creeps into his or her formal writing: 'This was the participant *what* the experimenter had to specially train.' This should be replaced by *whom* in this case.

While/whilst. Traditionalists prefer that these two words should be used in the sense of time (e.g. 'While shadowing the participant had to play the piano'), rather than as a substitute for *whereas* or similar words (e.g. 'Some theorists would agree with this interpretation while others would take another viewpoint'). However, it looks like this is another lost battle. Note that *while* is much more commonly used than *whilst*.

Who/whom and who's/whose. See **that/which/who(m)** on how to distinguish *who/whom*. The two words *who's* and *whose* can sometimes be confused. The form *who's* is a contraction of *who is* or *who has*, whereas *whose* is the possessive form of *who* (equivalent to *belonging to whom*), as can be seen in these two sentences: 'Who's that man over there?' and 'He's the man whose wife left him last year.'

Would. This is to note an incorrect usage that happens occasionally: 'If the participant had been given the correct information he or she *would of* been able to have completed the questionnaire.' This arises because of the contraction *would've* in speech and *would of* is confused with this. The sentence should be rewritten as: 'If the participant had been given the correct information he or she *would have* been able to have completed the questionnaire.'

12

IMPROVE YOUR EDITING SKILLS

Exercises in Proofreading and Making Corrections

Here is an opportunity to improve your own editing skills. In what follows, pieces of text are presented in the boxes, mostly taken from different sections of students' essays and research reports. Take a sheet of paper and cover up most of the page and slide it down until the first boxed sample is revealed. Try to see what is wrong with the text and, even better; try to rewrite it in some cases. If you slide further down you will get my own comments directly underneath each excerpt. The rest of the chapter (apart from the conclusion) consists of this arrangement. Most samples are easy to correct, but some harder examples are there as well. Doing an exercise like this should give you more confidence in picking up your own minor errors when revising your text.

Abstract

> The present study also aims to explore possible causes for the differences found. [This is a sentence in an abstract.]

Comment: This is an abstract so one can ill afford vague sentences like this. What specific causes? What specific differences?

> In the first section of this report the global structure of hypertexts is discussed. The second section describes the empirical study. [This is a sentence in the abstract to a lab report and is referring to the introduction section.]

Comment: One does not put in the abstract what is going to be discussed in the introduction. Instead, just get down to stating the main hypotheses. Then describe how the experimental design or other relevant detail.

> This comparison of how well students comprehend three different structures of hypertext offers new insights into the comprehension process.

Comment: This is too evaluative – let the reader be the judge of the worth of the results. Perhaps the writer thinks this self-compliment ('... offers new insights') will convince the reader and will improve the end mark? I doubt it.

Student: I think you've misinterpreted this one; the writer was merely trying to show that the study was original as it offered a new way of looking at the comprehension process.

John: Yes, maybe I'm getting too cynical in my old age; but it does leave an impression with me that the writer is trying to 'talk up' the results.

Introduction

> Over the last two decades more and more voices have gone up to call to address culture in health practices as a whole. [A reference is then cited.]

Comment: A little grandiloquent and slightly incomplete? This could be rewritten as: 'Since the 1980s researchers have increasingly called for health practitioners to consider the effects of culture.'

> The views of feminist psychology and why there was a need for a feminist overhaul of psychology. [This sentence is part of an introduction.]

Comment: This sentence is not grammatically correct – the subject, 'the views of feminist psychology', needs a predicate (see *predicate* in chapter 11); for example, 'will be examined'. However, even with this addition the sentence does not 'scan'. The two main ideas bound in this sentence by 'and' seem disparate. Perhaps it would be better to have two separate sentences: 'The views of feminist psychology will be examined. After that, the reasons for a feminist overhaul of psychology will be elaborated.' (Yes, I have used four extra words; perhaps you can do better.)

> Another such study looks at 'Gender differences in Early Risk Factors for Adolescent Depression among Low-Income Children' and looks for an explanation of why before adolescence, boys and girls have similar rates of depressive symptoms whereas there is an increase in depressive symptoms among adolescent females, with this increase in depressive symptoms persisting into adulthood. [This sample is at the beginning of a paragraph and is reproduced exactly as typed.]

Comment: This is easy to criticise. The obvious two aspects here are that the writer has not cited the study ('Gender differences …') properly and that the sentence is too long. The writer should have given the author and date of publication of the study rather than its title. The longer the sentence, the greater is the risk that it is not going to be grammatically correct or that the reader is going to have more difficulty in working out the overall sense or both. (Oops – I've just broken my own advice.) One of the aims of writers is to make their text easy to read. Incidentally, this is not the same as suggesting that writers should write only about easy subjects.

> Researches over the years have concentrated on this issue. They have found the basis and theories which help to explain and understand this perceptual process.

Comment: The first sentence could be combined with the second. As it is written, who are *they* who produced these theories? The studies need to be cited. Alternatively, we could rewrite this simply as: 'Research on this issue has tried to explain the perceptual processes that could be involved.' A minor aspect to note is that it is not correct to make research into a plural word ('researches'). Also, 'They have found the basis and theories…' has (at least) two problems. First, one does not *find* theories (if the research is quantitative), they are proposed. Second, as a reader I am not sure what 'the basis' is supposed to mean here.

> 2D:4D ratio is a widespread phenomenon that has been shown to be a physical marker of the amount of testosterone an individual has.

Comment: The main aspect that you probably noticed from this sentence is that the sentence begins with a number – '2D:4D' – that refers to the ratio in length between the second and fourth fingers. You might have thought that ending the sentence with a verb might be a mistake. It is not grammatically incorrect, but perhaps it seems slightly awkward.

Another problem would only be picked up if you happened to know about this area of research. It is to do with the beginning part where the writer is saying that the 2D:4D ratio is a widespread phenomenon. The author should have prefaced this with 'research into 2D:4D' as '2D:4D' by itself is just a measurement. The writer was suggesting there is much research on the 2D:4D ratio and besides it could reveal how testosterone affected this individual during an early stage in their development. This second part, unfortunately, is also inaccurate. The writer should have written that this ratio is used as a marker of the degree to which testosterone has been experienced prenatally.

Student: If you're going to be so fussy, how would you have written it then?

John: How about: 'The 2D:4D ratio is used widely as a marker of the degree to which testosterone has been experienced prenatally.'

Student: Ha! *Prenatally* isn't in the dictionary!

John: It depends on your dictionary. Let's change the last part to: '… has been experienced in the womb' instead – although the cost is two extra words.

> Those participants with a shorter index finger in relation to the ring finger are supposed to be an indication of an increased influence of testosterone over female hormone in the womb.

Comment: Here the writer of this long sentence has become confused. It sounds as though the participants are the indication, whereas it is the relationship of the relative lengths of the second and fourth fingers that is the indication. Therefore, a rewrite might produce: 'A shorter index finger in relation to the ring finger supposedly shows a relative increase of testosterone in the womb.'

> There is numerous research involving digit ratio with many different conclusions being drawn …

Comment: The writer should have written that there are 'numerous' (or in better, plainer English: 'many') studies or perhaps that there is 'much research'. This is the same problem as the distinction between 'fewer' and 'less'. If something is *numerous*, then it is countable. (See *countable/uncountable* in chapter 11.) We can count studies, and therefore can refer to 'numerous studies'; but we cannot count *research*.

> Baucom *et al.* (1985, as cited in Csatho *et al.*, 2002) said that females with high levels of masculinity had higher testosterone levels than feminine-sex-typed females. They furthered the results by showing females with higher levels of testosterone perceived themselves as self-directed, action orientated and resourceful compared to females with lower levels of testosterone, who viewed themselves as conventional and socialized.

Comment: There are a few points to note here:

1. The word 'said' (line 1) is used incorrectly – they did not say this, they wrote it. This should be written as 'found'.
2. The phrase '… than feminine-sex-typed females' perhaps would be better as: '… than females with high levels of femininity'. I would, however, prefer

to use ellipsis (see chapter 11) and write: '... found that amongst women, females in the masculine direction had higher testosterone levels.'

3. The extract 'They furthered the results by showing females with higher levels of testosterone perceived themselves ...' would be better written as: 'These more masculine females perceived themselves ...' (This shortens 14 words down to 6 and avoids 'they furthered ...') Although *furthered* is a permissible word, it is not being used suitably here.
4. The phrase 'action orientated' could do with a hyphen: 'action-orientated'. Better still would be 'action-oriented', which is plainer language.
5. The last sentence could probably be broken into two, with the second sentence being about the low-testosterone females being conventional and socialised. Incidentally, my Word grammar checker is suggesting that the 'who' in the last sentence of the student's excerpt should be changed to 'which'. The grammar checker can be useful, but in this case, it is wrong.

> Spelling and reading are both cognitive processes requiring the transformation of phonemes to graphemes, or graphemes to phonemes (e.g., Bradley & Bryant, 1983).

Comment: The word 'both' is equivalent to the use of logical *and*. At its core, this sentence is making a statement of the form: 'A *and* B are cognitive processes requiring X *or* Y'. What the writer meant (I hope) was that A is a cognitive process requiring X and that B is a cognitive process requiring Y. Furthermore, there is a similarity between X and Y in that they are both about the connections between phonemes and graphemes. So, rewritten it would make more sense like this: 'A similarity between spelling and reading is that they are both involved with processing connections between graphemes and phonemes. The difference between them is that they work in opposite directions: phonemes to graphemes for spelling and graphemes to phonemes for reading (e.g. Bradley & Bryant, 1983)'. Unfortunately, this rewrite has cost many more words – but at least it is makes more sense.

> Through the evidence that has been shown, it seems that there is more support for the dual-route account of word recognition, and is the most widely accepted.

Comment: The problem arises from the last phrase '... and is the most widely accepted'. This is repetitive in that it has already been stated that there is 'more support'. Besides, this phase should have been written '... and it is the most widely accepted'.

> The wealth of evidence is that people are accurate in their judgements of gender ... [This is followed by two references.]

Comment: The phrase 'wealth of evidence' is perhaps a little sweeping, especially as only two references are given. It might have been better to have preceded these references with 'for example,...'

> The increased acceptability of women in psychology has lead to increasing numbers of studies about women, for example, violence against women.

Comment: The word 'lead' should be 'led'. This type of spelling error happens often partly because the spelling checker does not pick it up. The phrase 'increasing numbers of studies' would be much more accurate as 'an increasing number of studies'. The example at the end is too truncated and would be better either in brackets as '(e.g. on violence against women)' or as '... for example, the work on violence against women'. Perhaps the writer had to trim to get the word count down.

> Energy levels generally increase the more active one is, obviously unless someone is too active and needs rest. Chrusial (2003) found that energy levels increased in the sample she used the more active they were.

Comment: If I were tinkering with the first sentence, I would edit this to read: 'Our energy level improves when we are more active. However, if we overexert ourselves, then obviously our available energy level reduces.' There are three more words used, but it reads better. I lose four words editing the second sentence, which could also be expressed better: 'Chrusial (2003) found that those with higher energy levels were also more active.' Note how 'in the sample she used' is redundant (all experimenters have a sample that they use).

The investigation concluded that depression was significantly lower...

Comment: Strictly speaking, the investigation, or the experiment, was not doing the concluding, it was the experimenter or experimenters. Thus, the writer should refer to him, her or them.

Ahmadi *et al.* (2002) looked at females who did sport and their depression levels, overall conclusions showed that physical activity positively correlates with lower mean scores on the Beck Depression Inventory.

Comment: This would be better as: 'Ahmadi *et al.* (2002) examined the levels of depression in females who took part in sports and found a correlation between activity and depression. Being more active correlated with being less depressed (as measured by the Beck Depression Inventory).' Note that in the original only a comma was used to separate two complete thoughts. The writer should have started a new sentence: 'Overall conclusions showed that...' The bit about the Beck is awkward. It is not all that important to the sentence, but it was important to the writer to mention it, as the Beck was going to be used in this student's study. In my rewrite, I tagged the Beck part on to the end of the sentence in brackets. Putting it earlier in the sentence could get in the way of the reader processing the gist. Another approach would be to state simply in the next sentence: 'They used the Beck Depression Inventory.'

This has been supported by Adams (1990) who claims that children develop the ability to produce connections between the letters of a word and the word's meaning...

Comment: This sentence is not strictly incorrect, but there are two aspects to note here. The first is that 'This has been supported...' is a stale and redundant way to start a sentence. A similarly bland (and often used) start would be 'It has been shown that...' However, the second and more important aspect is the use of the word 'claims'. This word has the connotation that this is an extravagant statement that has little basis in fact. I am sure the writer (i.e. the student, not Adams) did not mean to suggest this; but it is a commonly misused and emotive word. Of course, if the writer is using 'claims' in the right context, then it is acceptable.

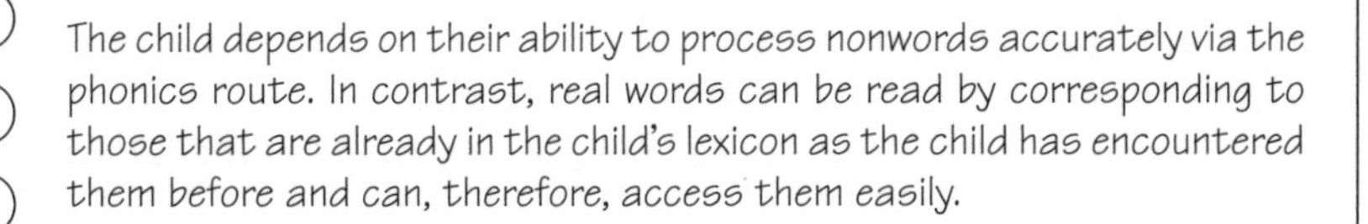

The child depends on their ability to process nonwords accurately via the phonics route. In contrast, real words can be read by corresponding to those that are already in the child's lexicon as the child has encountered them before and can, therefore, access them easily.

Comment: There are several aspects here, beginning with the first sentence: A minor problem is that the subject 'child', which is singular, disagrees with 'their', which is plural. I would suggest that this is a minor misdemeanour, because the writer is at least recognising the gender problem and avoiding the use of 'he or she'. A form such as this is becoming increasingly acceptable, but not to the purists, so it would perhaps be safer to put everything into the plural. The second sentence is about the workings of the lexicon, or *dictionary in our head*; but it is trying to get in too much information and appears complicated. An alternative might be: 'By contrast, real words activate representations in the child's developing lexicon; because this is a well-practised process, access to this lexicon is easier and therefore faster.'

Shepard and Metzler (1971) demonstrated this with a simple experiment which involved the participant to distinguish whether two 3D shapes were the same when placed at different rotations and sizes.

Comment: A minor proofreading problem is that the writer missed out *having* between 'participant' and 'to'. More importantly, Shepard and Metzler did not manipulate the size of their stimuli, they only changed the angle of required rotation between the stimuli.

Student: If one writes '... to distinguish whether two ...' shouldn't this be followed by 'were the same or not'?

John: Yes, it seems to disturb some people if the *or not* is missing, but I wouldn't worry about leaving it out as it helps conciseness. (See the entry for *ellipsis* in chapter 11.)

Caramazza, Capasso and Miceli (1996) studied patient L.B., hypothesizing that if reading and spelling use the same graphemic buffer mechanism ...

Comment: APA guidelines advise that identity-concealing labels for participants should have periods (as in 'L.B.'). However, the writer also needed (correctly) to put a comma after the introductory phrase and had therefore taken out the period after the letter *B*. Instead this should have been written: '... patient L.B., hypothesizing ...'

End Part of the Introduction

> It was predicted that there would be significant differences in cognition between males and females.

Comment: This is a vague hypothesis.

Student: So what would you put in its place?

John: Unfortunately, I've lost the original piece from which this excerpt is taken, but the cognitive tests where differences are expected should be mentioned and the direction of the difference stated. But the writer may have had other differences in mind; for example, an interactive difference such that the two genders would be different in some respects but not in others.

> The first hypothesis, consistent with previous research, is that the more the alphanumeric is rotated from the normal position, it will affect the participant's reaction time, there will be a difference between men and women's reaction times, and there will be a difference in reaction times between women who take the contraceptive pill and women who do not.

Comment: There is a lot wrong with this excerpt. However, the major problem is that the first hypothesis is not a hypothesis, but three hypotheses bundled together. I would rewrite it as follows, having previously stated that RT stands for *reaction time*: 'The hypotheses are that there will be: first, a linear increase in RT as a function of the angle of rotation of the alphanumeric characters; second, a difference between the sexes in RT in the rotation task; and finally, a difference between female contraceptive pill takers and non-takers in RT in the rotation task.' I have added an expectation in the first hypothesis and it would be useful to give a direction of expectation for the other two.

> ... it was therefore decided to investigate this effect by presenting participants with ...

Comment: 'Participants were therefore given ...' should do the job, using a third of the original words.

Method

> The sample consisted of mainly psychology undergraduates and these were randomly chosen as its an easy to apply method, gives everyone an equal chance of being selected and is representative of the student population.

Comment: Here the student is trying to express the idea that they randomly selected their participants from a student population, but a minority were not. (No further details of this minority are given.) This is all that needs to be stated: unless the instructor has asked for justification for everything that is done in the report, the reasons for randomisation can be assumed. Incidentally, with random selection every item (in this case, each participant) would have an equal chance of being selected, so there is circularity in this justification. Finally note the use here of *its*, which should have been *it's*. This, of course, is a contraction of *it is* and as contractions are not allowed, this should have been written in full.

> Due to the age of the children, using a bottle opener and striking a match were removed from the list. [This sentence is in the context of a description of a handedness test.]

Comment: It used to be considered incorrect to use *due to* in place of *owing to* as a preposition. However, nowadays either form is acceptable. If you want to avoid any possibility of dispute you could write *because of* or more long-windedly: 'It was because of the age of the children that ...' Another slight problem with this excerpt is that the two phrases 'using a bottle opener' and 'striking a match' should have been put in quotes (as in this present sentence) to show that they are test items. Similarly, 'were removed from the list' was a little ambiguous. This would have been the preferred sentence in its place: 'Because of the age of the children, two test items ('using a bottle opener' and 'striking a match') were removed from the handedness questionnaire.'

> Variables that are to be correlated with the activity groups decided using Baecke's Activity Questionnaire are; general health, ... [This is followed by a further list of variables.]

Comment: This is an awkwardly composed sentence. The writer was trying to suggest that the Baecke questionnaire was going to be used to create an activity variable by dividing the sample into different groups according to their activity levels (i.e. High Activity group = 5; Medium Activity = 4, etc.). Then this activity variable was going to be correlating with the other listed variables. A way of expressing this might be: 'An activity questionnaire was created based on the Baecke questionnaire.' (Then a sentence or two would describe the criteria used to achieve this.) 'The resultant activity variable was correlated with the General Health Questionnaire ...', etc.

There are two minor transgressions in the student's excerpt. One is that the description is in the future tense, when the past would be better (i.e. 'were correlated' would be better than 'are to be correlated') A second error, but a common one, is to misuse the colon. Here a semicolon (;) is used instead of the colon (:). (This gave this particular marker a dose of colonic irritation.)

Results

> As the above table shows, none of the relationships explored were significant.

Comment: There is not much wrong here except for the use of the word *none* (see the entry for this in chapter 11). The problem is that although the sentence *sounds* right, unfortunately to be grammatically correct it should be '... *was* significant'. (*None* is a singular word that is the subject of the verb *was*.) However, to most present-day ears this in turn makes the sentence sound wrong. A simple solution is to avoid the problem, like this: 'As Table 2 shows, all the relationships explored were non-significant.' Note also my reference to a specific table instead of 'the above table' here.

> The ANOVA revealed main effects of two significant three-way interactions. [No other description of the analysis of variance is given.]

Comment: When an ANOVA is described, all too often too little detail is given. This is an extreme case because as it has more than one three-way interaction it must have been at least a 4-factor ANOVA. So, where are the descriptions of the four main effects and the two-way and other interactions? To introduce the interactions with 'revealed main effects of' is confusing, as main effects are main effects and distinct from interactions, which are ... interactions. See Appendix 2 for an example of a report with an analysis of variance.

> ... the results showed a significant difference between the sexes on each of the two tracking different tasks. [The results of the *t* tests follow directly from here.]

Comment: Yes, there is a significant difference, but did the males perform better or worse than the females? It would also be preferable to give the means and standard deviations of each group on each of the tracking tasks. The sentence could have been written better as well.

> ... only attitude contributed significantly in the ...

Comment: This would be better as: '... only attitude contributed significantly to the ...'

Discussion

> Other problems with the experiment were that they were conducted on students who are not representative of the general population. Furthermore, the experiment was conducted on psychology students.

Comment: This is an excerpt discussing sampling in the context of the discussion section. There was no need for this writer to put this in their report as the same could be written in all reports on data based on testing psychology students. It is good practice to confine criticisms to the specific problems of that particular experiment. This kind of statement occurs frequently in student reports as mentioned elsewhere. Did you also spot the repetition of 'conducted'? Was the second sentence, stressing the use of *psychology* students, adding anything worthwhile?

The Essay

> This essay will discuss research which has identified a process by which words are stored in memory, evaluating two theories which attempt to account for how reading and spelling use these stores and how this accounts for the ability to read words which cannot be spelt.

Comment: This is a complicated sentence in the introductory paragraph to an essay. The important word 'which', which normally signals the beginning of a clause (as just shown; see *clause* in chapter 11), occurs no fewer than four times. The writer is trying to compress too much into the one sentence. There are three main ideas embedded in here. The essay is going to cover: (1) research into how words are stored in memory; (2) two theories accounting for how reading and spelling use these memory stores; (3) how the previous two points explain the situation in which words can be read but not be spelled. This would have been expressed better within three shorter sentences. We will not go into the accuracy of how memory processes are implied to be relevant to the differences between reading and spelling processes.

> The flavour of this relationship in a different context is demonstrated by Smith (2004)…

Comment: This should be: 'Other research supporting this relationship, but in a different context, is shown by…' However, a more concise approach might be: 'Smith (2004) similarly found that…' if space is tight. On the other hand, it gets monotonous if there is a sequence of sentences beginning this way.

> *In general an important behavioural difference is observed and an antecedent variable is sought to explain the difference.*

Comment: The repetition of *difference* in the same sentence is awkward. For instance, one could use the word *distinction* to replace the first instance of *difference*. (See the entry for *substitution* in chapter 11.)

As a general point when proofreading, look out for repetitions of words within sentences and across adjacent sentences and even in the openings to a sequence of paragraphs. I have just marked an essay in which about halfway through, a paragraph began 'one criticism raised…', the next paragraph began 'another criticism was…' and the next but one paragraph began 'another criticism of…' This student was making a list of criticisms at the rate of one for each paragraph, but the repetition was tedious. As noted elsewhere, repetition can be particularly noticeable if two occurrences of a rarely used word appear in close succession.

> …a number of studies have looked at attitudes of individual cultures, e.g. Hungarian… [A reference is then cited.]

Comment: Although it sounds wrong it should be *has looked* because the verb *has* is qualifying *number* not *studies*. This is the same problem examined earlier with the word *none*. This is another word to add to your 'to be avoided' list, for the same reason. Also, 'e.g.' should only occur within brackets.

> Another aspect that is worth mentioning was the believed to be value-free research. All those years psychological research was anything but value-free. It was from the beginning biased for males. [This passage starts a paragraph.]

Comment: The beginning could be more concise because the clause '... that is worth mentioning' is redundant. Some might think that this first sentence should not change tense from the present ('is') to the past ('was'). However, this is not problematic in this context. The phrase 'the believed to be' is awkward. The third sentence would be better with 'biased in favour of' in place of 'biased for'. The whole piece might be rewritten as: 'In the early development of psychology any gender-based research was biased in favour of males.' I would not write that research was 'anything but value-free' as I do not consider present-day research to be much less value-free either. However, that is just a personal view.

References

> Doran, Neal, McChargue, Dennis, Cohen, Lee. (2007). 'Impulsivity and the Reinforcing Value of Cigarette Smoking'. Addictive Behaviors, 32(1) 90–98. [This example was found in a student's References section. Spot the errors.]

Comment: This should have been presented as follows:

> Doran, N., McChargue, D., & Cohen, L. (2007). Impulsivity and the reinforcing value of cigarette smoking. *Addictive Behaviors, 32*, 90–98.

As mentioned before, the layout of the reference needs to be checked against the preferences of your instructor. For instance, British instructors might require an absence of a comma before the ampersand (&).

Concluding Remarks

I hope that on completion most of the errors in these extracts should have been spotted. A common problem with students' writings is carelessness. Careful rereading would have ensured that many of these errors would have been picked up. Other errors are simply because of having a relatively underdeveloped vocabulary. For instance, perhaps a writer does not know enough about the properties of a word such as *numerous*. They know, vaguely, that it could be a synonym for *many*, but one or two may generalise and think that it can also stand in for *much*, so they feel able to write something like 'numerous research'. Vocabulary can be accumulated simply by reading more about the subject, and can be refined by reading books like this that focus on problematic words. Similarly, grammatical knowledge will develop through further reading and, I hope, by the corrections that you will get from markers.

Language has rules and those rules are continuously bent by various users. If enough people diverge in a new direction, the rules change when the majority have adopted it. This causes grief to pedants, but our language has to keep moving with the times. There have been significant changes in the use of the language in psychology in the four decades of my own experience of the subject. Be prepared for the inevitable further changes in the future. However, try not to be a trendsetter and invent your own neologisms. Stick with the herd while you are still a student. Good luck in your writing and do not forget: always reread what you write and try to revise it a few days later. Most important of all: keep a positive frame of mind and keep writing.

Appendix 1

AN EXAMPLE STUDENT ESSAY

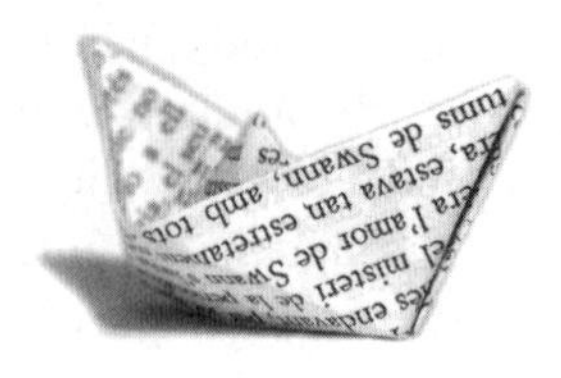

What is the effectiveness of the placebo in relation to an equivalent therapeutic intervention?[1]

Medical professionals need to know as much as possible about the psychological phenomenon known as the "placebo" to evaluate the effectiveness of their medical interventions.[2] Although it is unlikely to produce an effect equivalent to a corresponding medical intervention, the extent of the power of the placebo needs to be determined.[3] The placebo, as examined in this essay, is an inert substance that is given to a patient that could lead to an improvement in their condition due to their belief that they are being treated.[4] Nowadays double-blind randomized controlled trials are the gold standard in evaluating the effectiveness of a pharmacological treatment. This relies on both the patient and the researcher being unaware of (i.e., "blind to") the identity of the treatment drug and the placebo drug until the trial is completed. The design was introduced to control for the possibility that patients could recover purely because they believed that they were receiving a genuine therapeutic treatment. If the placebo response were feasible, it would imply that a belief can produce a physical response leading to recovery. We shall first examine the evidence for the placebo and then

Running commentary

Follow your tutor's instructions about how to submit. For example, the text should be double spaced (unlike the example to the left), have a title page, and so on. Obviously it would be wider on the page than shown here. The superscript numbers in the essay are purely to annotate comments for this right-hand column.

1. This is an evaluative essay title. It is not asking for an explanation of how the placebo effect works; instead the questioner wants to know about the extent of, or effectiveness of, the placebo.

2. The opening sentence provides a wider relevance to the question while still being connected to the topic.

3. This next sentence links in with the essay question and suggests that the potential of the placebo effect is not likely to be as much as a therapeutic intervention. However, the author agrees that the question of its extent needs to be answered.

4. This sentence provides a definition of the placebo and it is

look at arguments for the opposite side of the case, or at least, consider work constraining the areas where it might work.[5]

By the mid-twentieth century, there was strong evidence for the placebo.[6] Beecher (1955) produced a meta-analysis showing that about a third of the population responds positively to the placebo. Benson and Friedman (1996) showed in a review on later studies for other medical conditions that these also demonstrated placebo effects. For instance, a study by Benson and McCallie (as cited in Benson & Friedman, 1996) examined a particular treatment of angina pectoris.[7] This treatment is now considered ineffectual; nevertheless, success was at 70–90% because of the strong placebo context. However, once the profession became more doubtful, the effectiveness of this treatment reduced to 30–40%. The reduced expectancies had led to a large drop in effectiveness. It is also interesting to note from this work the implication of harnessing the placebo for current medical practice. For instance, by making clear to patients a strong confidence in the treatment.[8]

An example of the effectiveness of the placebo in more recent work is that by de la Fuente-Fernandez et al. (2001) on patients with Parkinson's disease. This showed that the expectation of motor improvement by means of placebo induced the production of endogenous dopamine in the striatum. This was a demonstration of how the placebo can promote a positive physiological effect.[9] Thus, this essay is not arguing against the existence of a placebo effect, rather it is concerned with assessing its relative strength. However, some researchers have taken an extreme position and have argued the placebo is nothing more than an illusion.

The case against the placebo effect was perhaps motivated by the implied criticism that the clinical interventions of medics are sometimes not much better than "quackery" if the placebo can be so effective.[10] Kienle and Kienle (2001) took a much more critical approach to the point of even suggesting the placebo might be just an "illusory" effect. Reexamining Beecher's meta-analysis and other studies that seemed to show placebo effects, Kienle

followed with background information on the placebo. A slight problem is that the narrowness of this definition excludes wider experimental contexts.

5. The final part of this introductory paragraph gives an overview of what is coming next, but not of the whole essay.

6. This is the topic sentence of the second paragraph. It is not a full introduction to the paragraph, but at least readers know that they are about to be find out about earlier work indicating a strong placebo effect.

7. This has the citation of a secondary source (i.e., a source not read by the essay writer but referred to by another author) in this sentence as the B & M study is a component of the Benson and Friedman review. Your tutor may have a different convention for the treatment of such references. Note that there is no reference for Benson and McCallie in the References section and that the date of B & M is not cited in the text.

8. These last two sentences are the author's evaluations.

9. This paragraph describes a physiological measure of the placebo effect that is referred to later in the conclusion. The following sentence is emphasising an important aspect of the perspective of the essay – that the placebo effect is considered to be a real one by the author, despite criticisms that are about to be covered.

10. We have finished with the pro-placebo part and are now going to look at the case against.

and Kienle concluded that because of errors of various kinds these effects were not demonstrated.

Their criticisms have validity when it comes to examining faulty argument or research design or both in placebo research.[11] In one study on hypertension that they cited (Coe, Best & Kinsman), a placebo effect was claimed because 62% of patients reported feeling better, even though there was no objective change in their underlying hypertension. This positive feeling of these patients had been induced by first giving them the toxic drug Veratrum, which produced adverse symptoms, followed by the placebo or treatment. The reason for the subjective improvement had probably been because of the stoppage of Veratrum. Another example of faulty design and interpretation is when placebo effects may be the result of additional treatment.[12] For instance, Moerman (cited in Keinle & Kienle, 2001) examined placebo effects in trials on patients with gastric complaints. However, the improvements in the placebo condition (10–90%) could be because of extra treatments such as: (1) hospitalization that led to reduced stress; (2) dietary, alcohol, and smoking advice; and (3) administration of antacids. One aspect Kienle and Kienle discuss is spontaneous remission. For example, treatment for a common cold using a placebo will seemingly produce a placebo effect as patients will recover anyway after about 6 days. Similarly, there can be regression to the mean whereby cases present to the doctor for treatment when at the peak of their illness and they subsequently improve. These and other cases they describe are convincing cases to account for false placebo effects in these particular studies, but it cannot imply that the placebo therefore does not exist.[13]

Kienle and Kienle went too far in their argument, however. They subdivided the construct into what might be called the "illusory placebo," which is the ineffective part and any part that is effective, which they call "error." For instance, they cited patient bias whereby "conditioned answers" were given or where there was "experimental subordination." They used the definition of Hornung (cited in Kienle & Kienle) in which the placebo is "an

The author is showing orientation against the anti-placebo position by suggesting it is motivated by defending the medical profession's respectability. Perhaps this is showing a little too much bias? The slightly negative tone continues in the paragraph.

11. In this paragraph a degree of balance is being restored and the positive aspects of K & K (2001) are being acknowledged.

12. This is a sentence linking two examples of faulty design. It is a fairly arbitrary decision whether to begin a new paragraph here.

13. Further evaluation by the author here again acknowledges the worth of K & K's analyses, but serves also to show the limitation. In other words, just because one has debunked the research that had purported to show X, it still does not imply that X does not exist. In order to do this, one needs experiments that are specifically designed to demonstrate that X does not exist.

inert preparation that looks like an active medication" (p. 36).[14] By doing so, they hoped to exclude any treatment intended specifically to use mind-body healing, as they considered these approaches as beyond their scope. One can appreciate that medical researchers want to remove anything "placebo-like" to find out the effectiveness of their treatments. However, this does not mean that these eliminated elements in themselves are illusory or ineffective for treatment.

To recap so far, evidence in the past for a placebo effect has been criticised because of poor experimental design or argument.[15] However, critics of the placebo, such as Kienle and Kienle, have gone too far by appearing to argue that when the placebo effect works this is error; and when it does not, this shows that it is illusion. This is not a falsifiable hypothesis. Work that is more recent can give a better indication of the extent of placebo effects, although this is not without problems as well.

Consider the placebo condition against a no-treatment condition. In the placebo treatment, patients believe that they are receiving a treatment during the trial.[16] By contrast, the patients in the no-treatment condition know that they are being left untreated. (They normally would have treatment after the duration of the drug trial, such as 6 months later.) If the placebo patients do better than the no-treatment patients, this should enable measurement of the placebo effect. This should be better than comparison of placebo with a treatment condition in which there is no corresponding baseline for comparison. It should be noted that the essay question is not strictly asking about comparing the placebo with a no treatment condition. However, it is potentially important to make this comparison in order to measure the effectiveness of the placebo.[17]

The comparison of placebo with no-treatment controls in a randomized paradigm was examined in detail by Hróbjartsson and Gøtzsche (2001, 2004). In these studies of 156 trials the placebo effect was found to be smaller than previously thought.[18] When they did find positive placebo effects it was when subjective measures (i.e., those

14. Note how this short quotation is formatted.

15. This is a useful signposting statement to make at the approximate midpoint of the essay. It is the beginning of a rough summary of what we have so far and a further evaluation follows. The paragraph concludes with an indication of what is to follow. If space is tight such a paragraph could be left out, but its inclusion does make the essay a little easier to read by giving information on structure.

16. This is just a minor point. The plural here and elsewhere is used to avoid "... the patient believes that he or she is receiving ..." or worse "... the patient believes that they are receiving..."

17. The essay question is asking: "What is the effectiveness of the placebo in relation to an equivalent therapeutic intervention?" As we are now examining the comparison of placebo to no-treatment conditions, it may be considered irrelevant to the question. This sentence has been put in to demonstrate the relevance of this particular line of investigation. This should reassure the marker that the writer has not lost sight of the question.

18. This sentence was previously: "In their 2001 study using 114 such trials and then later in 2004, when 42 further trials became available, they showed that the placebo effect was smaller than previously thought." This is an example of how detail can be cut down.

reported by patients) were used, particularly for reported pain. By contrast when parameters were measured by observers (e.g., blood pressure) there was no statistical evidence for a placebo effect. Reported effects sizes in 2004 were 0.3 versus 0.1 standard deviations (on placebo vs. no-treatment in each case) for the subjective versus objective measures, respectively, and this difference was statistically significant ($p < 0.01$).[19]

Hróbjartsson and Gøtzsche discussed some problems with their study. One is that of reporting bias: they argued that patients believe that they have been given a genuine treatment and even though they may not have experienced any benefit, may nevertheless wish to be positive. They suggested the 0.3 versus 0.1 (a factor of 3) difference, between subjective and objective measurement may be due mostly to this aspect of the placebo effect. Another problem is that despite the clear advantages of comparing placebo with no-treatment conditions a *co-intervention* problem could be that patients assigned to the no-treatment conditions might be more likely to try to find alternative treatments than the placebo controls. This would bring the no-treatment condition closer to the placebo in performance outcome. A way round this difficulty would be to ask no-treatment patients to elaborate on any alternative treatments that they may have used at the end of the study and then to evaluate this effect. However, presumably this is not standard procedure in medical research.[20]

It is important to distinguish the definition on the one hand of the effects of the placebo intervention confined to double-blind trials, and on the other the placebo effect per se. The latter term refers to the patient–provider relationship that has some undefined effect on the administration of a treatment. The Greek physician Galen (c. 200 AD) noted that the success of a cure depended on the degree of confidence of the recipient (Osler, 1892; as cited in Shapiro & Shapiro, 1997). The placebo effect is referring to effects that are psychologically mediated, such as the power of suggestion (Hróbjartsson, 2002). Although the comparison of placebo with the no-treatment counterpart represents

19. This paragraph is providing a direct answer to the essay question by showing in terms of effect size the effectiveness of the placebo for subjective measures as being 3 times greater than for objective measures.

20. The last two sentences provide more evaluation by the author with a suggestion on how this kind of research could be improved.

an advance in research on placebo interventions, even the untreated condition involves some interaction with practitioners. If the practitioner is assigning a patient to a no-treatment condition there could be something positive that the patients might gain from this experience (e.g., they might decide that their condition could not be so serious after all for them to be assigned thus).

The work comparing placebo and no-treatment might seriously underestimate the effects of the placebo in the clinical setting. Miller and Rosenstein (2006), discussing the Hróbjartsson and Gøtzsche (2001) study, pointed out that in the studies they examined of the placebo, the patients were informed about the experimental design. Thus they were aware that the treatment was going to be a placebo, a treatment or else they were going to be given no treatment. Therefore they would be uncertain whether they would receive the placebo in the placebo and treatment situations. Under these circumstances the placebo is unlikely to be so powerful as to have clinical relevance.

If patients have a belief that they are getting treatment for pain it can have a powerful effect compared to being uncertain whether or not they are getting treatment, as shown by Price, Riley, and Vase (2003). They found in a meta-analysis a large difference (-0.04 vs. 1.14) in weighted mean effect size (i.e., weighting according to sample size) between effects of placebo in clinical trials (in which the patients do not know if they are receiving placebo) compared with experiments evaluating placebo analgesia. Thus both types of placebo treatment were compared with no-treatment controls. Patients who knew there was a chance that they might or might not receive the treatment were substantially less affected than those who believed they were getting a treatment for pain relief.

In conclusion,[21] expectations for the power of the placebo had been high after the early work of Beecher (1955). Later critical work by Keinle and Kienle (2001) showed that often conclusions concerning the placebo have been affected by faulty experimental design, but they seem to deny any

21. In the conclusion the main thesis of the essay is being restated. These statements do not all necessarily address the question directly. For instance, the Beecher work is cited to indicate that the received view was that the placebo effect was a strong one. Later work has challenged this view, but in so doing perhaps some people have swung too much in the opposite direction.

effectiveness for the placebo. More recently the comparison of the placebo with no-treatment control conditions has helped improve our understanding. It appears that for most medical conditions the therapeutic effect of the placebo is small and not enough to be clinically effective. However, this may have underestimated the size of the placebo. The extent of the placebo effect appears to vary according to clinical conditions, but its effects should be easier to measure in the future using better research designs and physiological recordings.[22]

22. This is the concluding statement. This is normally one that requires some thought. This one is answering the question by countering it and saying that the extent of the placebo effect depends on the clinical condition. The second part is looking to the future suggesting that more accurate measuring of the extent of the placebo will come with better research designs and improved physiological research.

References

Beecher, H. K. (1955). The powerful placebo. *Journal of the American Medical Association, 159*, 1602–1606.

Benson, H., & Friedman, R. (1996). Harnessing the power of the placebo effect and renaming it "remembered wellness". *Annual Review of Medicine, 47*, 193–199.

de la Fuente-Fernandez, R., Ruth, T. J., Sossi, V., Schulzer, M., Calne, D. B., & Stoessl, A. J. (2001). Expectation and dopamine release: Mechanism of the placebo effect in Parkinson's Disease. *Science, 293*, 1164–1166.

Hróbjartsson, A. (2002). What are the main methodological problems in the estimation of placebo effects? *Journal of Clinical Epidemiology, 55*, 430–435.

Hróbjartsson, A., & Gøtzsche, P. C. (2001). Is the placebo powerless? An analysis of clinical trials comparing placebo with no treatment. *New England Journal of Medicine, 344*, 1594–1602.

Hróbjartsson, A., & Gøtzsche, P. C. (2004). Is the placebo powerless? Update of a systematic review with 52 new randomized trials comparing placebo with no treatment. *Journal of Internal Medicine*, 2004, *256*, 91–100.

Kienle, G. S., & Kienle, H. (2001). A critical reanalysis of the concept, magnitude and existence of placebo. In D. Peters (Ed.), *Understanding the placebo effect in complementary medicine: Theory, practice and research* (pp.31–50). London: Churchill Livingstone.

Miller, F. G., & Rosenstein, D.L. (2006). The nature and power of the placebo effect. *Journal of Clinical Epidemiology*, 331–335.

Price, D. D., Riley III, J. L., & Vase, L. (2003). Reliable differences in placebo effects between clinical analgesic trials and studies of placebo analgesia mechanisms. *Pain, 104*, 715–716.

Shapiro, A. K., & Shapiro, E. (1997). *The powerful placebo: From ancient priest to modern physician*. Baltimore, MD: Johns Hopkins University Press.

Appendix 2

AN EXAMPLE STUDENT QUANTITATIVE LAB REPORT

Students' preference to study with or without music: is this due to differences in the potentially distracting effects of music and speech while learning?[1]

Abstract

Previous research has found that roughly half of students prefer to study with background music. The present study examined whether these "music learners" chose to study this way to use music as a potential mask to produce the most effective study environment. Music learners and silent learners memorized word lists and then after a delay performed a recognition task under different conditions of continuous distraction. Music learners, in contrast to silent learners, were more disrupted by speech, but less affected by music. However, this interaction just failed to reach significance. Music learners may prefer their mode of study to mask out the potential distraction of speech. By contrast, silent learners may not need music because although they too are distracted, the level of distraction is unchanged across the different distracter types. This gives moderate support for the hypothesis that students who prefer to study with a background of music prefer to do so in order to mask out the potential distraction of speech.[2]

Running commentary

Follow your tutor's instructions about how to submit. For example, it should be double spaced (unlike the example to the left), have a title page, and so on. Obviously, the text would be wider on the page than shown here. The superscript numbers in the report are to annotate comments for this right-hand column.

This write-up is based on Neil Spence's undergraduate dissertation data which I supervised at the University of Leicester, UK. Neil has kindly agreed to let me do this.

1. This title is a bit long. To shorten it 'is this due to differences in the potentially distracting...' could have been omitted. However, the longer title allows the hypothesis to be stated while at the same time including the main variables (study preference, distraction from music and speech).

2. Consult chapter 4 for advice about the construction of an abstract – and for the rest of the sections in this report. Within the first two sentences, the nub of the problem is presented.

When learning material for an examination students presumably develop their preferred strategies for achieving the best result.[3] Gurung (2005) examined different ways of learning information including the type of environment that students had during private study. Among other variables, external factors such as background noise and the presence of others were examined and it was noted that those revising in the presence of music performed less well than when revising in silence. A distraction such as music affects the quality of learning. The present study investigates whether students study with a musical background because for them the cost of this distraction is outweighed by the benefits of masking potential other distractions, especially speech.[4]

Previous research on the effects of various types of distraction has shown that they hinder performance. For example, compared with silent conditions, distractions such as television (Pool, Koolstra & Van Der Voort, 2003), classical music and verbal prose (Flowers & O'Neill, 2005) and office noise (Banbury & Berry, 1998) all hinder performance on cognitive tasks.[5]

A potential distracter during studying may be more potent according to how close it is to the primary task.[6] For example, we may find the sound of a conversation much more disruptive while trying to read a difficult section of text than the background noise of busy traffic. Salamé and Baddeley (1982) accounted for this effect with the proposal of a detector system that picks out sounds that are similar to vocal patterns and integrates them into concurrent mental processes. Banbury, Macken, Tremblay and Jones (2001) in a review of auditory distraction concluded that short-term memory is vulnerable to interference from external sounds.

Crawford and Strapp (1994) found that half the students they questioned preferred to study with music.[7] They gave these students a number of cognitive tasks (e.g., maze tracing, memory testing) of different cognitive levels under conditions of silence and music. They found contrasting performances between those who studied with music and the silent learners. The silent learners were more accurate during silence whereas the music learners were

The task is described. The main result and the conclusion follow. You may need to start a new page for the introduction that follows.

3. The introduction of the general area starts with a sentence on the proposition that students aim to develop a learning strategy that works best for them. Soon the distractions of background noise such as music while studying are introduced.

4. The introductory paragraph finishes with the statement of the research problem.

5. This paragraph briefly outlines some previous research on the effects of distraction. Notice that it is pitched at a general level.

6. The topic sentence of this paragraph is reminding the reader that a central aspect of this paper is about studying and serves to introduce the Salamé and Baddeley theory as well.

7. This opening sentence moves the introduction on to the fact that half of learners like to study with music. This paragraph outlines a difference between the two types of learner (i.e. those who have silent study vs. those studying with music) and ends with the problem that music learners are adversely affected by music, but they still employ it.

better during musical distraction. Previously Etaugh and Ptasnik (1982) had found a similar result during a comprehension exercise. Such results might suggest that people adopt a method of studying that enables them to learn information that suits them the best. However, this does not explain the paradox that music in itself is also a distracter.

To obtain a fuller picture of how distraction influences different learners, we need to examine the effects of speech as a distracter as well as music. A potential resolution of this problem is that although music is distracting, speech may be even more distracting for the learner who prefers a background of music. Music could help to attenuate these different distractions.[8]

The present study compared students who prefer to study while listening to music with those who normally study in silence under different distraction conditions. A task was devised to simulate their learning situation while studying in a simplified but controlled manner. They had to learn lists of words and then had to recognize them while simultaneously undergoing one of four different distraction conditions. The first of these was a control condition in which the task was done under silence and the other three were speech alone, music alone, and music plus speech. Those who study with music are expected to perform better during music than the silent learners and all participants should be adversely affected in the speech condition. Suppose that music learners study the way they do to maximize the effectiveness of their learning environment according to their capabilities. We should expect that they not only do better (relative to silent learners) during the music distraction condition, but that they are more impaired with speech alone and less impaired when music and speech occur together.[9]

Method

Participants

There were 48 university students (8 males and 40 females, mean age of 19.13 years, SD = 1.00, range

8. The reason for including speech distraction is outlined very briefly here. This paragraph also serves the role of explaining the relevance of the study to the context of the research described so far.

9. In this last paragraph, we are briefly describing how the research question is going to be examined. Importantly it ends by outlining our expectations according to our hypothesis. Our hypothesis in general terms is that students study with or without music depending on how it affects their personal overall performance. Thus they study in a way that suits them the best. There is also a more specific version that relates to predictions in performance, as outlined in the last sentence.

18 to 22 years) who volunteered for the experiment as part of a course requirement for Psychology. All the participants had English as their first language. The participants were divided into two groups according to their preferred method of studying (with music vs. silence) to create the music study group (4 males and 18 females, mean age of 19.09, SD = .92 years) and the silent study group (4 males and 22 females, mean age of 19.15, SD = 1.08 years). Their age ranges were 18 to 21 and 18 to 22 years, respectively.[10]

Materials

The source materials for the auditory part of the experiment were eight contemporary songs as well as an excerpt from an audiobook for the speech distraction part. Tracks from a diverse range of genres were selected. This helped the music learning participants, in particular, to choose music more similar to what they used while studying. Details of the musical selections and participants' preferences are shown in Appendix 1. This shows, for instance, that 29.2% of participants chose a track by Jack Johnson. The audiobook excerpt was from Brown (2003).[11]

The words used for the memory task were matched on word length and word frequency for four lists of 40 words (e.g., *soap, relief, verify*).[12] Four laminated sheets each containing a different list of 40 words arranged in two columns were prepared. The four corresponding test sheets consisted of a sample of 26 of the original words and 13 matched foils, randomly arranged in two columns. Appropriate spaces were provided on these sheets so that they could put a tick or a cross next to each item according to whether it was old or new. The accuracy of performance in the memory task was calculated by the number of hits minus the number of false positives (adjusted for chance by multiplying by two) expressed as a percentage.

Design[13]

The two independent variables were type of distraction (at four levels) and type of study preference

10. The participants are described and the description of the method of selection is important, as well.

11. Apparatus could have been mentioned in a section entitled 'Materials and Apparatus'. However, the technical requirement of the apparatus was regarded as too straightforward to warrant mention. (It only involved playing a recording through headphones.) The materials are much more important with detail of the participants' choices of music being given in an appendix. Some might think that the numbers of choices for each track is an actual result and therefore ought to go into the Results section. However, presenting these data in the results would be a distraction from the main results. They are better suited to being examined in the context of the appropriateness of the method. More could be written about the data in Appendix 1. However, space is too restricted for a report of this nature.

12. You would give the full lists of words in an appendix.

13. Your tutor may advise that you should incorporate the Design section into other subsections of the method.

(at two levels). All participants experienced the distraction conditions as follows: (a) silence (b) music of their choice (c) speech consisting of an excerpt from the audiobook and (d) music of choice and speech experienced simultaneously. The same piece of music was played for conditions (b) and (d); similarly, the same excerpt of speech was played for conditions (c) and (d). Order of presentation was counterbalanced for each participant according to a Latin Square design. Each distraction condition was experienced only once. The other independent variable was whether the participant studied with or without music. Performance in the recognition task was the dependent variable.

Procedure

Participants were asked whether they listened to music when they were studying. The procedure and relevant ethical aspects of the experiment were then explained to them.[14] They were then given a printed list of 8 tracks of contemporary music. At the same time, they were told that they would be participating in a memory task while listening to the track that they were about to select. The songs were recognizable to most participants; therefore, no excerpt of these songs was given at this point. Their choice was subsequently used for both the two music distraction conditions.

In the first phase of each trial in all the auditory conditions, the participants put on headphones and they were allowed to adjust the volume to a suitable level during this 30-second period. In the second phase, experienced by all participants, they were given a laminated sheet showing 40 words that had to be memorized during a 90-second period. These were then taken away and there was a 30-second delay while they did nothing. Immediately after this in the third and final phase, they were given a test sheet and they indicated by a tick or cross on this sheet whether each word was in the previous list or new. In all the auditory conditions, from the first to the final phase of each

14. This description of the instructions might be considered to be a little vague, but the tasks here were straightforward. You would need to be more explicit for more complicated tasks or if there was anything that was ethically relevant to your study.

trial, the auditory distraction was on continuously. To ensure this, the track was on repeat for the trial duration.

Results

An alpha level of .05 was used for all statistical tests.[15] The log transformed percentage recognition data were analyzed with a 4 × 2 (type of distraction × study style) mixed analysis of variance with distraction type serving as repeated measures. These data were log transformed because the music plus speech distraction condition failed Levene's test of equality of error variances on the untransformed data. The log transformed data passed Levene's test.[16] In the ANOVA the main effect of the distracters was significant, $F(3,138) = 9.582, p < .001$, but the effect of study style was not, $F(1,46) = 0.085, p = .772$. The interaction failed to reach significance, $F(3, 138) = 2.430, p = .068$.[17] Figure 1 shows the performance of the two groups across the distraction conditions.

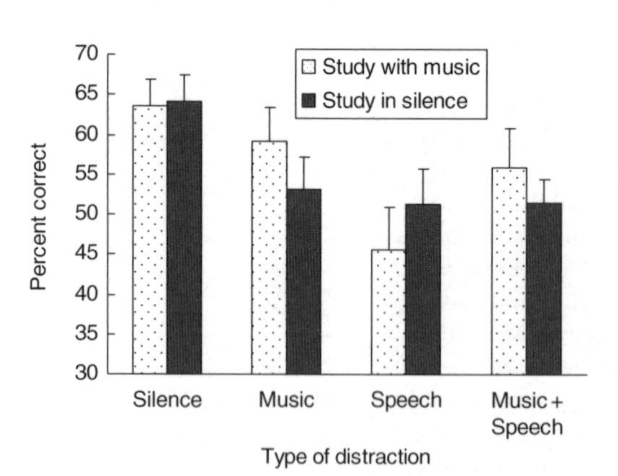

Figure 1 The mean percentages correct and standard errors (shown by the error bars), corrected for guessing, as a function of type of distraction in a memory task for participants preferring to study with music or in silence.[18]

15. By making this statement, this means we can then state the exact a posteriori probability for our tests, where necessary.

16. The first paragraph of the Results section opens with a description of the major analysis of the experiment. Note how the description of the analysis of variance (or ANOVA) makes it clear what the dependent variable is (the recognition data), what the components are (study style & distraction), what the levels are (2, 4), which are repeated measures and which are independent (there is no need to be explicit what the independent is, as it can only be study style) and the type of ANOVA (mixed). A very minor point: note also that the order of the description of the independent variables is kept the same throughout (from Method section to Results), that is, type of distracter first and then the study style.

17. The interaction fails to reach below the 5 per cent level of probability, which makes the result marginal. If the probability level was at (say) 10 per cent or higher that would be the end of the matter. However, at this level it is still worth looking at effect sizes to look at the extent of this marginal interaction. At least this way, there is more to discuss. Throughout the discussion, however, this weakness in the level of interaction means that the nature of the results is described only tentatively. Incidentally, this experiment had sufficient power in that an adequate number of participants were tested; therefore, lack of numbers cannot be used as a reason why significance was not reached.

18. There are several things to

Dependent t-tests on the log transformed data for all six combinations of two-way pairings among the four distraction types with alpha set at .0083[19] (based on a Bonferroni correction of alpha = .05) revealed significant differences in half of these pairings. These were silence versus music, silence versus speech, and silence versus music plus speech. The t-tests were $t(47) = 2.895, p < .01$; $t(47) = 3.826, p < .001$; and $t(47) = 3.791, p < .001$, respectively. Effect sizes (using Cohen's d here and elsewhere) for these same comparisons were moderate to high at 0.439, 0.757, and 0.586, respectively. Thus, the main effect for distraction type in the analysis of variance was produced by the superiority of performance during silence compared to the other conditions involving music, speech, or music plus speech. Furthermore, in terms of effect size, speech alone produced the greatest distraction overall.

The interaction between study preference and type of distraction just failed to reach significance. Nevertheless, further effect size differences were explored as inspection of Figure 1 shows some evidence of an interaction between the type of distraction and study preference, excluding the silent condition. Effect sizes between the two types of learner were 0.312, 0.249, and 0.229 for the music only, speech only, and music plus speech conditions, respectively. The interactive aspect of these differences, although slight, was that the music learners performed better in the two distraction conditions involving music, whereas in the speech distraction condition the music learners were worse than the silent learners. The effect size analysis shows that the largest difference between the two groups (at a moderate level of effect size) is when there is music as the only distraction.

The mean times (with ranges in brackets) to complete the recognition phase for the silent, music, speech, and music plus speech conditions were: 54.4 (30 to 100), 59.4 (32 to 92), 60.1 (28 to 115), and 59.5 (32 to 110) seconds, respectively.[20] There was a significant main effect across these times according to a one-way repeated measures ANOVA, $F(1, 47) = 6.17, p < .05$. The silent condition was

note about the figure. You may be required by your tutor to show the figure at the end of the paper rather than in the Results section. Standard errors were used here to show the variation across the conditions. There tends to be a convention to use these instead of standard deviations. Note that a bar graph rather than a line graph was used to indicate that these are separate conditions. Finally, a graph was used instead of a table as it shows nicely the nature of the interaction and the extent of it.

19. A zero is not put before the decimal point in this decimal fraction because this number cannot be greater than 1. Furthermore, this particular decimal is expressed to four decimal places to give sufficient precision as the first two (to the right of the decimal point) are zero.

20. Note this method of listing information on means and ranges across conditions. Unfortunately, it can lead to long sentences. If there were much more information like this, then a table would be better. The result discussed here is a minor one and is not followed through in the Discussion section.

faster than the rest and paired-samples t tests on the other three conditions compared with silence with a Bonferroni correction setting alpha at .0125 found only one significant difference. Thus participants were significantly slower during recognition with speech than recognition in silence, $t(47) = 2.88, p < .01$.

Discussion

The results from the present study give mild support for the hypothesis that students study with or without music in order to produce the best study environment for their capabilities. Study preference has a weak interactive influence on memory performance under different distraction conditions. In particular, the music learners were less affected by the distraction of music alone, but more affected by speech alone in relation to themselves. Processing music may have become more automated for them so that it represents less competition in cognitive resources. Part of this result for the music study group concurs with the findings of Crawford and Strapp (1994). They found that music learners (defined in the same way as the present study) when performing during music were more accurate on a series of cognitive tasks compared to silent learners.[21]

In the present study, there was not a complete mirror in the results for the silent learners comparing their own performance across the different distractions. For them, all types of sound encountered in the experiment were equally distracting. Although they do not listen to music while studying, the impact of music for them is at the same level as for speech and speech plus music. This pattern would still be in accord with the proposition that students select their learning environment to minimize distraction. For silent learners, there is no need to have music on while studying. However, it should also be noted that silent learners are more distracted by music than music learners. Nevertheless, this aspect is further support for the proposition

21. This is the section for the discussion of the hypotheses in relation to the results. The first sentence is an overview of how the hypothesis, more generally stated, is given mild support. Had the interaction been stronger, we could have made this a correspondingly stronger statement. This is followed at a more detailed level concentrating on the results from the perspective of the music learners. Towards the end of the paragraph, there is some integration with previous research that had been mentioned in the introduction.

that students lessen the distraction of their study environment. By studying in silence, they are going to be distracted by speech, music, or a combination of the two in equal measure. The cost of this approach is that should they hear any music, it is going to affect them more because they are less used to it when they study.[22]

The support for the idea that learners choose their potentially best study environment found in the present experiment agrees with work by Campbell and Hawley (1982). They showed that silent learners preferred silent areas within a library, whereas music learners preferred quiet areas in the library where low conversation was permitted. However, music may have other qualities that induce students to prefer music to silence. For example, Schellenberg, Nakata, Hunter and Tamoto (2007) showed that music enhances mood and in the current experiment, allowing them to choose their own style of music could have helped this.

It needs emphasizing that this discussion of the interaction between the two groups is based on effect sizes within a marginal interaction.[23] The main statistically significant finding combining groups was that in comparison with the other distracting conditions, silence was consistently the easiest condition for memorizing and retrieving the verbal stimuli, whereas speech alone was the most distracting. The effect size between this speech condition and silence was the largest and supports previous research showing the distracting effect of speech (e.g., Banbury & Berry, 1997; Salamé and Baddeley, 1982). Similarly, music was distracting as previously found (e.g., Flowers & O'Neill, 2005).

The present study allowed participants to choose their own music across a diverse range of styles to reflect more accurately the musical conditions that would be closer to their own study environment. It was not easy to equate information load and 14 students chose the Jack Johnson track (see Appendix 1). This was a male vocalist with a background guitar with a slow and soft rhythm suggesting an inclination to choose music that was less distracting. Thus, while providing a more realistic

22. Similarly, in this paragraph the findings relating to the silent learners are discussed.

23. This is just to make sure that the reader is fully aware that we are discussing findings that are not statistically significant. This also serves as a transition to discuss the one finding that has found statistical significance. However, this is not a particularly important finding in terms of developing the discussion on the main hypotheses.

reflection of the music learners' personal study habits, it unfortunately meant that information load was not consistent across all participants. This may have contributed to the marginal nature of the interaction.[24]

In conclusion, all participants were significantly affected by the various distracters during a word-learning task relative to silence. In addition, there was a slight interaction that showed that music learners were less affected by music alone but more affected by speech alone; whereas the silent learners were distracted in equal measure. This pattern gives moderate support for the hypothesis that students who prefer to study with a background of music prefer to do so in order to mask out the potential distraction of speech. By contrast, silent learners may not need music because although they too were distracted by speech, they did not demonstrate these differential distracting effects. However, there could be other explanations for this result that need further investigation; for example, music may be used by music learners to make their studying more enjoyable by enhancing their mood.[25]

24. This is the one paragraph that discusses the main problem of the experiment that could have contributed to the interaction not quite reaching statistical significance. Other weaknesses could have been mentioned, but space is precious. For instance, perhaps the experiment should have been completely presented by computer to allow more precise control over the presentation conditions. However, this was a student's experiment and time was limited. Furthermore, is learning word lists a good simulation of normal study conditions? Perhaps you can think of other problems?

25. This conclusion summarises the main arguments. In the last sentence, we look to the future to see what needs to be investigated further.

References

Banbury, S., & Berry, D. C. (1997). Habituation and dishabituation to speech and office noise. *Journal of Experimental Psychology: Applied*, *3*, 181–195.

Banbury, S., & Berry, D. C. (1998). Disruption of office-related tasks by speech and office noise. *British Journal of Psychology, 89*, 499–517.

Banbury, S., Macken, W. J., Tremblay, S., & Jones, D. M. (2001). Auditory distraction and short-term memory: Phenomena and practical implications. *Human Factors, 43*, 12–29.

Brown, D. (2003). *The Da Vinci code.* New York: Doubleday. Audiobook read by Jeff Harding.

Campbell, J. B., & Hawley, C. W. (1982). Study habits and Eysenck's Theory of Extraversion–Introversion. *Journal of Research in Personality, 16*, 139–146.

Crawford, H. J., & Strapp, C. M. (1994). Effects of vocal and instrumental music on a reading comprehension test for extraverts and introverts, *Perceptual and Motor Skills, 62*, 283–289.

Etaugh, C., & Ptasnik, P. (1982). Effects of studying to music and post-study relaxation on reading comprehension. *Perceptual and Motor Skills, 55*, 141–142.

Flowers, P. J., & O'Neill, A. A. M. (2005). Self-reported distractions of Middle School students in listening to music and prose. *Journal of Research in Music Education, 53*, 308–321.

Gurung, R. A. R. (2005). How do students really study (and does it matter)? *Teaching of Psychology, 34*, 239–241.

Pool, M. M., Koolstra, C. M., & Van Der Voort, T. H. A. (2003). Distraction effects of background soap operas on homework performance: An experimental study enriched with observational data. *Educational Psychology, 23*, 361–380.

Salamé, P., & Baddeley, A. D. (1982). Disruption of short-term memory by unattended speech: Implications for the structure of working memory. *Journal of Verbal Learning and Verbal Behavior, 21*, 150–164.

Schellenberg, E. G., Nakata, T., Hunter, P. G., & Tamoto, S. (2007). Exposure to music and cognitive performance: tests of children and adults. *Psychology of Music, 35*, 5–19.

Appendix

The musical selections (with the frequencies of selection shown in brackets for silent learners and music learners, respectively) were by Britney Spears, "Baby one more time" (3, 0); Girls Aloud, "Love machine" (2, 2); Green Day, "American idiot" (2, 2); Jack Johnson, "Better together" (8, 6); Kaiser Chiefs, "Every day I love you less and less" (3, 3); Lily Allen, "LDN" (4, 1); McFly, "Five colours in her hair" (1, 2); and Nelly Furtado, "Maneater" (3, 6).

REFERENCES

Abrams, D., Eller, A. & Bryant, J. (2006). An age apart: The effects of intergenerational contact and stereotype threat on performance and intergroup bias. *Psychology of Aging, 21*, 691–701.

Adams, M.J. (1990). *Beginning to read: Thinking and learning about print.* Cambridge, MA: MIT Press.

Ahmadi, J., Samavat, F., Sayyad, M. & Ghanizadeh, A. (2002). Various types of exercise and scores on the Beck Depression Inventory. *Psychological Reports, 90*, 821–822.

Allen, D. (2002). *Getting things done.* New York: Penguin.

American Psychological Association. (2001). *Publication manual of the American Psychological Association* (5th edn). Washington, DC: American Psychological Association.

Beech, J.R. (2001). A curvilinear relationship between hair loss and mental rotation and neuroticism: a possible influence of sustained dihydrotestosterone production. *Personality & Individual Differences, 31*, 185–192.

Beech, J.R. & Harding, L.M. (Eds.) (1990). *Testing people: a practical guide to psychometrics.* Windsor, UK: NFER-Nelson.

Beech, J.R. & Harris, M. (1997). The prelingually deaf reader: A case of reliance on direct lexical access? *Journal of Research in Reading, 20*, 105–121.

Beech, J.R. & Mackintosh, I.C. (2005). Do difference in sex hormones affect handwriting style? Evidence from digit ratio and sex role identity as determinants of the sex of handwriting. *Personality and Individual Differences, 39*, 459–468.

Beech, J.R. & Mayall, K.A. (2005). The word shape hypothesis re-examined: evidence for an external feature advantage in visual word recognition. *Journal of Research in Reading, 3*, 302–319.

Bishop, D.V.M. (2002). Cerebellar abnormalities in developmental dyslexia: Cause, correlate or consequence? *Cortex, 38*, 491–498.

Bolker, J. (1998). *Writing your dissertation in fifteen minutes a day: A guide to starting, revising, and finishing your doctoral thesis.* New York: Henry Holt and Company.

Bradley, L. & Bryant, P.E. (1983). Categorizing sounds and learning to read: A causal connection. *Nature, 30*, 419–421.

Bryant, T. (2004). *Self-discipline in 10 days: How to go from thinking to doing*. Seattle, WA: HUB Publishing.

Buzan, T. (2002). *How to mind map: the ultimate thinking tool that will change your life*. London: HarperCollins.

Caramazza, A., Capasso, R. & Miceli, G. (1996). The role of the graphemic buffer in reading. *Cognitive Neuropsychology, 13*, 673–698.

Chruscial, H.L. (2003). Physical activity, mood and self-esteem: A mediational model of maternal self-efficacy and energy. *Dissertation Abstracts International: Section B: The Sciences and Engineering* (Vol. 63, 11-B), p. 5548.

Cohen, J. (1988). *Statistical power analysis for the behavioral sciences* (2nd edn). New York: Academic Press.

Covey, S.R. (1989). *The 7 habits of highly effective people*. London: Simon & Schuster.

Csatho, R., Osva, A., Bicsa, E., Kara, K., Manning, J. & Kallai, K. (2002). Sex role identity related to the ratio of second to fourth digit length in women. *Biological Psychology, 62*, 147–156.

Doran. N., McChargue, D. & Cohen, L. (2007). Impulsivity and the reinforcing value of cigarette smoking. *Addictive Behaviors, 32*, 90–98.

Fiore, N. (2007). *The now habit*. New York: Tarcher.

Frith, C. (2007). *Making up the mind: how the brain creates our mental world*. Oxford, UK: Blackwell.

Glaser, B.G. & Strauss, A.L. (1967). *The discovery of grounded theory: Strategies for qualitative research*. New York: Aldine.

Halliday, M.A.K. & Hasan, R. (1976). *Cohesion in English*. London: Longman.

Hartley, J. & Benjamin, M. (1998). An evaluation of structured abstracts in journals published by the British Psychological Society, *British Journal of Educational Psychology, 68*, 443–456.

King, S. (2000). *On writing: A memoir of the craft*. London: Hodder & Stoughton.

Kline, P. (2000). *Psychometrics primer*. London: Free Association Books.

Kucera, H. & Francis, W.N. (1967). *Computational analysis of present-day American English*. Providence, RI: Brown University Press.

Miller, G.A. (1956). The magical number seven, plus or minus two: Some limits on our capacity for processing information. *Psychological Review, 63*, 81–97.

Poletiek, F.H. (1996). Paradoxes of falsification. *Quarterly Journal of Experimental Psychology, Section A: Human Experimental Psychology, 49*, 447–462.

Popper, K.R. (1959). *The logic of scientific discovery*. New York: Harper and Row.

Reicher, S. (2000). Against methodolatry: Some comments on Elliott, Fischer, and Rennie. *British Journal of Clinical Psychology, 39*, 1–6.

Reisberg, D. & McLean, J. (1985). Meta-attention: Do we know when we are being. distracted? *Journal of General Psychology, 112*, 291–306.

Rutter, M. (2007). *Genes and behaviour: nature–nurture interplay explained*. Oxford, UK: Blackwell.

Seligman, M.E.P. (1975). *Helplessness: On depression, development and death.* San Francisco: W.H. Freeman.

Shepard, R.N. & Metzler, J. (1971). Mental rotation of three-dimensional objects. *Science, 171*, 701–703.

Strauss, A. & Corbin, J. (1990). *Basics of qualitative research: Grounded theory procedures and techniques.* London: Sage.

Thoits, P.A. (1986). Social support as coping assistance. *Journal of Consulting and Clinical Psychology, 54*, 416–423.

Thoits, P.A. (1995). Stress, coping and social support processes: where are we? What next? *Journal of Health and Social Behavior, 37*, 53–79.

Thoits, P.A., Hohmann, A.A., Harvey, M.R. & Fletcher, B. (2000). Similar-other support for men undergoing coronary artery bypass surgery. *Health Psychology, 19*, 264–273.

Truss, L. (2003). *Eats, shoots and leaves: The zero tolerance approach to punctuation.* London: Profile Books.

Veith, E.M., Sherman, J.E., Pellino, T.A. & Yasui, N.Y. (2006). Qualitative analysis of the peer-mentoring relationship among individuals with spinal cord injury. *Rehabilitation Psychology, 51*, 289–298.

Willig, C. (2001). *Introducing qualitative research in psychology: Adventures in theory and method.* Maidenhead, UK: Open University Books.

INDEX

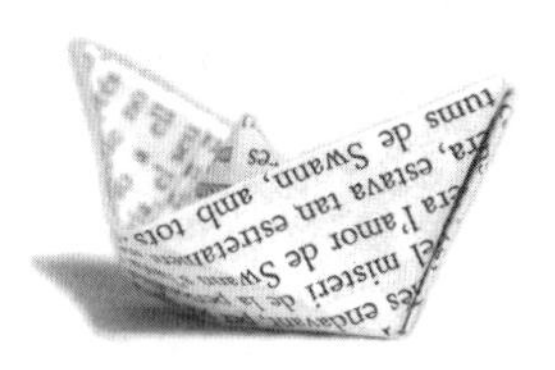